D1519032

Missionary of Moderation

Henry Melchior Muhlenberg

Engraving by James W. Steel after Charles Willson Peale. *The Historical Society of Pennsylvania.*

Missionary of Moderation

Henry Melchior Muhlenberg

and the Lutheran Church in English America

Leonard R. Riforgiato

Lewisburg
Bucknell University Press
London and Toronto: Associated University Presses

© 1980 by Associated University Presses, Inc.

Associated University Presses, Inc.
4 Cornwall Drive
East Brunswick, New Jersey 08816

Associated University Presses
69 Fleet Street
London EC4Y 1EU, England

Associated University Presses
Toronto M5E 1A7
Canada

Library of Congress Cataloging in Publication Data

Riforgiato, Leonard R   1939-
Missionary of moderation.

Bibliography: p.
Includes index.
1. Muhlenberg, Henry Melchior, 1711-1787.
2. Lutheran Church—Clergy—Biography. 3. Clergy—
United States—Biography. 4. Lutheran Church in the
United States—History. I. Title.
BX8080.M9R53   284.1'092'4   [B]   78-75203
ISBN 0-8387-2379-9

Printed in the United States of America

This book is dedicated to my parents,
John and Jeanette Riforgiato

Contents

Preface

There are several valid reasons for writing a biography of Henry Melchior Muhlenberg, colonial Pennsylvania Lutheran clergyman and founder of the Lutheran church in America. In the first place, Muhlenberg has been virtually ignored by church historians despite his importance for American Lutheran history. Though abundant source material on his life and works is extant in the form of the *Hallesche Nachrichten* and his own journals, there is no satisfactory scholarly biography of the man. Those works which do treat him suffer either from denominational triumphantism or a one-sided emphasis on the establishment of his ecclesiastical polity. None attempts to place the man against the background of his own theology, as well as against his times.

William J. Mann's standard biography, *The Life and Times of Henry Melchior Muhlenberg* (1887), is little more than a factual summary of the journals which were still unpublished when he wrote. Mann, moreover, deeply committed as he was to the pietistic faction of American Lutheranism, takes great pains to plant his subject firmly in the Halle tradition. He thus misses the complex nature of Muhlenberg's brand of pietism by oversimplifying his ideas. Writing as he did in the nineteenth century, Mann also falls victim to his times by portraying Muhlenberg as a staunch defender of American democracy, which he decidedly was not. The picture Mann presents, therefore, is neither exact nor objective. The only other biographies of note, W. K. Frick, *Henry Melchior Muhlenberg, Patriarch of the Lutheran Church in America* (1902) and Margaret R. Seebach, *An Eagle of*

9

the Wilderness: The Story of Henry Melchior Muhlenberg (1924), are derived from Mann and so suffer from the same defects. Paul A. W. Wallace's *Muhlenbergs of Pennsylvania* (1950) is a popularized history more concerned with his children than with Muhlenberg himself. What he does say of Muhlenberg is not original.

Muhlenberg does figure prominently in several doctoral dissertations. Charles H. Glatfelter's "The Colonial Pennsylvania German Lutheran and Reformed Clergymen" (1952) emphasizes his efforts to compromise with the spirit of voluntarism, while Richard Charles Wolf's, "The Americanization of the German Lutherans" (1947) concerns itself with Muhlenberg's contribution to the process of anglicization. Neither presents a picture of the whole man.

A second reason which might justify writing on this topic is the neglect of the religious history of the middle colonies in general and of the Lutherans in particular. Unlike New England Puritanism, which has been the chief preoccupation of religious historians, middle colony Lutheranism has been considered outside the mainstream of American religious history. Most histories of the Lutheran Church in this country, as Henry Eyster Jacob's *History of the Evangelical Lutheran Church in America* (1898), were written before the turn of the century by clergymen or laymen within the Lutheran tradition. Too often they are mere chronicles of the pastoral acts of clergymen. Lars P. Qualben's *The Lutheran Church in Colonial America* (1940) is, in reality, an uncritical outline of Lutheran history intended for Sunday school classes. Only Abdel Ross Wentz's *Basic History of Lutheranism in America* (1955) comes close to an adequate history. But, as its title suggests, it is not an exhaustive work. Its treatment of colonial Lutheranism is particularly sketchy.

Several controversial studies have appeared. Johannes J. Mol's *The Breaking of Traditions: Theological Convictions in Colonial America* (1968) argues, unconvincingly, that the pietistic commitment to a transcendental God, in contrast to orthodox emphasis on the institutional church, better enabled Muhlenberg to adjust to the new American environment. Since, however, Muhlenberg also insisted very strongly on the institutional character of the church, Mol's conclusions are somewhat dubious. Dietmar Rothermund, in his *Layman's Progress* (1961), presents Muhlenberg as much more of a politician than he actually was. His description of Muhlenberg as a crafty political manipulator is simply not borne out by the evidence. There is, therefore, justification for a new historical treatise on Muhlenberg and colonial American Lutheranism.

This work does not pretend to exhaust either subject. Rather it attempts to correct the traditional picture of Muhlenberg as a pragmatic, opportunistic organizer. By investigating his educational formation, it seeks to discover influences which caused him to develop a theology of moderation which effected a viable compromise between Lutheran orthodoxy and pietism. It claims that this theology underlay and motivated all his organizational actions, indeed every position he took whether in secular or religious matters. Thus his emphasis on liturgical revivalism caused him to reject both left-wing Moravian enthusiasm and right-wing Berkenmeyer orthodoxy. His emphasis on the need to channel the godly life within institutional frameworks, along with his theological conception of the ministerial office, led him to establish an orderly ecclesiastical polity. Finally, his concept of the roles played by church and state in the economy of salvation prevented his deep involvement in political matters unless they affected the welfare of the church or the souls committed to his care.

It is, therefore, the contention of this work that Muhlenberg was more than a pragmatic opportunist. Rather, throughout his ministerial career, he pursued a course of action which was consistent with his theological beliefs.

Acknowledgments

I am indebted to the library staffs of the following institutions for the help I received during my research for this study: the Lutheran Theological Seminary at Gettysburg, Lutheran Theological Seminary at Philadelphia, the Pattee Library of the Pennsylvania State University, and the library of the Shenango Valley campus of the Pennsylvania State University.

My gratitude also goes to the late Professor Theodore Tappert of the Philadelphia seminary for taking the time to discuss with me the ideas underlying this study; to Dr. Thomas Knight, Associate Dean for Commonwealth campuses of the Pennsylvania State University College of Liberal Arts for providing a research grant which enabled me to complete the work; to Dr. Harold Sargent, Director of the Shenango Valley campus of the Pennsylvania State University for the support and encouragement he gave while I readied the manuscript for publication.

Finally my special thanks go to my former graduate school adviser and present colleague, Dr. John B. Frantz, Associate Professor of History at the Pennsylvania State University. His friendship, enthusiasm, helpful criticism, and concern carried me through this project.

Missionary of Moderation

[1]
The Origins of Muhlenberg's Thought

Henry Melchior Muhlenberg, the Patriarch of colonial American Lutheranism, was born on September 6, 1711, in the town of Einbeck (Eimbeck) in the Duchy of Hanover, whose sovereign was the future King of England. Upon the death of Queen Anne, the last of the Stuart family, in 1714, none of whose seventeen children survived her, the Duke of Hanover ascended the British throne as George I. In a sense, Muhlenberg was already a naturalized citizen of the British Empire before undertaking his American ventures in 1742.

In the early eighteenth century, Einbeck was a small, unimportant, rustic village whose days of glory were long past. The origins of the town can be traced to the establishment in the eleventh century of the *Alexander Stiftskirche,* a shrine which, since it purportedly contained a drop of Christ's blood, soon became a popular site of pilgrimage. The town later grew up around the shrine.[1] During the Middle Ages Einbeck formed a connection with the Hansa Confederation and developed into a prosperous commercial center of some 12,000 inhabitants; its present population is 30,500. It was especially noted for its six hundred breweries which provided Germany with *Einpöckisches Bier* from which bock beer derives its name.

The onset of the Reformation, however, ended Einbeck's commercial promise. Martin Luther soon won a following for his ideas within this Hanoverian town as is evidenced in that Luther-

17

ans were serving on the town Council in 1528.[2] In the same year, Einbeck also received its first Lutheran pastor, one Conrad Bolen, who served in the *Markt Kirche*. By 1580, Einbeck officials had subscribed to the Formula of Concord.[3] Still, it was not easy to slip from traditional Catholic moorings. Between 1618 and 1648, Germany was convulsed by a series of politico-religious conflicts known collectively as the Thirty Years War during which Catholics and Protestants slaughtered one another in the name of God and for the sake of political power. Despite its strong fortifications, Einbeck fell victim to Catholic armies after a protracted siege.[4] It never recovered fully from this disaster and, by the time of Muhlenberg's birth, evidences of the devastation were still plainly visible.

Despite his obvious importance for American colonial religious history, virtually nothing is known of Muhlenberg's early life and family background. However, attempts have been made to implant the Muhlenbergs within the ranks of German aristocracy. According to this line of reasoning, the family traced its origins from one Ziracka, a Wendish and Sorbic prince, who was converted to Christianity about the year A.D. 950. Since he resided in Mühlberg (from the German word for mills, *Mühlen*) in Prussian Saxony, the family name was changed to von Mühlenberg. The ancestral Prince von Mühlenberg was received into the German nobility as a vassal of the Bishop of Naumburg and his son, Bonifacius von Mühlenberg, later accompanied one of the Emperors Otto on an Italian expedition, thus winning valuable concessions for the family. During the Thirty Years War, the branches of the family tree were either exterminated or impoverished. Hence, by 1650, the Muhlenbergs no longer appear on the roll of the nobility of the Empire.[5]

Intriguing as such genealogical speculation may be, it is merely academic in Muhlenberg's case. His immediate origins spring from the background of Einbeck's *petite bourgeoisie*. His father, Nicholas Melchior Muhlenberg, was a burgher, brewer, and cobbler.[6] He is listed in the Einbeck church records as a deacon and *Vorsteher*.[7] Muhlenberg's mother, Anna Maria Kleinschmid, was the daughter of an officer in the royal army.[8]

The Muhlenbergs seem to have had nine children: Johann

Daniel and Engel Maria, both born before 1700; Ilse Marie, born September 11, 1700; Heinrich Christoph, born July 13, 1702; Christina Hedwig, born July 16, 1705; Johann Arend, born May 16, 1709; Melchior Heinrich, baptized September 6, 1711; Maria Catharina, born April 6, 1714; and Maria Catharina, born September 19, 1722.[9] This last child was given the same name as her older sister who died in 1718. Though baptized Melchior Henry, Muhlenberg reversed the order of his names by the time he entered the university.

Muhlenberg's early education seems to have followed the pattern of German youth of modest means. In 1718 at the age of seven, he began his schooling in the local German and Latin schools. In his twelfth year he was received into the Evangelical Lutheran church through the sacrament of confirmation at the *Neustadter Kirche* in Einbeck.[10] At the same time he began private instructions from the pastor primarius of the *Neustadter* church, Valentin Benkhard, a convert to Lutheranism from Roman Catholicism. Prior to his installation in Einbeck in 1708, Benkhard had been superior of Cloister Triffenstein near Augsburg. His appointment to the Lutheran pastorate at Einbeck, arranged by the Hanoverian court, stirred up heated opposition which led many to withdraw from the *Neustadter* church. By the time of his death on August 24, 1743, however, Benkhard appears to have won the love and respect of his parishioners.[11] At any rate it is interesting to note that Muhlenberg could have been influenced by the thought of this man, well versed in both Catholic and Lutheran theology.

In the same year as his confirmation, 1723, the Muhlenberg family fortunes changed drastically with the death of his father, Nicholas Melchior, from apoplexy or a stroke.[12] Young Muhlenberg was now obliged to discontinue his education, in which he had advanced to the third form, and seek work to supplement the family income. In later years, in typical pietist fashion, he was to attribute the first stirrings of grace in his process of awakening to these two almost simultaneous events—his confirmation instructions under Benkhard and the sudden death of his father.[13] Nevertheless, by his own admission, these first feeble sparks of grace were quickly quenched in a life of self-indulgence. It is somewhat difficult to picture the dour clergyman of later life as a boisterous, hell-raising youth, but such is Muhlenberg's claim. A combination of over-indulgence by his doting mother and the deprivation of paternal authority, combined with the company of young friends "with poisoned minds" tended to keep young Henry in a somewhat rebellious state.[14]

By his eighteenth birthday, Muhlenberg sufficiently regained his self-composure and control to resume his education. Though he still labored during the day, he devoted his evenings to the study of the organ under Mr. Alberty and of math under Cantor Kuhlmann.[15] At this time, he seems to have entertained some idea of pursuing a career as an organist. By 1722, however, he was receiving private tutoring in Latin and Greek from Johann Joachim Schüssler, the rector of the *Rathschule (schola senatoria)* of the *Neustadter Kirche* in Einbeck.[16] Schüssler convinced him to quit his job and enroll full-time in the Latin school where he entered the highest form.[17] To help pay his tuition and fees, he sang in the school choir. Evidently young Muhlenberg acquired a fairly extensive background in music for, in addition to his choir activities, he became adept at playing the organ and the clavichord.[18] He also secured a broad knowledge of classical Latin and Greek. Muhlenberg, however, was far from being a humanist for he condemned the classics "since the real Latin language can be learned nowhere else but from heathen authors, inquisitive youth swallows the heathen abomination along with it."[19]

In Easter 1733, Muhlenberg was accepted as a student at the Zellerfelde Latin school or lyceum, an eight-hour walk from Einbeck.[20] At this time the school was directed by Rector Raphelius who retained this position until 1740 when he joined the faculty of the University of Rostock.[21] In addition to receiving both public and private instructions from the four man teaching staff, Muhlenberg instructed eighteen younger students in catechesis, writing, mathematics, and the clavichord to earn funds for his upkeep.[22] During the year he was at Zellerfelde, Muhlenberg progressed far enough in Latin to enable him to study Cicero, Caesar, Virgil, Horace, and Terence and to acquire an understanding of the Greek New Testament. For the first time, too, he began the study of French and Hebrew.[23]

During the autumn of 1734, Muhlenberg returned to Einbeck to resume private tutoring from Rector Schüssler.[24] The following year, 1735, the new royal university was opened at Göttingen. Since the university was supported by a public tax, each town in the Duchy was able to nominate candidates for free room and board in proportion to the stipend which it contributed. Einbeck's contribution was sufficient to allow it to appoint a single scholar for one year's duration, and due to Schüssler's intervention, this scholarship was granted to the twenty-four-year-old Muhlenberg who took up residence at Göttingen on March 19, 1735.

Muhlenberg's spiritual condition at this stage of his life was, according to his later recollections, somewhat wanting, for as he stated, "there was in me nothing but darkness and death and . . . an inclination and disposition toward evil."[25] Since Göttingen was of such recent vintage, it attracted a great variety of wild young men from diverse nations.[26] Young Henry cast his lot with these *Renommissten* and *Stutzern,* sowing his wild oats freely until he learned that another band of rowdies had slain a school guard during an evening brawl.[27]

Muhlenberg's course of studies during his first year likewise reflected the dilettante outlook of a youthful *bon vivant.* He studied for logic under Professor Hollmann, Hebrew and pure mathematics under the Vice-Rector of the University, Professor Waener (a popular teacher because he would perform tricks in class), and Greek under Professor Gesner.[28]

Events were shaping up, however, which were to transform Muhlenberg's life, lead to a genuine conversion experience, and set him on the path to the ministry. Three young transfer students, Einbeck natives all, arrived from Halle University and struck up a friendship with their fellow townsman.[29] From what little Muhlenberg says of them in the journals and his autobiography, it is evident that these young men introduced him to the Halle brand of pietism, emphasizing the manner and possibility of translating Christian beliefs into actual daily practice.[30] At about the same time, Göttingen received the first of its theology professors, Dr. Oporin, who exercised a critical influence on Muhlenberg's life. Oporin, the author of a two-volume book entitled *The Ancient and Only Rule for a Convincing and Effective Manner of Preaching* (1736–1737), written in opposition to the influx of Wolfian philosophy into clerical sermons, was also of the pietist school of thought.[31] Muhlenberg enrolled in Oporin's courses in dogmatic and moral theology where he experienced a conviction of his sinfulness, felt shame and contrition, and developed a hunger and thirst for the righteousness of Christ.[32] In other words, he underwent a conversion experience, but, unlike the experiences advocated by August Hermann Francke and even more so by the radical pietists, Muhlenberg's conversion seems to have been a gradual process of enlightenment, not an instantaneous transformation. During his later ministerial career, Muhlenberg's rejection of instantaneous conversion as a normative experience placed him in the ranks of moderate pietism.

Oporin's interest in his student led him to tender him the job of secretary or *amanuensis*. This enabled Muhlenberg to cut himself off from his more disorderly companions by moving into Oporin's house. It also afforded him the opportunity for intensive theological progress under the direction of his mentor.[33] Equally important to the development of the fledgling theologian were the contacts he made with the German nobility who occasionally visited Göttingen and whose patronage was essential to the furtherance of his career. In 1735 the founder of Göttingen, the High Sheriff von Münchausen, befriended the young man and provided him with a grant to support three years of study at the university.[34] More important still was the friendship of the XI Count Reuss who made Muhlenberg the chaplain of his Göttingen residence and involved him in the pietistic *Bettestunde* or conventicles held there.[35] Yet another patron was Count Ernst von Wernigerode.

In 1736 Muhlenberg joined with two other theological students to found a small school for poor children whom they instructed in their spare time.[36] Opposition soon developed from the resident pastors of Göttingen who viewed the school as a dangerous innovation, unsanctioned by either church or state, and conducted by unordained seminarians. These men lodged a complaint with the central government in Hanover, but the court steward and counselor of the XI Count Reuss von Greiz, Herr Riesenbeck, remonstrated in the seminarians' behalf. As a result, the school was granted official sanction, provided it was placed under the control of the theological faculty of the university.[37] With this sanction the school flourished until it reached a total enrollment of 120 pupils.[38]

Eventually, in 1737, Muhlenberg entered the *Seminarium Theologicum* and took his turn catechising and preaching in the university church.[39] Again external influences were to change the course of his career for, toward the close of 1737, two preachers from the Jewish mission fields, Messrs. Wideman and Mantius, arrived at Göttingen and struck up a friendship with him. They extended to Muhlenberg an invitation to join them in their work of grace with the condition that he first enroll at Halle in the Jewish Institute conducted by Professor Callenberg.[40] Muhlenberg quickly wrote to Riesenbeck of his burning desire to labor among the Jewish missions and begged for patronage support.[41] Due to Riesenbeck's intercession, Muhlenberg was summoned to Kostritz in the spring of 1738 by the XXIV Count Reuss, Heinrich, and by Count Erdmann Heinrich Henckel von Donnersmark.[42] Actually his patrons had intended to appoint him to a vacant deaconship at Greitz, which they served as trustees, but, upon discovering that the young theologian was not yet ready for such a responsibility, they dispatched him to Halle in May, 1738, to obtain a degree under the direction of Dr. Francke.[43]

By the time Muhlenberg entered the Francke institutions at Halle in 1738, they had already long been established as a leading center of pietism. At the time the institutions were directed by Gotthilf August Francke, the son of the illustrious August Hermann Francke, who had indelibly stamped his character on Halle and the Halle brand of pietism.

The University of Halle had been founded in 1674 by Elector Friedrich III of Brandenburg-Prussia.[44] Historical circumstances soon converted it into a center of German pietism. At this time, the Hohenzollerns were trying to unite their dispersed lands both politically and religiously. Because the polemical conflicts between Lutheran orthodox and Reformed threatened this unity, Frederick III (after 1701, Frederick I, King of Prussia) tended to favor the ecumenical, nonpolemical, pietist movement.[45] In 1691, through King Frederick's influence, Philipp Jacob Spener, the controversial founder of German pietism, was offered and accepted a call to Berlin as Provost of the *Nikolarkirche*.[46] Through Spener's intercession, a theological school, strongly pietistically oriented, was added to the University of Halle in 1692.[47] It was Spener too who gave August Hermann Francke refuge. In 1692 Francke became pastor at Glaucha, a suburb of Halle. By 1698 he had joined the theological faculty at Halle as professor of Semitic languages.[48] Meanwhile he gradually evolved the design of the great orphanage at Halle which he founded in 1698. Eventually the Francke institution boasted, in addition to the schools for orphans and children of the nobility, a printing house, publishing plant, dispensary and clinic, as well as the Canstein Biblical Institute.[49] In time Francke came to dominate the theological faculty by virtue of his accomplishments at the institutions and his position as pastor of Halle's *Ulrichskirche*. Francke, then, was in a position to mold the many seminarians who passed through the University of Halle, many of whom later spread his theological-spiritual heritage in Halle mission stations within Germany and throughout the German diaspora. Though Francke died in 1727, his spiritual ideals were furthered by his son and successor, Gothilf August. Moreover, Halle's dominance was assured in 1729 when the Prussian King Friedrich Wilhelm I decreed that every Brandenburg-Prussian seminarian had to spend at least two years in its school of theology.[50] Here too, August Hermann Francke's influence was paramount for he had taught the king when he was crown prince.

It was within the orphans' institute at Halle that Muhlenberg received his final theological training. He began his duties as an instructor in the *Weingarten* school for the youngest children, rapidly advancing to the middle school and then to the great orphanage itself as instructor for eight boys.[51] In addition, Muhlenberg taught Greek and Hebrew classes at Halle's theological school and served as inspector of the institute's hospital, from which experience he learned the medical and pharmaceutical practices which he used to great advantage in the English colonies.[52] Within a year, Muhlenberg was requested to return to Göttingen to resume supervision of the charity school he had founded earlier. His Halle mentors, however, dissuaded him, informing him that they planned to send him to a new mission field at Bengale in the West Indies.[53] Still events precluded the Indian missions for in July, 1739, the XXIVth Count Reuss sent a call to Muhlenberg to the church at Grosshennersdorf in the Oberlausitz which he finally accepted.[54] Considering the count's insistence and the generosity he had shown to him, Muhlenberg had no other choice. A formal call was issued on August 12, 1739, and, shortly thereafter, following an examination by the consistory, Muhlenberg was ordained in Leipzig.[55]

Grosshennersdorf, where Muhlenberg assumed pastoral duties in the fall of 1739, is situated in Saxony only a few miles from Herrnhut, the center of Count Nikolaus Ludwig von Zinzendorf's restored Church of the United Brethren which figured so prominently in Muhlenberg's American ventures. Indeed, Baroness Henriette Sophie von Gersdorf, under whose beneficence Muhlenberg labored, was Count Zinzendorf's aunt, the sister of his mother.[56] For a time during his youth, the count had lived with this aunt, but something had happened to strain their relationship, for, while Zinzendorf blazed new theological trails for himself the baroness remained a Hallensian pietist. At Muhlenberg's first meeting with the count in Philadelphia in 1742 it was evident not only that Zinzendorf and the baroness were estranged but that Henriette Sophie had colored Muhlenberg's view of her nephew.

The baroness had, from her munificence, erected at her Grosshennersdorf estate several charitable institutions patterned after the Halle model. Her orphanage had four sections: a *pädagogium* for the scions of impoverished nobility; a school for poor boys; one for their female counterparts; and an old folks home for destitute widows. In addition there was a small congregation composed of Bohemian exiles from the Catholic

Counter-Reformation to whom the baroness had given refuge.[57] Muhlenberg took charge of all these works of charity. The funds for maintaining them, however, came solely from the patrimony of the baroness. By 1740 the financial strain proved too great and she was forced to sell her estate to the Reich Supreme Court Justice Baron Carl Gottlob von Burgsdorf.[58] Because of his reduced income resulting from the new owner's cutback in charities, for a time Muhlenberg considered accepting a call to a vacant deaconship in Gorlitz but abandoned this on the baroness's insistence.[59] Instead, he set out for Einbeck to see whether he could receive some of his family inheritance to enable him to continue in the Grosshennersdorf position.

On route he stopped at the home of his old patron, the XXIVth Count Reuss, in Kostritz and diplomatically informed him of his reduced circumstances. This news was relayed to Francke by Baron von Braun who had been present at Kostritz during Muhlenberg's visit. When Muhlenberg arrived at Halle on September 6, 1741, Francke was prepared to offer him a way out of Grosshennersdorf in the form of a call to the United Congregations of Philadelphia, New Hanover, and New Providence which had been extended through the offices of Court Preacher Frederick Michael Ziegenhagen in London.[60] With the consent of his patrons, Counts Reuss and Henckel and Baroness von Gersdorf, Muhlenberg accepted the call and readied himself for the voyage to Pennsylvania. He brought with him to the New World a pietistic theology which would leave an indelible stamp on American Lutheranism. His pietism, however, in comparison to the various forms the movement assumed, was of a distinctly moderate and churchly nature.

Although pietism as a distinct manifestation of the Christian life and the individual's response to the Christ event did not appear in Europe until post-Reformation times, it was not an entirely unique religious phenomenon. Its origin lay within an experiential tradition which reached back through Anabaptism and medieval mysticism to the primitive Christian communities of the apostolic and patristic ages.[61] In its post-Reformation form, pietism invaded all four great Christian churches: Lutheran, Reformed, Church of England, and Roman Catholic.

Among the German Lutherans and Reformed, it was known as pietism. Dutch Reformed called the movement precisionism, the Anglicans knew it as puritanism, while the Roman Catholics labeled it Jansenism. All were, however, variations of the same religious impulse, though with obvious differences.

As a rule, pietism appeared not as a distinct sect or credal statement, but as a reemphasis on long neglected experiential elements within the doctrinal systems and theological heritage of the established churches. Pietistic adherents had no desire to depart from hallowed Reformation heritage but merely wished to complete the process of reform by refurbishing Christian life. They developed no common set of doctrines, advocated no single type of church polity, nor imposed any standardized forms of liturgical worship for none of these were essential to their main concern, the encounter with Christ.[62] Still there were certain elements common to all pietists.

Chief among these was the interpretation of Christianity in terms of a meaningful relationship of the believer with God which resulted in a feeling of contentment and a state of righteousness. The individual entered into an experiential I=Thou relationship with the Almighty. He was essentially a *Hörer des Wortes,* a role that demanded response in the form of personal commitment to a moral life lived in accord with the will of God. By a process of interior identification, the individual lived in God and God indwelled in him or her.[63] In theological language this found expression as the indwelling of Christ or the engrafting of branches to the vine. It was the Pauline concept of the mystical body in which each member of the Church, used in an all-inclusive sense of the People of God, shared a living, organic relationship to the Head who was the Word.

A second element common to all forms of pietism was religious idealism. This struggle for a life of perfection was symbolized in the concept of the Two Ways, ultimately derived from Judaic wisdom literature and perhaps proximately derived from the imagery of the Johannine Apocalypse, the Epistle of Barnabus, and the *Didache.* The Two Ways were, of course, the way of Christ—good and light—and the path of Satan—darkness and death. Each person must opt for one or the other. There could be no compromise between the two, or the sacrificial atonement of Christ's death on the cross was rendered meaningless. A true Christian was one who chose the path of light, but even here pietists made a distinction between believers—those who accepted the faith intellectually—and possessors—those who put faith into practice in their daily lives. Only the latter were true Christians, for only they had achieved justification by a faithful adherence to the sacrifice of Christ.[64] Once commitment was given, justification entered human experience in conversion and sanctification.[65] The possessing Christians would then live lives of near perfection while their sanctification expressed itself in a response to God's will through good works. They would, moreover, wish to communicate what they possessed to others, an impulse which found an outlet in the missionary zeal of European pietism.[66] This missionary impulse was heightened by a somewhat chiliast strain implicit in pietism and its consequent rejection of the material world, the *sarx* of Paul. Christians, therefore, had to foster and continually nourish this spirit of responsiveness to God's goodness and grace. This pietists did through conventicles and liturgies that served to stimulate piety and personal response. Especially helpful to this purpose was hymnody and exhortive sermons.[67]

Finally, pietism strongly emphasized biblical law in counterdistinction to orthodox rationalism. Pietistic rules for the moral life came straight from the pages of the New Testament, while its stress on the regulation of Christian conduct was an attempt to enforce the Pauline ethic without compromise.[68] It was, in essence, an ethical movement. Although orthodoxy, under the influence of rationalism, gradually reduced faith to intellectual assent to abstract theological propositions, pietism defined faith existentially, as practice and personal commitment. In some cases, experience eclipsed reason altogether and certain pietistic offshoots rejected all doctrine and law save that found in scripture. Since every person could achieve a personal relationship to God and, under the inspiration of the Holy Spirit, was able to discover divine law in the Bible, radical pietists felt little need for an educated clergy, turning instead to lay preachers. In the more churchly manifestations of pietism, this emphasis resulted in a renewal of the doctrine of the universal priesthood of all believers.[69] The pastoral office, too, underwent a modification. The pastor was no longer seen as the guardian and dispenser of revealed truths but rather as a model of true Christian life through whose example and exhortations the laity would be led to experience faith.[70]

The rise of German Lutheran pietism must be seen in relation to the historical situation in sixteenth-century Germany. Thirty years of constant warfare had shattered all order and produced a pessimistic view of life with an attendant immorality.[71] A leveling tendency was operative in church life, denominational differences were blurred. From orthodox ranks a reaction set in known as *Verkonfessionalisierung,* the struggle for doctrinal purity. Doctrine now hardened into rigidly held dogma.[72] As a result, Lutheranism suffered from an ossification of its theological arteries, for faith became merely assent to dogma, while good works were roundly denounced as nonessential to the godly life in an obvious misinterpretation of Luther.[73]

Any reaction must itself ultimately provoke a counter reaction. Such was the case with the *Verkonfessionalisierung* which was later answered by Lutheran pietism. The roots of the movement can be found in the writings of the young Luther himself who, in turn, was influenced by medieval German mysticism.[74] As a youth Luther exhibited definite mystical tendencies inspired, in part, by his contact with the works of the Friends of God.[75] Stressing as he did personal union with Christ, achieved through suffering and self-denial which results in love of God, Luther himself prepared the way for the mystically oriented pietist movement. Though he later edged away from his earlier mysticism, Lutheran pietists could justly lay claim to a foundation of their ideas in the leader himself, as indeed they did.

Although not himself a pietist, the seeds of the Lutheran phase of the movement are contained in the speculations of Stephen Pastorius (1536–1603). Both John Arndt and Spener exhibit traces of dependence on his writings.[76] For Pastorius, the righteousness of Christ was imputed to the sinner in baptism.[77] It was a believer's duty to enter into communion with the living Christ, thus accepting his calling. Such communion results in a blessed life achieved through moral rectitude and self-denial. Theological insights such as these merely earned for Pastorius a condemnation by the Ministerium of Danzig.[78]

Philipp Nicholai (1556–1608) carried Pastorius's reasoning further, developing the mystical union between Christ and the believer. Through baptism man became one with the nature of Christ.[79] In this unity the Holy Spirit dwells within the Christian soul, causing it to will only what God wills and moving it to love God above all else. Spiritual rebirth enabled a Christian to commit himself or herself entirely to Christ, separating himself from mere professing, not possessing Christians. Thus an individual came to know the Trinity through the experience of God's love for him, manifested in His gracious act of union and communion.[80]

The real father of Lutheran pietism was John Arndt (1555–1621). He "transformed the doctrine of the Word, as Luther understood it, into an ethical doctrine, and thereby changed the experience of justification into one of sanctification."[81] Arndt viewed human salvation and spiritual renewal as the effect of God's activities, a gracious act not based upon any merit inherent in the sinner. Unlike orthodox Lutherans, however, he deemphasized the finality of this redemptive act, stressing instead the continual interaction between Redeemer and redeemed. Christ's work within the individual must be accompanied by a reciprocal act of trust in and commitment to the Word on the part of that individual.[82] Baptism was the prerequisite for this loving communion with Christ but not the final answer. Communion had to be constantly fostered by a life morally lived, worthy of a hearer of the word. Once individuals placed their trust in God, they achieved an identity of nature with the divine and a renewal of life. Dying to the world, the renewed Christians were now capable of rendering love to God through good works shown toward their fellow humans.[83]

If Arndt was the father, Philipp Jacob Spener (1635–1705) was the organizer of Lutheran pietism. Influenced by Arndtian and Reformed pietism, as well as by Waldensianism and Labadism, Spener spearheaded the demand for reform within

the Lutheran church.[84] In brief, he demanded certain changes, enunciated in his *Pia Desideria* (1675), among them ministerial efforts to spread the word of God through the use of entire biblical expositions in preaching as well as through the use of conventicles.[85] He urged acceptance and propagation of the doctrine of the priesthood of all believers and championed an emphasis on the practice of Christian life rather than on dogmatic knowledge. Doctrinal disputations, he felt, should be avoided since they served to factionalize the church. Finally he sought the establishment of *collegia pietatis*, or seminaries, where candidates for the ministry could be trained in Christian morality and edifying preaching techniques. Thus Spener offered the first concrete program of pietistic reform.[86]

As did Arndt, Spener felt that the essence of Christianity consisted in the living, personal relationship between God and the sinner. Given this, Spener opposed interference by civil authorities in purely religious matters as well as the *ex opere operato* interpretation of the sacraments which rendered nugatory the individual's role in renewal and frustrated the furtherance of pious practices.[87] Above all, Spener felt one had to avoid so over-emphasizing justification that the need for an active holy life was obviated. As for purity of doctrine, Spener found meaning in doctrine only if it led people to God and a godly life.

Since he held to the priesthood of all believers, Spener opted for a presbyterial polity with a trained *collegium presbyterium* to help the pastor in his work for souls.[88] Basically Spener followed the theology of Arndt, still professing, as he did, that he was an orthodox Lutheran.

Though Spener's call for reform was, at first, welcomed by orthodox theologians who had themselves been for some time denouncing the very same deficiencies, the rapid spread of pietism soon aroused hostility and suspicion. The innovation which received most opposition was the conventicle. Since it operated outside the official church, it contained within itself the seeds of separatism. Moreover, based as it was on the concept of the priesthood of all believers, and elevating as it did the role of the layman in matters religious, it was feared that the conventicle would lead to anticlericalism and voluntarism.[89] These dangers were soon realized as pietism began to split up into various wings or factions.

The group closest to Spener remained the Halle brand of pietism proposed by August Hermann Francke. Puritanical in outlook, it was opposed to the world and critical of worldly pleasures. Halle likewise advocated strict rules to regulate the conduct of its members. Francke, moreover, gave a novel twist to Spener and Arndt's concept of awakening. The conversion experience was, for Francke, an instantaneous, once-for-all breakthrough of grace. It was experienced at a definite moment in time and space and should later be described to the gathered congregation. This tended to divide sharply those who had had such a conversion experience (the regenerate) from those who could offer no proof of it (the unregenerate). It led moreover to an intolerance of those considered to be unconverted.[90]

Equally distinctive was Francke's downgrading of the intellect and reason as a source of awakening. The emotional and spiritual aspects of conversion became primary and normative. Though Francke himself remained a scholar, his followers tended to fall into intellectual aridity. Given Francke's concept that the conversion experience should express itself in concrete activities for the benefit of souls, Halle developed an acute mission consciousness which was paralleled by its emphasis on practical works of charity, schools, orphanages, and dispensaries.

Yet another brand of pietism developed at Württemberg. Here the separatist tendencies, down-played at Halle, assumed great force. Württemberg pietism, unlike the Halle variety, remained intellectually alive, especially in its efforts to unite science and theology. This attempt ultimately gave rise to chiliastic features and philosophical-mystical tendencies. Also, whereas Halle pietism appealed primarily to the nobility, Württemberg drew most of its adherents from the clergy and middle classes. This gave it a populistic, evangelistic flavor lacking in the north German variety. Nor did Württemberg emphasize the moral rules and regulations advocated by Halle.[91]

The third major branch of pietism was represented by the Moravian Brethren and Count Zinzendorf. This carried to an extreme the pietistic tendencies toward ecumenism, dogmatic indifference, and mission consciousness. The future course of pietism was, to a large extent, determined by the constant clashes between Zinzendorf and Halle.[92]

Finally there emerged a splinter group of pietistic separatists known collectively as radical German pietists. Among these were the Philadelphians, Schwenkfelders, Boehmists and others, all of whom were united by the theosophy of Jacob Boehme which emphasized separatism, universalism, Sophia-mysticism, anti-trinitarianism, the inner light, continuous revelation and inspiration, freedom of the will, and the new birth. In opposition to the three churchly branches of pietism, these left-wingers of the movement ultimately left the established churches to seek their religious ideals.[93]

Pietism then was a many-sided religious phenomenon and, while Henry Melchior Muhlenberg can with justification be considered a pietist, it is difficult to assign him to any one branch of the movement. There are certain evidences to support the contention that Muhlenberg's family background was itself pietistic. Much has been made of the fact, for example, that one of his brothers was named after John Arndt, the founder of the movement. Certainly, too, Muhlenberg was subjected to pietistic influences in his pre-Halle training. Dr. Oporin was, without a doubt, an adherent of Spener's school and all of Muhlenberg's principal patrons held some connection to Halle. Francke would never have dispatched Muhlenberg to the New World missions had he not been sure that he was a worthy representative of pietism. To be sure, Muhlenberg objected to the tag "pietist" and emphatically denied that he was one but so did Spener. The word had been coined as a derogatory term for the followers of the new movement so it is understandable that they should reject it. It also failed to convey any one meaning but frequently referred to the radical, separatist pietists. This gave Muhlenberg, who was himself a strong church person, further reason to reject the term. Regardless of this, it is evident that he was considered a pietist and that he held to some pietistic ideas.

Shortly before he sailed to America, for example, Muhlenberg was denounced to the Ministerium of Hanover for holding pietistic conventicles in Einbeck in violation of Hanoverian law which forbade them.

There is extant an interesting document defending pietism which has been linked to Muhlenberg by some scholars. It is a response to a book published by Balthasar Mentzer in 1740, *Worte der Ermahnung,* attacking the pietists. Among other charges, Mentzer accused them of teaching doctrines contrary to scripture, of hypocritical self-satisfaction in condemning all who disagree with them, and of pharisaical aloofness.[94] He also strongly criticized pietistic notions of sanctification, in particular the claim that the redemptive act was not complete in itself but only insofar as the sinner is converted and sanctified and that a person can attain on this earth complete sanctification and sinlessness.[95] Mentzer likewise took offense in pietistic contentions that an unconverted minister cannot disseminate the word of God efficaciously and that scripture cannot work an effect without a special intervention of the Holy Spirit.[96] Finally Mentzer denounced what he termed 'peculiar doctrines' held by pietists, that God's call to persons is temporary and ceases after a time, that faith must have works to operate efficaciously, and the whole gamut of chiliastic ideas.[97]

Balthasar Mentzer was answered in a pamphlet dated 1741 at Leipzig and Gorlitz under the title "Missive addressed to the Rev. Dr. Balthasar Mentzer, First Court Chaplain of the King of Great Britain, the Elector of Brunswick and Lüneburg; Consistorial Counsellor and General Superintendent of the Duchy of Calenberg; asking for the proofs of his *'Ermahnungsworte'*; and commenting on the special kind of meetings that are held for Christian edification." It was signed simply, D. M. From the beginning this pamphlet was attributed to D(iaconus) M(uhlenberg).[98] There seems to be no reason to doubt this conclusion though positive proof to support Muhlenberg's authorship cannot be produced. Certainly the work is not contrary to Muhlenberg's character. The response is not that of a systematic theologian for it passes over the doctrinal objections raised by Mentzer. Rather it is the work of a man concerned solely with the

promotion of godliness in the practice of life. If Muhlenberg were indeed its author, as this writer is inclined to believe, this ranks as one of the few extant theological works to come from his pen.

The style of the pamphlet is moderate and reasonable, reflecting several points of view strongly held by Muhlenberg in his later life. There is, moreover, nothing in its contents which would contradict his basic beliefs. The author readily admits that abuses have crept into pietism as into any movement. Some of its branches had, indeed, fostered separatism which D. M. strongly condemns.[99] But, he pointed out, separation had in part been occasioned by the mishandling of awakened souls by unconverted preachers. Awakened souls, prone to enthusiasm, posed a special problem for pastoral counseling. They were like children "who, when they have got a penny, carry it off to the fair, expecting that it will buy everything that pleases their fancy."[100] They also fall into the error of condemning those who have not experienced a like eruption of grace, for the internal condition of the soul is not always evidenced by externals.[101] But, rather than suppress the experience of grace in awakenings, the author preferred that these stirrings of the spirit be channeled by experienced and learned pastors. While the laity had a great part to play in matters of faith, it was still up to the pastor to orchestrate the whole, to guide activities within acceptable churchly norms. For this reason, the pastor must himself be regenerate, must have undergone a conversion experience, else he could not presume to direct others in matters of which he is ignorant.

As for doctrinal differences, the pamphlet claimed that pietism had merely recovered the original positions of Luther which were submerged in the polemics of orthodox dogmatism.[102] The author, in response, offered a concise compendium of the essence of the theology taught by pietists:

> These godly men held up the Bible again, and preached in demonstration of the Spirit and of power. They proclaimed that all men should acknowledge their sins, as sins, according to the teaching of the law, and should repent of them; that under this conviction of sin, and with hungering and thirsting

souls, laboring and heavy laden, they should humbly go to Christ, and, as poor, wretched sinners, worthy of condemnation, should be justified by faith. Further, they insisted on it, that, after justification, faith must prove itself by its spiritual fruits and its good works.[103]

D. M.'s harshest words are reserved for unconverted preachers, hirelings, wolves in sheep's clothing, belly worshipers who care more for their own comfort than for the welfare of the flock entrusted to them. Such men had, he claimed, crept into the ministry because of a misunderstanding of the nature of the call. Their office was based merely on the external, mediative call by the church. This, D. M. asserted, was essential, but more was needed. There were two other aspects to a valid call: the candidate must have natural gifts in proportion to the task entrusted to him, and he must possess the spiritual gifts necessary to the office.[104] Such men could be produced by proper training not merely in the fundamentals of the law but in experiential knowledge of faith. While he did not deny that unconverted preachers could do some good despite themselves, this was limited and dependent on the grace of God. If they were dead, they could not efficaciously preach the word which was the primary ministerial obligation. Instead they merely preached abstract concepts stultified by a philosophical coating. Correct preaching was simply heart talking to heart. A pastor mediated the word not through technical jargon but through the power of the Spirit of God.

On the whole, this response to Mentzer reflects a type of pietism conformable to the teachings of Luther. The pastor occupies an important place in the process of salvation. But while he is expected to have a command of theology as a scientific discipline, he must also be versed, through personal experience, in the science of the heart. Extremes of the awakening process are condemned as is the tendency toward separatism. And while Muhlenberg stresses that works must follow justification, he nowhere denies that a person achieves salvation by faith alone. Similar to Luther himself, he holds that works must of necessity result as a testimony to the faith of the believer. A conversion experience is required, but there is no

evidence that this must be a sudden, definite event which may be used as proof of conversion. Indeed, the author states that externals need not necessarily indicate the interior condition of the soul. Muhlenberg was a pietist in the generic sense of the term; nevertheless, he cannot be classified as a Halle pietist, or indeed as a pietist of any particular stripe. Perhaps the best way to describe him would be to call him a moderate churchly pietist.

When Muhlenberg boarded the ship to America, he had already formed his theological and ecclesiological positions. From then on the gifts cultivated in his youth were put to the test time and again. From his university days at Göttingen and his schooling in Einbeck and Zellerfelde, Muhlenberg acquired a broad linguistic and theological background. His training was adequate to produce a first-rate theologian, but his chosen arena of work would leave him little more than time for pragmatic decisions. He was an opportunist as can be seen in his dealings with his patrons and was possessed of abundant diplomacy as well. From Halle he acquired a knowledge of charitable works and medical ministrations which he put to good use in his New World mission. His experiences at the charity schools in Göttingen, Halle, and Grosshennersdorf impressed him with the importance of a Christian education for youth. His training imbued him with a pragmatic pietism which was tempered by the moderation of his cautious personality. And his acquaintance with the powerful in both church and state in Germany bolstered his position in the colonies as he tried to establish a viable Lutheranism in the New World.

NOTES

[1] Henry Melchior Muhlenberg, *Heinrich Melchior Muhlenberg, Patriarch der Lutherischen Kirche Nordamericka's. Selbstbiographie, 1711–1743. Aus dem Missionsarchive der Franckischen Stiftungen zu Halle* (Allentown: Brobst, Diehl & Co., 1881), edited by W. Germann, pp. 185–86, n. 6. Hereafter referred to as *Selbstbiographie.*

[2] William J. Mann, *The Life and Times of Henry Melchior Mulenberg* (Philadelphia: G. W. Frederick, 1887), p. 2.

[3] Ibid.

[4]Ibid., p. 1.
[5]Ibid., pp. 3–4.
[6]*Selbstbiographie*, pp. 183–84.
[7]Mann, p. 3.; see also Henry Melchior Muhlenberg, *The Journals of Henry Melchior Muhlenberg in Three Volumes*, trans. by Theodore G. Tappert & John W. Doberstein, vol. I (Philadelphia: Muhlenberg Press, 1942), I. Hereafter referred to as *I Journals*. W. Germann received a letter from Senior Lic. Elster at Einbeck who examined the church archives of the *Neustädter (St. Marien) Kirche* for records pertaining to the Muhlenberg family. A few references were discovered relating to a Nichol. Melchior Mühlenberg listed as a *Bürger, Brauer* and *Diaconus. Brauer* was merely an honorary title given to Einbeck citizens indicating that they possessed the ancient town right of conducting a brewery should they so desire. In Muhlenberg's case, the right was never exercised. *Diaconus* did not refer to a spiritual office but to a lay position within the church. Another entry lists the children of Nic. Melchior Möhlenberg. Given the uncertain spellings of names practiced in those times, this too, in all probability, refers to Muhlenberg's father. *Selbstbiographie*, p. 183, n. 1.
[8]*I Journals*, p. 1.
[9]*Selbstbiographie*, pp. 183–84.
[10]*I Journals*, p. 1.
[11]*Selbstbiographie*, p. 185, n. 2.
[12]Ibid., p. 183; *I Journals*, p. 1; Mann, p. 3.
[13]*I Journals*, p. 1.
[14]Ibid.
[15]Ibid.
[16]*Selbstbiographie*, p. 185, n. 4.
[17]*I Journals*, p. 2.
[18]Mann, p. 6.
[19]*I Journals*, p. 2.
[20]*Selbstbiographie*, p. 195, n. 6.
[21]Ibid., pp. 195–96, n. 6. It is possible, too, that Raphelius had pietistic leanings. At least Germann states that he was hauled before the Consistory of Hanover to explain a tract he had published on the Sabbath.
[22]*I Journals*, p. 2.
[23]Ibid.
[24]Ibid.
[25]Ibid.
[26]*Selbstbiographie*, p. 5.
[27]Ibid.
[28]*I Journals*, p. 3; *Selbstbiographie*, p. 5.
[29]*Selbstbiographie*, p. 6.
[30]Ibid.: *I Journals*, p. 3.
[31]Mann, p. 9.
[32]*I Journals*, p. 3.
[33]*Selbstbiographie*, p. 6.
[34]Ibid.; *I Journals*, p. 4 records the year as 1737.

[35]*I Journals,* p. 4; there were two branches of the Reuss family, which dates from the twelfth century in Thuringia. The older Reuss line had its capital at Greiz, while the younger line centered about Gera.

[36]*I Journals,* p. 4.

[37]Ibid.; *Selbstbiographie,* p. 7.

[38]Mann, p. 11.

[39]Ibid.; *I Journals,* p. 4.

[40]*Selbstbiographie,* p. 8.

[41]Ibid.

[42]*Selbstbiographie,* p. 198, n. 9; and p. 199, n. 10.

[43]Ibid., p. 9.

[44]Mann, p. 9.

[45]Carl Mirbt, "Pietism," in the *New Schaff-Herzog Encyclopedia of Religious Knowledge,* IX, 1911 edition, p. 55.

[46]Ibid.

[47]Ibid.

[48]Martin Schmidt and Wilhelm Jannasch, *Das Zeitalter des Pietismus* (Bremen: Carl Schünemann Verlag, 1965), p. 66.

[49]Ibid.

[50]Ibid., p. xxxvi.

[51]*Selbstbiographie,* p. 10.

[52]*Selbstbiographie,* p. 10.

[53]Ibid., p. 11.

[54]Ibid.

[55]Mann, p. 17; *I Journals,* p. 5.

[56]*Selbstbiographie,* p. 202, n. 13.

[57]Ibid., p. 13.

[58]Ibid., p. 202, n. 13.

[59]Mann, p. 20.

[60]Ibid., pp. 21–22.

[61]Cf. E. Ernst Stoeffler, *The Rise of Evangelical Pietism* (Leiden: E. J. Brill, 1965), p. 6. Stoeffler's book is the only one of its kind in English, for English and American historians, theologians, and sociologists have sadly neglected pietism. Though he does produce some convincing evidence for interplay between Reformed and English Puritan pietism, he fails to show any real connection with the Lutheran variety. Moreover, he really fails to disprove convincingly the contention that what he terms evangelical pietism did not arise from local characteristics within the histories of the English, Dutch, and German churches. Bullinger and Bucer seem to be central to his argument of transition, but he merely states this as a fact in a relatively brief passage without fully developing the idea. Certainly it is tempting to seek some connection between Puritanism and pietism which bear such close affinities to each other. It is possible, however, that in so emphasizing their similarities, Stoeffler has chosen to ignore their differences which are considerable.

[62]Stoeffler, p. 13.

[63]Ibid., p. 14.

[64]Ibid., p. 17.

[65]Ibid.

[66]Cf. Ernst Benz, "Pietist and Puritan Sources of Early Protestant World Missions," *Church History* 20 (June 1951): 28–55.

[67]Stoeffler, p. 19.

[68]Ibid., p. 21.

[69]Ibid., p. 22.

[70]Schmidt and Jannasch, p. xlv.

[71]Cf. Theodore G. Tappert, "Orthodoxism, Pietism and Rationalism, 1580–1830," chap. 2 in Harold C. Letts, ed., *Christian Social Responsibility: A Symposium in Three Volumes, Vol. 2. The Lutheran Heritage* (Philadelphia: Muhlenberg Press, 1957), pp. 38–39.

[72]Arthur M. Bowser, "The Great Awakening of the Evangelical Lutheran Church in the Middle Colonies, 1742–1764," master's thesis. Pennsylvania State University, 1968.

[73]Tappert, pp. 44–45; Stoeffler, p. 16.

[74]Stoeffler, p. 16.

[75]Schmidt and Jannasch, p. xxv; Stoeffler, p. 191.

[76]Stoeffler, p. 196.

[77]Ibid., p. 194.

[78]Ibid., p. 196.

[79]Ibid., p. 198.

[80]Ibid., p. 199.

[81]Ibid., p. 203; see also Martin Schmidt, "Pietism," *Encyclopedia of the Lutheran Church* 3 (1965): 101.

[82]Stoeffler, p. 207.

[83]Ibid.

[84]Cf. Mirbt, pp. 54–55.

[85]For a modern edition of this book, see Theodore G. Tappert, ed. and trans., *Pia Desideria* (Philadelphia: Fortress Press, 1964).

[86]Cf. Mirbt, pp. 56–57.

[87]Stoeffler, pp. 235–36.

[88]Nicholas Kurtz, *Church History,* vol. 3, trans. John Macpherson (New York: Funk & Wagnalls, 1890), p. 111.

[89]Mirbt, p. 55.

[90]Mirbt, pp. 57–58; see also John T. McNeill, *Modern Christian Movements* (Philadelphia: the Westminster Press, 1954), chap. 2, "German Pietism," p. 64.

[91]Mirbt, pp. 58–59; McNeill, pp. 69–70.

[92]McNeill, p. 68; Mirbt, p. 59.

[93]For a history of these left-wing movements, see Chauncey David Ensign, "Radical German Pietism (ca. 1675–ca. 1760)," Ph.D. dissertation, Boston University, 1955. For yet another view see Ronald A. Knox, *Enthusiasm: A Chapter in the History of Religion: With Special Reference to the XVII and XVIII Centuries* (New York: Oxford University Press, 1950). Although Monsignor Knox, an outstanding English Catholic historian, was writing in a polemical and unsympathe-

tic vein, the book is of value for it traces enthusiasm from the rise of the primitive church and shows its various manifestations in all churches.

[94]C. W. Schaeffer, trans., "Muhlenberg's Defense of Pietism," *Lutheran Church Review* 12 (1893). 351–52.

[95]Ibid., p. 352.

[96]Ibid.

[97]Ibid., p. 353.

[98]This, for example is asserted by the *Acta Historica Ecclesia* with which assertion Schaeffer concurs.

[99]Schaeffer, p. 356.

[100]Ibid., p. 357.

[101]Ibid., pp. 358–59.

[102]Ibid., p. 360.

[103]Ibid., pp. 361.

[104]Ibid., p. 369.

[2]

American Lutheranism before Muhlenberg

By the time of Muhlenberg's arrival in English America in 1742, Pennsylvania had emerged as the focal point of German immigration and hence of Lutheran activity. Nevertheless the Lutheran church in America actually began in other colonies, such as New York.

In 1609 Henry Hudson, sailing for the Dutch East India Company in search of the elusive all-water route to Asia, chanced upon the river which now bears his name. Using Hudson's discovery as a basis for colonial claims, the Dutch sent other expeditions to the same area in 1610, 1611, and 1613. At some point during the last of these voyages, they erected Fort Nassau (later Fort Orange) in the vicinity of what is now Albany, while a few rude huts rose on Manhattan Island to serve as centers for Indian trade. Thirteen shipowners from Amsterdam organized the New Netherland Company in 1614, receiving an exclusive three-year trading monopoly in the new Dutch colonial possessions. When their charter expired in 1617, however, it was not renewed by the authorities in Holland. Instead a new venture, the Dutch West India Company, organized by William Usselinx, was chartered by the States General in 1621 with an exclusive monopoly on all colonization and trade in the new world. By 1624 some thirty families, mostly Dutch Reformed but with a scattering of German and Scandinavian Lutherans, sailed to New Netherlands, the majority of whom located at Fort

42

Nassau.[1] Two years later, Peter Minuit, recently appointed director general of New Netherlands, landed on Manhattan Island with still more immigrants. Once he had completed his fabled bargain purchase from the Indians, Minuit established the new and commercially promising settlement of New Amsterdam. The dominant church element in the colony was Reformed, though there were some Lutherans.[2]

From its inception, New Netherlands pursued a restrictive and oppressive religious policy which rivaled that of the New England colonies. By the Provisional Regulations for the Colonists of 1624, it was stipulated that no form of divine worship other than the Reformed variety was to be tolerated, while only the Dutch Reformed Church could be established by law.[3] Despite this handicap, Lutheran settlers continued to arrive and, in addition to older settlements at Fort Nassau and New Amsterdam, soon established themselves at Loonenberg (Athens), Hackensack, Esopus (Kingston), and Bergen (Jersey City).[4] Meanwhile, in 1646 crusty old Peter Stuyvesant was appointed director of New Netherlands. Three years later New Netherland Lutherans first petitioned the Amsterdam Consistory for a pastor to serve their religious needs as well as for the right to publicly exercise their religion.[5] Fearing involvement in the complex colonial political and religious situation, the consistory failed to act upon their request.

In 1653 the Lutherans again broached the matter of religious toleration, presenting two petitions to Governor Stuyvesant to be forwarded to Holland, one addressed to the directors of the Dutch West India Company, the other to the States General. Again they requested freedom of worship and permission to call and maintain a minister of their own religious persuasion.[6] A third petition asked the New Amsterdam Consistory to provide a minister at a stipulated salary, adding somewhat optimistically that they had Stuyvesant's promise "not to obstruct us if we ourselves could obtain permission from the supreme authorities."[7] Under great pressure from the colonial Reformed clergy, the Dutch authorities refused the petitions outright.[8] Instead the consistory advised New Netherlands Lutherans not to seek public official sanction for their project but to arrange matters for themselves quietly, hoping for tacit permission and toleration from the directors.[9] Consequently Paulus Schrick, a lay leader of New Amsterdam Lutherans, began to conduct private religious services in the colony in 1655. Tacit permission for this violation of law was not forthcoming for, on February 1, 1656, the New Netherlands Council issued an edict forbidding either public or private conventicles and imposing stiff fines on both preacher and participants.[10] Lutherans protested the severity of this act to the directors in Holland who in turn chided Stuyvesant for his stiff-necked attitude and urged him to tolerate private, though not public, Lutheran worship.[11]

The Lutherans were determined to have public worship as well. Perhaps encouraged by the Dutch conquest of New Sweden in 1655 and the subsequent tolerance accorded their Lutheran coreligionists within the Delaware provinces, the Amsterdam Consistory dispatched the Rev. John Ernst Gutwasser to New Amsterdam in June, 1657. Gutwasser, however, never had an opportunity to begin his ministry for he fell ill soon after landing. Upon his recovery in 1659, he was deported from the colony.[12] Stuyvesant's actions in this affair, though not the heavy-handed methods he employed, won hearty approval from the directors and effectively ended, for a time, Lutheran struggles for religious freedom.[13] In 1662 Stuyvesant issued yet another sweeping proclamation banning the preaching of any but Reformed doctrine "either in houses, barns, ships or yachts, in the woods or fields."[14]

However, the days of Dutch control of New Netherlands were drawing to a close. English encroachments on Dutch territory in what is now Westchester County and on Long Island had continued for some time. The English coveted New Netherlands both for its splendid deep water port of New Amsterdam and as a means of completing a territorial linkage between their northern and southern colonial holdings. Imperial officials reasoned that ownership of this vitally strategic area would also eliminate an irritating escape hatch from the Navigation Acts and thus terminate illegal colonial trade outside the empire. The British therefore moved against New Amsterdam on September 7, 1664, forcing Peter Stuyvesant to surrender the colony to a superior force without a struggle. With this event the Dutch colonial empire in North America ceased to exist.

King Charles II granted these new English holdings to his younger brother James, Duke of York and later King James II. Both the colony and its chief city were renamed New York in his honor. James appointed Colonel Richard Nicolls to rule in his stead as New York's first governor. Among Nicholls's first official acts was the institution of British civil and criminal codes embodied in the "Duke's Laws." Included among them was a provision guaranteeing freedom of conscience to all who professed themselves to be Christians with the exception of Roman Catholics.[15] Sensing an end to the disabilities under which they had labored for so long, New York Lutherans quickly requested and were granted by Governor Nicolls, permission to call a regular minister through the consistory of Amsterdam. After a delay of five years, their request was finally answered in the person of the Reverend Jacob Fabritius who arrived in New York City on February 19, 1669.[16]

A Silesian by birth, Fabritius had ministered in Hungary prior to the Turkish invasion of that country. Unfortunately, he soon proved himself unsuited for his New World post. He quarreled continuously with the civil authorities and occasioned great scandal and dissension among his parishioners by his imprudent actions including excessive tippling. By 1670 New York Lutherans could tolerate no more and urgently petitioned the consistory for his removal. The following year, still having received no satisfaction from Holland, they presented their grievances to Governor Lovelace. Finally Fabritius resigned to labor in New Sweden. He was replaced in 1671 by Reverend Bernardus Arensius, a Dutchman.[17]

Arensius proved to be both competent and faithful, serving his charges well until his death in 1691. Because of the enormous territorial extent of his parish, Arensius spent the summer months at New York City and the winters at Fort Nassau, now called Albany. For eleven years after his death, New York Lutherans remained pastorless until, in 1702, they prevailed upon the Reverend Andreas Rudman, Swedish provost and pastor of the Gloria Dei (Old Swedes) Church at Wicaco, to visit them. Though failing health prevented him from assuming further ministerial burdens in New York, Rudman did arrange to extend the New York call to Justus Falckner, a resident of New Hanover near Philadelphia. Falckner, the son of a Lutheran pastor at Zwickau, Saxony, had previously studied theology at Halle. Instead of seeking ordination, however, he migrated to Pennsylvania in 1700 with his brother Daniel, an agent for the Frankford Land Company, then engaged in the development of Germantown in Pennsylvania.[18] On November 24, 1703, Rudman and his two Swedish Lutheran assistants, the Reverend Andreas Sandel, and the Reverend Eric Tobias Björk, acting under authority granted by the archbishop of Upsala, ordained Justus Falckner to the Lutheran ministry at Gloria Dei Church. This marked the first Lutheran ordination ceremony in the New World.[19]

Falckner labored in New York until his death in 1723. In addition to New York City and Albany, his parish included congregations at Loonenberg, Klinckenburg (Four Mile Point), and Pieter Lassens (near New Hamburg) in New York, as well as Hackensack, the Raritan Valley, and Ramapo (Mahwah) in New Jersey.[20] During his ministry, the flood tide of Palatine immigration arrived in New York considerably increasing the Lutheran population of the colony.

This mass migration of German Palatines initiated one of the most fascinating periods in colonial history. Certainly it must rank among the greatest mass folk movements in modern history. Though estimates vary widely, it is likely that between May and December of 1709, some 13,500 Palatines migrated from their Rhineland homes to the British Isles.[21] There were diverse reasons for this human flood. In the first place, the unfortunate people of the Palatinate dwelt in the fulcrum of incessant warfare. From 1618 to 1648, this area was ravaged by both Catholic and Protestant armies fighting the Thirty Years War. The Treaty of Westphalia terminated the conflict in 1648 by arriving on the formula *"cuius regio, eius religio,"* which stipulated that the populace should adopt the religion of the ruling prince of any given territory. But peace was purchased at a heavy toll in blood and treasure. Whole areas of the Palatinate suffered virtual depopulation from war, disease, and famine, while the widespread destruction of homes, crops, and livestock brought on an economic and social crisis which rent the whole fabric of society.[22] Nor did permanent peace result from the Westphalia treaty. Although the French continued sporadic raids throughout the 1670s, in 1680 and again in 1688–89, the armies of Louis XIV poured across the Palatinate in force pursuing a scorched-earth policy which caused additional devastation. Peace finally came in 1697 only to be shattered anew ten years later in the War of the Spanish Succession.[23]

Nature herself added to these man-made hardships for the winter of 1708–1709 was one of the longest and most bitter in memory. So cold did it become that even the sea froze along the coast lines, while food and fuel were in short supply.[24] Adding to these woes were the inefficiency and corruption of the petty princes of the Palatinate states, who, in slavish imitation of the splendor of Versailles, constructed a luxuriously extravagant court life which could only be supported by the imposition of heavy taxes on an already overburdened and impoverished populace.[25] A land hunger which looked to America as a source of new, fertile farm land unavailable in the Palatinate also encouraged emigration.[26]

Yet another decisive factor was the advertising and promotion techniques engaged in by land companies and proprietors who sought to attract settlers to their colonial grants. Too often these gardens of Eden turned out in reality to be overrun with brambles, while the terms of settlement, which looked so reasonably attractive on paper, proved to be almost impossible to fulfill. Among others, William Penn's *Account of the Province of Pennsylvania in America* (1681), Daniel Pastorius's *Umständige geographische Beschreibung* (1700), and *Curieuse Nachricht von Pennsylvania* (1702) by Daniel Falckner, stirred up considerable interest in the New World with their glowing accounts of conditions in America and of the opportunities open to those who would grasp them.[27] Perhaps the most influential of these circular reports was Joshua Kocherthal's *Aussführlich, und unständlicher Bericht von der berühmten Landschafft Carolina, in dem engelländischen America gelegen* (1704). Though Kocherthal had never himself visited the Carolinas, the attractive picture he painted of conditions there was an important factor in the ensuing migrations.[28] This was reinforced by his hints that Queen Anne herself was favorable to German migration and ready to provide moral and financial support. There seemed to be some basis to this for Anne had married a German Lutheran, Prince George of Denmark, and had provided him with a Lutheran court chaplain, the Reverend Anton Wilhem Boehme.[29] In reality, however, Anne had given no such assurances.

Parliament, infused as it was with the mercantile spirit and hence eager to attract population to its American empire, had in 1709 passed a naturalization act which allowed foreign Protestants who would take an oath of allegiance to the British crown and receive in public the Anglican communion to become citizens of the empire.[30] But Parliament was completely unprepared for the massive migration which followed.

In 1708 the Reverend Joshua Kocherthal, a Lutheran minister, petitioned the crown to settle a group of refugee Palatines in the American colonies. This request was granted by the Board of Trade which decided to locate the group on the Hudson River "where they might be useful to this kingdom, particularly in the production of naval stores, and as a frontier against the French and their Indians."[31] Governor Lovelace of New York transported Kocherthal's group, which had landed on Long Island in December, 1709, to the mouth of the Quassaick Creek on the Hudson, the site of the present city of Newburg.[32]

Meanwhile, further numbers of Palatines poured into England. By October, 1709, there were 13,500 of them, 3,500 of whom were Roman Catholic and thus suffered deportation back to the continent.[33] Still 10,000 remained placing a severe strain on the resources of the government. Some were housed in warehouses or private homes; others sought shelter in temporary tent cities which sprang up around London. Since no plans had been made for their support or colonization, they suffered mightily from want and deprivation. Private charity supplemented government doles to some extent and, at first the English people responded warmly to their plight. But the mood gradually turned ugly. The British lower classes were enraged at the diversion of government funds from their own needs and armed mobs attacked Palatine camps. When the government attempted to settle the Germans within the British Isles, riots broke out.[34] Finally, in October, 1709, Parliament issued a proclamation circulated throughout the Rhine Valley prohibiting further immigration into Britain.[35]

The British attempted various schemes to settle the Palatines. Some they sent to Ireland. Others they placed in English counties on the inducement of a government subsidy of three pounds sterling per head to any who would welcome them. Still others they settled in New Bern in the Carolinas.[36] The majority, however, boarded ship for New York.

At this time, the kingdom of Sweden held a virtual monopoly on the world production of naval stores. Thus, contrary to the tenets of sound mercantilistic policy, the English navy found itself dependent on a rival power for a vitally strategic raw material. It occurred to the Board of Trade that it could solve both the Palatinate problem and the lack of naval stores in one stroke. Plans developed to settle the Palatines on the Hudson River where they could, as indentured servants, work off their obligations to the crown by the production of naval stores. The terms of indenture were harsh. Settlement was allowed only on lands chosen by New York's governor. The Palatines could not leave the settlements without his permission and, while there, had to work on the production of naval stores, like it or not. When they had fulfilled the indenture, though no set time was stipulated, the governor would grant each person forty acres of land free of quit rents for seven years.[37]

The first group of 2,800 arrived in June of 1710. By October they were established ninety-two miles above New York City on a 6,300 acre tract along the west bank of the Hudson and a 6,000 acre east bank tract purchased by the province from Robert Livingston.[38] In 1711 there were seven German villages, with approximately 2,000 Germans, along the Hudson, the chief of which were East and West Camp.[39]

Governor Robert Hunter's tar scheme was doomed to failure. Farmers by trade, the Palatines deeply resented forced labor in manufacturing. Moreover, government subsidies in foodstuffs were poor in quality and insufficient in quantity. When the Tories came to power in the English parliamentary elections of 1710, they immediately moved against the Palatine plan. Presenting the proposed Palatine settlement plan as a plot to undermine the established church by introducing large numbers of aliens into the empire, the Tories eventually won the queen over to their side.[40] In February, 1712, Parliament repealed the Naturalization Act of 1709 and voted to discontinue further subsidies to the Palatine project.[41] Governor Hunter continued to support the Palatines from his own income at a total expenditure of £ 32,144 until September 12, 1712.[42] After this date all payments were terminated and the Palatines were given leave to settle anywhere in New York or New Jersey with the governor's permission. Evidently Hunter wished to control migration should the naval stores project be revived in the future.

Much to Hunter's anger and dismay, many Palatines moved into the Schoharie Valley, without his permission, purchasing from the Indians the land which was once part of the now repudiated extravagant grants. In 1714 Hunter ceded this territory to seven Albany partners who in the following year demanded that the Palatines purchase, lease, or vacate their farms. After a period of violence and continued opposition to the partners' claims, the Palatines sent deputies to London to plead their cause in 1718. Among these men was John Conrad Weiser, the father of Muhlenberg's future father-in-law. Imprisonment for debt was their only reward. The crown ordered the Palatines to pay up or vacate. Some stayed in the Schoharie Valley eventually coming to terms with their landlords. Others moved to the Stone Arabia or Palatine bridge patents in New York. Still others settled in the Raritan Valley of New Jersey. In 1723 a group of fifteen Schoharie German families moved to the Tulpehocken region of Pennsylvania at Governor Keith's invitation. Fifty more families arrived there in 1729, including the family of Conrad Weiser. New York's harsh and unjust treatment of the Palatines occasioned this shift in immigration patterns.

With the spread of Palatine settlements in New York and New

Jersey, ministerial burdens increased accordingly. By 1711 Kocherthal had settled at New Town (West Camp) from which he served Lutheran congregations in Queensbury (East Camp), Schoharie, and Rhinebeck.[43] The remainder of the congregations were served by Justus Falckner until June 24, 1719 when Kocherthal's death placed the entire burden on Falckner's shoulders.[44] Falckner died in 1723 leaving New York without a regularly ordained resident Lutheran pastor. For a time between 1724 and 1734, Justus's brother, Daniel Falckner, ministered to the Raritan congregations though it is doubtful that he ever received ordination.[45] Finally in 1725 the Reverend Wilhelm Christoph Berkenmeyer accepted a call to New York and New Jersey from the Hamburg consistory, thus opening a period of relative stability for the Lutherans of those provinces.

At approximately the same time as the Lutherans were settling along the Hudson River, others were moving into the area surrounding the Delaware River. The brief history of this Swedish colony in the New World originates with William Usselinx, the organizer of the rival Dutch West India Company. In 1624 Gustavus Adolphus, king of Sweden, commissioned Usselinx to begin a Swedish company whose purpose was to promote trade with Asia, Africa, and America. Somewhat of a visionary, Usselinx decided to expand the concept of his proposed company into a great cooperative Protestant trading and colonization association. With this in mind he sought French, Spanish, Portuguese, and Dutch support but to no avail.[46] Before he could sign the final charter for the company, Gustavus Adolphus fell at the Battle of Lützen in 1632. Usselinx then unsuccessfully sought support from the Germanic Protestant League and cooperation from the Dutch West India Company. Finally Samuel Blommaert and Peter Minuit, the former director general of the New Netherlands colony, organized a trading company with joint Dutch and Swedish financial backing, receiving in 1637 a charter from the Swedish government to colonize and trade along the Delaware River. Minuit himself commanded the first two ships of this expedition, the *Kalmar Nyckel* and the *Fogel Grip,* which sailed into the Delaware in March, 1638.[47] Land was purchased from the Indians and Fort

Christina was erected on the site of present-day Wilmington, Delaware. A second expedition in 1639–40 brought to the colony the Reverend Reorus Torkillus, a thirty-year-old native of Fässberg, who continued his ministry among the Lutherans of New Sweden until his death in 1643. To him belongs the distinction of being the first regularly ordained Lutheran clergyman in the American colonies.[48] When Dutch stockholders withdrew their backing in February, 1641, the company was reorganized as an exclusively Swedish venture known as the New Sweden Company. John Printz, an exceptionally capable administrator, now received an appointment as governor. On February 15, 1643, he arrived in the colony in the company of a new Lutheran pastor, the Reverend John Campanius Holm.[49] Unlike its neighboring Dutch rival, the colony of New Sweden, while conscientiously providing for the spiritual needs of the Lutheran majority, granted freedom of worship to the Reformed minority.[50]

In all probability Torkillus had already built a rudimentary church in Fort Christina from which he conducted divine services. Governor Printz, however, removed the seat of colonial government from Christina to the island of Tinicum in the Delaware River, about nine miles southwest of the present city of Philadelphia.[51] Holm accompanied the governor to Tinicum and there erected a church in 1643.[52] In accordance with his instructions, Holm energetically catechized the Indians, even translating Luther's *Small Catechism* into their language; but his New World ministry was shortlived. In 1647 the Reverend Lars Carlson Lock, a Finn, arrived to replace Holm who returned to Sweden the following year. Lock received additional help in 1654 with the arrival of two more pastors, the Reverend Matthias Nertannius and the Reverend Peter Hjort.[53]

At this time relations rapidly deteriorated between the colonies of New Sweden and New Netherlands. The Swedes had settled on land which the Dutch claimed through the voyages of Henry Hudson. In an attempt to prevent a possible Dutch enforcement of this claim, Governor Printz erected a series of block houses at Varkens Kill (Salem Creek), Upland, New Gothenburg on Tinicum Island and Fort New Krisholm near the mouth of the Schuylkill River. Peter Stuyvesant countered these aggressive moves by constructing Fort Beversrede across the Schuylkill in present Philadelphia. Though the Swedes captured and burned Beversrede in May and again in November of 1648 they were unable to dislodge the Dutch. Stuyvesant then erected Fort Casimir (New Castle) in 1651 to control the approaches to New Sweden and choke off supplies to the colony. Three years later John Classon Rising, who had succeeded Printz as governor, temporarily captured Fort Casimir. The following year Stuyvesant led an expedition which recaptured Casimir and took Fort Christina thus ending Swedish rule in North America.

Though for political reasons the Dutch decided to allow their new Swedish subjects along the Delaware free practice of their Lutheran religion, they permitted the presence of but one Lutheran pastor in the region. Consequently both Nertannius and Hjort were deported, leaving Lock alone in his labors.[54] In 1664 after the British seized New Sweden from the Dutch, all restrictions were again lifted from the Lutherans. Seven years later the Reverend Jacob Fabritius, who had just resigned his New York pastorate, arrived on the Delaware. Lock and Fabritius divided the colony into two parishes to promote more efficient administration, Lock taking the upper parish with churches at Tinicum and Wicaco (1669) while Fabritius labored in the lower parish of New Castle and Tranhook (Fort Christina, Wilmington).[55]

On August 24, 1682, the duke of York conveyed to William Penn the region along the western shore of the Delaware, which included much of New Sweden. From this time on, the colony's fortunes were closely bound to those of its larger neighbor, Pennsylvania. This area, which became the colony of Delaware, had a separate colonial assembly sitting at New Castle but was under the jurisdiction of the governor of Pennsylvania. With the onset of Penn's enlightened rule, German and English settlers entered the area, swelling the Lutheran population accordingly though there was no corresponding increase in the ministerial supply. Fabritius's active ministry came to an end in 1683 when he became totally blind. Lock's death five years later in 1688 left

New Sweden without a regularly ordained Lutheran minister for the first time since the inception of the colony. For eight years the colonists petitioned the Swedish crown for replacements. Because New Sweden had passed from its control and the number of Swedes migrating to the New World was minimal, the Swedish government had seemingly lost interest in the project. Eventually in 1696 King Charles XI of Sweden dispatched the Reverend Andreas Rudman, the Reverend Erick Björk and the Reverend Jonas Auren to the colonies.[56] Rudman served as provost of the Swedish pastors, taking up residence at Gloria Dei Church in Wicaco while Björk went to Wilmington. Jonas Auren served a Swedish-Finnish congregation at Elk River, Maryland, until 1706 when he transferred to Racoon in New Jersey.[57] In failing health, Rudman appealed to Upsala for a successor. One appeared in 1702 in the person of the Reverend Andreas Sandel who took over duties at Gloria Dei. From July, 1702 to November, 1703, Rudman ministered to Lutherans in New York City, then returned to semiretirement in Philadelphia where he died in 1708.[58] After his death, Björk held the office of provost until his return to Sweden in 1714. He was replaced by the Reverend Andrew Hesselius and the Reverend Abraham Lidenius.[59] Hesselius succeeded Björk at Wilmington where he remained until 1723.[60] Lidenius labored at Racoon and Pennsneck, New Jersey until 1724. Both then returned to Sweden.[61] In 1719 the Reverend John Lidman replaced Sandel in Wicaco, ministering there until 1723. The Reverend Samuel Hesselius, brother of Andrew, labored first in Neshaminy and Manathanium near Pottstown then in 1723 replaced his brother at Wilmington. He, too, returned to Sweden in 1731.[62] Other Swedish pastors who labored in America prior to Muhlenberg's arrival included the Reverend John Enberg, who succeeded Samuel Hesselius at Wilmington in 1732, the Reverend John Dylander, pastor at Wicaco from 1737 until his death in 1741, and the Reverend Peter Tranberg, pastor at Racoon and Pennsneck from 1725 to 1740, then minister at Wilmington until his death in 1748.[63]

Although it is evident that Swedish Lutherans in America were well provided with a ministerial supply, the Swedish Lutheran church failed to sink deep roots in American soil and eventually merged into the Episcopal church. One obvious reason for this was the termination of large-scale Swedish immigration after New Sweden fell to the Dutch. The most important causes, however, lie in the very nature of the Swedish Lutheran church. In essence it was much more closely linked to the Church of England than to its religious counterparts in Germany. As in England, the king of Sweden functioned as chief bishop and head of the church, exercising his spiritual authority through the Archbishop of Upsala. Like the Anglicans, too, the Swedes retained the episcopal hierarchy of old Roman Catholicism along with the variety and richness of its liturgical life. Authority was invested in strictly hierarchical lines. Though one of the colonial ministers always served as provost, his position was merely executive, not legislative. Decisions touching on substantive matters could only be reached in Sweden, and despite the slowness of communications, Wicaco could not take action until it had been ordered from Upsala. It is true that the colonial Swedish pastors did perform a unique ordination ceremony at Philadelphia in 1703, but they did not do so on their own authority but on authorization from Sweden. Like the Anglicans, the Swedes made no attempt to establish a native clergy for this would lessen the bonds of authority from Upsala. Moreover, colonial Swedish pastors did not, for the most part, come to the New World to settle but instead looked upon their tenure of office in America as a stepping stone to higher ecclesiastical rewards in their European homeland. As a result, their pastorates were short-lived, and ministerial stability was never really achieved.

The middle colonies of New York, New Jersey, Delaware, and later Pennsylvania, contained a significant number of Lutherans served by pastors sent from Europe. Quite the opposite was true in New England where, prior to the American Revolution and for some time thereafter, Lutherans were a negligible element. New Englanders neither attracted nor welcomed German immigration. For this reason German Lutherans migrated to the more religiously and ethnically heterogeneous middle and southern colonies.

One exception to this rule was the colony at Waldoborough in the region of Maine, settled in 1739 by a group of German immigrants under the leadership of Samuel Waldo. Forty Lutheran families from Saxony and Brunswick moved there in 1740 accompanied by their minister, the Reverend Tobias Wagner, a Württemberg clergyman. Wagner remained until 1743 when he moved with his family to Pennsylvania, ministering for a time in the Tulpehocken region. Meanwhile ministerial duties were performed by a layman, Johann Ulmer, at whose urgings the congregation erected a church. In 1762 the Reverend John M. Schaeffer, a former pastor in New York City, accepted a call to Waldoborough.[64]

The southern colonies, however, proved more receptive to Lutheran immigrants than did New England. For the most part German Lutheran immigration to the two northernmost of these, Maryland and Virginia, came indirectly through the province of Pennsylvania. As the best farm lands in eastern Pennsylvania were occupied, subsequent immigrants from Germany and some long-established residents of the province who desired larger land holdings, began to cross the Susquehanna and push southward through the Shenandoah Valley. Both the governments of Virginia and Maryland eagerly encouraged this movement by offering cheap land on easy terms in their western frontier regions. British prohibition of settlement west of the Susquehanna further strengthened this southern migration.

At some time in the early 1730s a small community of Lutherans settled at Monocacy Creek, near the present town of Frederick, Maryland. They formally organized a congregation in 1738 which was moved to the flourishing town of Frederick in 1752. Prior to Muhlenberg's arrival, from 1734 to 1743, the Reverend John Caspar Stoever, Jr. occasionally served the Monocacy congregation from his Pennsylvania base, but efforts to procure a permanent pastor failed.[65]

Other Pennsylvania Germans located on the Conococheague Creek, about eight miles southwest of present Hagerstown, Maryland. There they built a union church in cooperation with their Reformed neighbors but were also unable to get a permanent pastor. Instead they were periodically visited by the Reverends John Nicholas Kurtz, John Caspar Stoever, Jr., and Charles Frederick Wildbahn. Shortly before the outbreak of the Revolution, the congregation merged with one established at Hagerstown in 1769.[66]

Baltimore attracted several Lutheran families shortly after its founding in 1730. This Lutheran community, which by 1750 was the largest in Maryland, proved something of an exception to the rule since its growth came from direct migration from Europe and not as the result of a Pennsylvania overspill.

Hebron Church, founded in 1717 in Spottsylvania, now Madison County, Virginia, was the first Lutheran congregation in that colony. Its origins reach back to twelve Palatinate families who fled north to escape Indian massacres in North Carolina and from a colony of Alsatians and Palatines, originally bound for Pennsylvania, but purchased as indentured servants by Governor Alexander Spotswood of Virginia and settled by him on his lands along the upper Rappahannock River.[67] Further migrations from Pennsylvania swelled the congregation to approximately three hundred by 1737.[68] Though there is some evidence to support the theory that an itinerant Pennsylvania minister, the Reverend Anthony Jacob Henkel, occasionally ministered there, the congregation's first regular pastor was the Reverend John Caspar Stoever, Sr., who arrived in 1733 shortly after his ordination by the Reverend John Christian Schultze at New Providence in Pennsylvania. In the following year Stoever and two laymen traveled to Europe in search of financial and ministerial assistance for the parish. Court Preacher Ziegenhagen warmly entertained them in London and gave them letters of introduction to aid their cause in Holland and Germany.[69] In Hamburg they prevailed upon a young seminarian, George Samuel Klug, to accept a call to Virginia. Shortly after his ordination in 1736, Klug sailed for Hebron while Stoever remained behind at Darmstadt to study theology under a relative, the Reverend John Philip Fresenius. He died aboard ship during the return voyage to America in 1739. Klug then remained in Hebron. From this base he ministered to Lutherans scattered throughout the Shenandoah Valley until his death in 1764.[70]

The first Lutheran clergyman to dwell in the valley was the

Reverend Henry Burcher Gabriel Wartmann who became pastor of the Upper Peaked Mountain congregation in 1757, serving in addition congregations at McGaheysville and Fort Run (Rader's). About the year 1760, Wartmann moved to St. John's parish in Charleston, South Carolina, left vacant by the death of the Reverend John George Friedrichs. At approximately the same time, a small congregation was organized at Winchester, Virginia which requested Muhlenberg to ordain its catechist, Charles Fredrick Wildbahn. The Pennsylvania Ministerium first temporarily licensed and then ordained Wildbahn. In addition to congregations at Winchester and Shepherdstown in Virginia, Wildbahn served two congregations in York County, Pennsylvania, four in Frederick County, Maryland and three in Washington County, also in Maryland.

Unlike George Klug, Wildbahn maintained close relations with Muhlenberg's Pennsylvania Ministerium. Klug's orthodoxy prevented him from much contact with the pietistic Hallensians. After his death, however, the Hebron congregation secured from the Pennsylvania Ministerium, the ordination of its catechist Johannes Schwarbach. When Schwarbach's ministry ended, he was replaced in 1775 by another of Muhlenberg's men, the Reverend Jacob Franck, former cantor and teacher in the school of Zion Church in Philadelphia. In 1772 Muhlenberg's own son Gabriel Peter received Anglican ordination and ministered for a time to a congregation at Woodstock, Virginia.

German colonization south of Virginia began as early as 1674 when a colony of Dutch and German Lutherans from New York established themselves on James Island, South Carolina, though they never organized a formal congregational structure or built a church.[71] A second abortive effort at German settlement came in 1710 when several hundred Palatines were shipped from England to settle at New Bern in North Carolina between the Neuse and Cape Fear rivers.[72] During the following year, the settlement was exterminated by recurrent Indian attacks. About the year 1735, Pennsylvania Germans began to filter down the Shenandoah Valley into the central and western portions of North Carolina. Eventually they organized congregations at Zion Church (Rowan County), St. John's (Cabarrus County), and

Salisbury, but they were unable to secure the services of a minister until the arrival of the Reverend Adolphus Nussman in 1773.[73]

Further sporadic colonization attempts continued in South Carolina. Between 1710 and 1734, a small group of German Lutherans had settled in Charleston. They were served by periodic visitations from Georgia pastors but did not organize themselves into a congregation until 1755.[74] There were also a few Lutherans residing in the settlement begun at Purysburg, South Carolina in 1732, but again no congregation eventuated. Swiss Germans founded a colony at Orangeburg, South Carolina, near the Edisto River in 1735. Two years later they received a regularly ordained Swiss Lutheran minister, the Reverend John Ulrich Geissendanner, and soon after erected the first Lutheran church edifice in the Carolinas.[75] From Orangeburg, German settlers pushed west so that before the outbreak of the Revolutionary War additional congregations had been established at Hard Labor Creek (Abbeville County), Amelia Township (Orangeburg County), and Indian Swamp (Barnwell County).[76]

Georgia, the last of the original thirteen English colonies to be founded, was the only southern colony to contain an important Lutheran element whose origins did not reach back to a Pennsylvania background. This colony, which served as a buffer between the English seaboard possessions and Spanish Florida, was granted by the crown to James Edward Oglethorpe who envisioned it as a haven for paupers and debtors, as well as for all those suffering from religious persecution except Catholics and Jews. Its chief city, Savannah, was laid out in 1733. The following year the first shipload of Salzburg Lutherans arrived seeking refuge from persecution in their native Austria.

Sporadic periods of persecution of Protestants had broken out in this predominantly Catholic city prior to the turn of the century. In 1684, for example, the archbishop of Salzburg presented Lutherans with a choice of conversion to Catholicism or banishment, with attendant loss of property and children. According to one estimate, over one thousand Lutherans were banished and six hundred children seized until the death of the archbishop ended the persecution.[77] Hostilities were once more renewed when Leopold Anton, count of Firmian, succeeded to the archbishopric in 1728. Three years later, on October 31, 1731, he issued the *Emigration Patent* ordering all Protestants to leave his diocese.[78] Most of the displaced persons trekked north to Germany, arousing deep sympathy from their German coreligionists over their plight. In particular the Reverend Samuel Urlsperger, senior of the Ministerium of Augsburg, rallied to their cause. Through his intervention, the Anglican Society for the Propagation of Christian Knowledge lent financial support to transport ninety-one refugees to Georgia. They were granted free passage, provisions to last them through one season in the New World, and land grants which were held free for ten years with a small quitrent attached thereafter.[79]

On March 18, 1734, the Salzburgers reached Georgia, ultimately settling at Ebenezer, twenty-five miles up river from Savannah. With them they brought two Halle pastors provided by Francke, the Reverends John Martin Boltzius and Israel Christian Gronau.[80] In time the colony prospered, especially after it was moved from its original location, which proved both unhealthy and inconvenient, to a new site six miles east in 1736.[81] Further immigration swelled the population, agriculture flourished, cotton and indigo were successfully raised, and the beginnings of an industrial base laid in the cultivation of silk and the manufacture of cloth and wooden wares. By 1741 there were approximately twelve hundred inhabitants in the settlement. Spiritually, too, Ebenezer flourished. Boltzius founded churches, schools, and an orphanage patterned after the Halle model. This latter institution received the financial support and enthusiastic endorsement of no less a person than George Whitefield, the Anglican evangelist, who first visited Ebenezer in May, 1738. Soon Ebenezer became the center of Lutheran activities in the southern colonies. From here, Boltzius, Gronau, and their successors made circuit rides to minister to fellow Lutherans in such places as Charleston and Purrysburg.[82]

Gronau died in 1744 to be replaced by another Halle man, the Reverend Herman Henry Lemke. After 1750 the Reverend Christian Rabenhorst appeared on the scene with some

Württemberg immigrants. Ebenezer's idyllic stability lasted until Boltzius's death in 1765, followed by the death of Lemke three years later. In their places came the Reverend Christopher F. Triebner who soon occasioned a deep division within the colony by his imperious and dictatorial policies.[83] Only the personal intervention of Henry Melchior Muhlenberg in 1774 prevented the complete dissolution of the colony. But the onset of revolution rendered nugatory all his efforts. British armies invaded and destroyed the settlement, scattering its surviving inhabitants throughout Georgia. Rabenhorst died in 1776 while Triebner finally declared his sympathies to lie with the Tories. Thus ended the most successful Lutheran venture in the southern colonies.

Though not the first area of Lutheran settlement in colonial times, William Penn's colony became, before the Revolutionary War, a great magnet for successive waves of German immigration and the home of the most numerous Lutheran church in America.

In 1681 Penn, a devout Quaker and the son of Admiral Sir William Penn, received a proprietorship from Charles II over what came to be called, in his honor, Pennsylvania. A deeply religious man, Penn looked upon his colony as a holy experiment in good government and freedom of conscience, ideals which he embodied in his first Frame of Government. So successful was the experiment that Pennsylvania soon outstripped all other English colonies in population while its chief city, Philadelphia, first laid out in 1682, ranked second only to London as the largest metropolis in the British empire. In addition to his managerial skills, Penn possessed a fine advertising sense. Through written word and personal visitations, he extolled the virtues and opportunities of his province, especially in Germany, and his efforts soon bore fruit.

The Frankford Land Company purchased from the proprietor in 1682 some twenty-five thousand acres of land which lay northwest of Philadelphia. The following year the company land agent, a controversial pietistic jurist named Francis Daniel Pastorius, arrived in Pennsylvania to begin the foundations of Germantown, laid out in 1685.[84] On October 6, 1683, the first

wave of German colonists reached Pennsylvania aboard the ship
Concord. Though the majority were German Mennonites, there
were a few Lutherans present among these first settlers of
Germantown.

In June, 1694, a small group of forty German mystics known
as Rosicrucians, or the Brethren of the Rosy Cross, took up
residence on the Wissahickon River near Philadelphia.[85] This
sect, later known as the Hermits of the Wissahickon, had been
founded by the Reverend John Valentine Andreae, a German
Lutheran court preacher, on the mystical-spiritualism of Jacob
Boehme and the Philadelphian ideals of Jane Leade. Its name
symbolized the union of science (the rose) with the cross (Christianity). The Wissahickon chapter came to Philadelphia under
the leadership of Baron Johannis Kelpius. Included in its company, too, were a questionable Lutheran preacher, Henry Bernhard Koester, and the Falckner brothers, Daniel and Justus.[86]
Apparently Koester gathered together the Lutherans of the
Philadelphia area about the year 1694 and held intermittent
services there though he made no attempt to organize a congregation.[87]

More important to the history of Lutheranism in Pennsylvania
were the Falckners, sons of a Lutheran clergyman from Saxony.
Daniel, born in 1666, had studied theology at Erfurt before
migrating to Pennsylvania in 1694. Five years later, while on a
return visit to Germany, the Frankford Land Company appointed him to replace Daniel Pastorius as its land agent. Daniel
then returned to Philadelphia, this time accompanied by his
brother Justus, in 1700.[88]

Justus, born on November 22, 1672, began his theological
studies at the University of Halle in 1693. Upon their completion, however, he chose not to enter the ministry but instead
accompanied his brother to Pennsylvania.[89] Both brothers settled in the region known as Falckner's Swamp or New Hanover.
Justus became acquainted with John Rudman, the Swedish
provost of Gloria Dei Church, who tendered him a call in 1703
to serve the New York Lutherans. On November 24, 1703, in
Gloria Dei Church, Wicaco, Rudman, Björk, and Sandel con-

ferred ordination to the Lutheran ministry upon Justus Falckner, the first such ceremony in the New World. It appears that this act was performed under authorization from Upsala and was not intended to serve as a precedent for future independent ordinations by colonial clergymen which would lead to a native ministry independent of Europe.[90] Justus immediately moved to New York leaving the Swedish Lutheran pastors alone in the Pennsylvania field. With the increase in immigration, especially after 1708, the colony's German Lutheran population increased rapidly and the need for German Lutheran pastors soon became critical. As more Germans entered the province, they moved to new settlements beyond Philadelphia. One such was New Hanover.

New Hanover, or Falckner's Swamp, had originally been part of the land grant conveyed by Penn to the Frankford Land Company in 1701. German Lutherans had begun to settle in the area shortly after 1700. In 1708 the area was sold to John H. Sprogel. Eleven years later, Sprogel presented fifty acres of land to an already existing New Hanover congregation for a church and school, though it is probable that such structures were extant in rudimentary form prior to this. There is also some evidence to suggest that Daniel Falckner performed ministerial functions there prior to 1708, the year when he was dismissed by the Frankford Land Company on charges of fraud. The congregation erected a log church in 1721 and a more substantial building twenty years later, a year before Muhlenberg's arrival.[91] In point of age, then, New Hanover ranks as the mother church of Pennsylvania Lutheranism.

New Providence, also called the Trappe, was likewise settled shortly after the turn of the century. Though it is probable that a sizable congregation gathered here at an early date, the church records only date back to 1729. After 1733 a congregational structure emerged complete with elders and deacons though no church was built until after Muhlenberg assumed the pastorate. Instead, services were held in a barn.[92]

The origins of a regular German Lutheran congregation at Germantown are likewise sunk in obscurity. A German Reformed church had been erected in 1719 which was likely shared by the Lutherans. By 1730 Germantown Lutherans began construction of their own church and organized a congregation.[93]

Philadelphia Lutherans received spiritual care from the Swedes at Gloria Dei and, from 1688 to 1691, from the Reverend Jacob Fabritius, formerly of New York, who preached to them in German. They do not, however, appear to have had a congregation or church of their own. Church records in Philadelphia began in 1733 while services were conducted in a former carpenter shop shared with the city's German Reformed congregation.[94]

The history of what were later to be the United Congregations committed to Muhlenberg's care cannot be separated from the name of the Reverend John Caspar Stoever, Jr. On September 11, 1728, John Caspar Stoever, Junior and Senior, sailed into Philadelphia harbor aboard the ship *James Goodwell.* Stoever, Sr. was born in 1685 in Frankenberg, Hessal, the son of a merchant, while his son and namesake was born in 1707.[95] Both father and son migrated to Pennsylvania to escape the persecutions of the Jesuit-led Catholic Counter-Reformation. Both settled at first in New Providence and, though he was not ordained, John Caspar Stoever, Jr. performed ministerial acts in the vicinity of New Providence, Philadelphia, and New Hanover as early as 1729.[96] In 1730 he moved to New Holland In Lancaster County which served as his ministerial base. Seeking to legitimize his actions, Stoever, Jr. journeyed to the Raritan Valley in New Jersey during the summer of 1731 to request ordination by Daniel Falckner. Falckner did listen to a trial sermon by Stoever but, for reasons unknown, refused to confer ordination.[97] Undaunted, Stoever returned to his illicit ministrations in Pennsylvania.

On September 25, 1732, the Reverend John Christian Schulze, born June 11, 1701, at Scheinbach in the Margrave of Ansbach, arrived in Philadelphia where he gathered the Lutherans into a congregation and then persuaded the congregations already extant at New Hanover and Providence to attach themselves to it.[98] He then convinced these united congregations to send him to Europe as their agent to raise funds for church and school buildings. To look after pastoral concerns during his absence, Schulze ordained both Stoevers on April 8, 1733, in a barn at New Providence.[99] Schulze left Philadelphia the following October, never to return, while John Caspar Stoever, Sr., accepted a call to Hebron, Virginia. For two years, Stoever, Jr. labored in the Philadelphia area. Then in 1735 he moved back to New Holland where he continued his ministry.

Unlike Muhlenberg, Stoever was an itinerant, moving about from place to place, preaching, baptizing, administering the sacraments, and initiating church records. He never showed any interest in establishing permanent congregational or synodical organizations was but content to plant the seed of faith, leaving its cultivation to others. Nevertheless, his contribution to colonial Lutheranism was important for he laid the foundations on which Muhlenberg later built.

In 1733, Stoever began church records for congregations at Lancaster, New Holland, Muddy Creek, Bernville, Tulpehocken, and York.[100] Until 1742 he was the only pastor to these congregations, but he was still unable to settle permanently. In 1740 he moved again to a site on the Quitopahila, a few miles west of Lebanon, Pennsylvania, from which he continued to work until his death in 1779.[101]

While Stoever was itinerating, John Christian Schulze and his two lay companions, Daniel Weisiger and Johann Daniel Schoner, were traveling throughout Europe in search of funds. They had departed from Philadelphia armed with a letter of introduction by the *Vorstehers* of the United Congregations authorizing them to act as their agents in securing funds for needed churches and schools. Affixed to this testimonial was a statement dated May 1, 1733, by Governor Patrick Gordon of Pennsylvania, guaranteeing its veracity and the good character of its bearers.[102]

Schulze and his companions first visited the Rev. Frederick Michael Ziegenhagen in London where they received a cordial welcome and pledges of support from the mission-minded court preacher. Ziegenhagen also gave Weisiger a letter of introduction to a fellow pastor in Hanover, strongly urging support for the fund-raising project.[103] Weisiger himself published a brief account of the conditions prevalent in the Pennsylvania congregations. He complained that the lack of schoolteachers and pastors had caused many to fall away from the Lutheran faith and that, though a few schools had been opened in Philadelphia, they were insufficient. He pointed out though there were approximately five hundred German Lutheran families in the three congregations, they did not of themselves possess sufficient resources to carry out a building program. Finally Weisiger appealed for aid to bring to fruition the work of God in Pennsylvania.[104]

Through the intercession of Ziegenhagen, Dr. Gotthilf August Francke of Halle promised to supply the congregations with pastors on the following conditions: (1) Ordination would be conferred on the pastors before their departure for America. In the meantime the congregations had to dispatch to Halle a regular call, signed by all the elders, before the ministers would be sent. (2) The United Congregations had to pledge, in advance, to obey and support the pastors sent to them. (3) A definite salary had to be agreed upon beforehand, payable in cash, not produce, at regularly stated intervals so that the pastors could devote themselves to the spiritual needs of the congregations without the necessity of entering into business activities to sustain themselves and their families. The congregations also had to provide traveling expenses to Pennsylvania, guarantee return fare to Germany should the pastors be unsatisfied with the conditions they encountered, and agree in advance to accept whomever Francke sent.[105]

Weisiger evidently assured Francke that the Pennsylvania congregations would meet these rigid conditions for in a letter from Rotterdam dated August 21, 1734, he wrote that he expected the arrival of the regular call shortly and that he planned to sail home with the Halle pastors.[106] Matters, however, did not proceed that smoothly.

Both Francke and Ziegenhagen grew suspicious that Weisiger was pocketing some of the funds raised for Pennsylvania. On September 3, 1734, Weisiger reported to Counselor Cellarius, in charge of fund raising in England, that he owed Melchior Scholtz, a merchant at Harlem in Holland, six hundred thalers which the united congregations had borrowed for building purposes. Noting that he would be unable to collect in Holland, Weisiger asked Cellarius to forward all monies collected to Scholtz who would deduct his due and transmit the remainder to Philadelphia. He further noted that Schulze had written to him asking that he be relieved of his collection work since his dishonesty had been uncovered. Scholtz was to take Schulze's place as collection agent.[107] Francke was puzzled by Weisiger's request for payment of six hundred thalers but more disturbed by the rumor that he had approached Bishop Augustus Gottlieb Spangenberg, who was preparing to lead a band of Moravian missioners to America, for the purpose of obtaining Moravian preachers for the united congregations. This charge Weisiger solemnly denied, vowing that he relied only on Halle for true, upright pastors.[108]

Weisiger then sailed home but still the call from the Pennsylvania congregations had not reached Halle. On March 11, 1735, Francke wrote to Weisiger informing him that he had raised four hundred thalers which he had forwarded to Ziegenhagen and expressing wonder that no call had been sent, nor had the congregations signed the *Formular der Vollmacht*. This Francke insisted upon for he stated that he had heard that Pennsylvania Lutherans were wont to show disrespect to their pastors, that they promised all sorts of support in their ministry but then reneged on their promises, that they exposed their preachers to need and anxiety, and that the pastors could not go to the government to redress their grievances.[109]

Shortly after this Francke received an answer from the *vorstehers* of the United Congregations. Denying that there was any truth to the charges made in Europe of their mistreatment of ministers, they suggested that Halle dispatch the Reverend John Martin Boltzius from Georgia to investigate the situation in Pennsylvania and then report back to Europe. Lamenting the lack of teachers and preachers which led to a weakening of religion in the province, they reported that a layman from Halberstadt, Johann A. Langerfeldt, now preached on alternate Sundays in a house shared with the Reformed in Philadelphia. Finally they asked for a preacher but made no mention of Francke's terms.[110]

In early fall of 1735, Francke informed Ziegenhagen that he had been shown a letter written by Christopher Sauer, a German printer in Philadelphia, to a friend of his in Halle, in which Sauer charged that Schulze had received Governor Gordon's approval of his mission by bribing a lawyer named Ludwig Mathes and that neither Schulze nor his companions had ever intended to turn over all they collected but rather to divert portions of the funds to their personal use. Francke admitted that he, too, harbored suspicions of Weisiger's intentions, especially since he had received no word from him since his return to Philadelphia.[111]

Ziegenhagen answered that he had long concurred in Francke's fears of Weisiger but did not feel that the collection was a complete fraud. He further stated that he had received a letter from the United Congregations requesting that a pastor be sent but that his salary be paid by the Society for the Propagation of Christian Knowledge since they had no funds for this purpose. The court preacher had written, in return, that unless they sent a formal call with a definite salary, no pastor would be sent. He also had demanded an account of the funds, books, and medicines sent over with Weisiger from European contributors since he suspected him of fraud and added that, until the matter was cleared up, he would not release one penny more of the monies already collected.[112]

On February 5, 1736, Ziegenhagen informed Francke that he had learned that Weisiger had delivered to the United Congregations neither the money nor the books collected but insisted that the books were in the care of a Mr. Van der Putten in Rotterdam and that he had not collected enough money even to cover the six hundred thaler loan from Scholtz. Ziegenhagen intimated that Weisiger had, instead, used the money to fund the establishment of a shop in Philadelphia and further suggested that Francke advertise in the German newspapers that Schulze, who he felt was still at large with his collection book, was no longer authorized to raise funds.[113] Francke answered that Schulze had already been arrested in Augsburg so there was no need to advertise an unwholesome incident which might prejudice further mission collections. As for the proposed pastor,

Francke decided that the recalcitrance of the United Congregations in the matter of the formal call and stipulated salary, combined with the general state of disorder existing among them, made it impossible for Halle to send anyone. He added that Zinzendorf and his family had set out for Holland but it was uncertain whether or not his ultimate destination was the West Indies as rumored.[114]

The United Congregations finally answered Francke on December 6, 1736. Again they requested that Boltzius be sent to investigate their condition. Claiming that division and dissension within the congregations prevented them from sending either a call or stated salary, they proposed that either Francke or Ziegenhagen send them a pastor, pay his traveling expenses and salary for one year from the money collected in Europe for the Pennsylvania mission, and request him to investigate and report conditions there. They further proposed that they invest the remainder of the collection funds in land, or they would lend it out at interest, using the revenues thus accrued for the support of a teacher and pastor. They also denied that any proof existed of wrongdoing by Weisiger.[115]

Under the same date, the United Congregations wrote to Ziegenhagen explaining further their reluctance to agree to Francke's conditions. Because of the widely scattered nature of the Lutheran settlements within the three congregations, they claimed agreement on such a call was impossible, though one could be extended once order was restored. But for the restoration of order, it was first necessary to have a pastor to do the ordering. Secondly, they claimed that Francke's insistence on a salary made them suspect that Halle was more interested in providing a good living for one of its men than in sending a preacher content with gospel poverty. Pennsylvania, they pointed out, could not support a minister in European luxury and, while they were willing to promise him a subsistence level of living, they refused to accede to any of Francke's demands for written guarantees. They then requested that Ziegenhagen make arrangements to support the pastor for one year since they were unwilling to bind themselves in advance, sight unseen, to someone they might find unsuited to their needs.[116]

To this Francke categorically refused to agree. Pointing out that their lack of order and the hardships of colonial existence made theirs an undesirable ministerial field, he indicated that the promise of a good and stable position alone could induce a man to forsake a comfortable European community for frontier life. While promising that he would send Boltzius to investigate as soon as conditions in Georgia allowed, Francke informed the congregations that they could not expect him to send them a pastor on the terms they offered.[117]

Here matters stood until 1739 when the United Congregations addressed a final letter to Ziegenhagen. Once again they accused Francke and him of having more interest in the material well-being of a minister than in the spiritual welfare of their souls. Restating their oft-repeated objections to a formal call, and reiterating their desperate need for ministerial aid, they again asked Ziegenhagen to send them a pastor without a call and to provide him with both traveling expenses and salary for two years. Finally they requested a definite answer from him in one year after which they would appeal to other sources for a pastor.[118] Halle did not change its position, despite the threat, so the United Congregations petitioned the Consistory of Hesse-Darmstadt for a minister.

On August 25, 1742, Valentine Kraft landed in Philadelphia claiming to have been sent by the consistory. He had, however, no testimonials to back up this claim.[119] Kraft was indeed an ordained minister, but he had recently been dismissed from his post by the authorities in the duchy of Zweibrücken. Once in Pennsylvania, Kraft assumed pastoral duties within the three congregations, even attempting to erect a consistory, with himself as head, which included some vagabond itinerants then acting as ministers in the province without authority to do so.[120] When Muhlenberg finally did arrive in December, 1742, Kraft was the first barrier he had to hurdle in establishing his authority.

From the foregoing account of the verbal struggle between the Pennsylvania congregations and Halle over the question of a pastor, it is clear that colonial Lutheranism in the province had developed certain characteristics which differed from those of its European counterparts. The chief reason for this divergence was that the people had preceded the pastor. Immigration into the middle colonies had taken place haphazardly. There individuals and families had come alone or in small, scattered groups, often as indentured servants, to settle in remote frontier areas. Once sufficiently established, they joined with their neighbors, organized a congregation, purchased land, and built a church. Then, on their own initiative, they sent out a call for a pastor. Since the congregations had organized independently of the ministry, and since they owned the ecclesiastical buildings and paid the minister's salary, they tended to look on their pastors as help hired to do them a service. They thus demanded an active voice in ecclesiastical affairs. This modification in the relationship between laity and clergy, known as voluntarism, which sprang up in a society where state and church were separate, was to bedevil Muhlenberg throughout his career.[121] The need to accommodate and combat this phenomenon was one of the factors which caused him to seek out a middle way.

NOTES

[1] Lars P. Qualben, *The Lutheran Church in Colonial America* (New York: Thomas Nelson & Sons, 1940), pp. 126–27.

[2] Ibid.

[3] Harry Julius Kreider, *Lutheranism in Colonial New York* (New York: Privately printed, 1942), p. 14.

[4] Qualben, pp. 128–29.

[5] Kreider, pp. 14–15; see also Henry Eyster Jacobs, *A History of the Evangelical Lutheran Church in the United States* (New York: Christian Literature Co., 1893), p. 50.

[6] Kreider, p. 15.

[7] Ibid.

[8] Ibid., p. 16.

[9] Ibid.

[10] Ibid., p. 17.

[11] In a letter dated June 14, 1656, the directors wrote to Stuyvesant: "We would have been better pleased if you had not published the placat against the Lutherans, a copy of which you sent us, and committed them to prison; for it has always been our intention to treat them quietly and leniently. Hereafter you will

therefore not publish such or similar placats without our knowledge, but you must pass it over quietly, and let them have free religious exercises in their houses." (Quoted in Jacobs, p. 51)

[12]Kreider, pp. 18–20; Qualben, p. 132.

[13]In this matter the directors wrote Stuyvesant: "That you have sent back here the Lutheran preacher is not contrary to, but rather in accordance with, our good intentions, although you might have proceeded less vigorously. . . . [our aim must be] not to alienate, but rather attract, people of different belief. We shall leave it to your prudence, and trust that henceforth you will use the least offensive and most tolerant means, so that people of other persuasions may not be deterred from the public Reformed Church, but in time may be induced to listen, and finally gained to it." (Quoted in Jacobs, pp. 53–54)

[14]Qualben, p. 133.

[15]Jacobs, p. 56.

[16]Kreider, p. 23.

[17]Kreider, pp. 24–26; and Jacobs, p. 59.

[18]Kreider, pp. 30–31.

[19]Ibid., p. 31.

[20]Ibid., pp. 33–34.

[21]See Walter Allen Knittle, *Early Eighteenth Century Palatine Emigration* (Philadelphia: Dorrance & Co., 1937), pp. 65–66. Various estimates have placed the number of immigrants as low as 2,000 and as high as 32,000. (P. 1)

[22]Richard Charles Wolf, "The Americanization of the German Lutherans, 1683–1829," Ph.D. dissertation, Yale University, 1947, pp. 30–31. Cf. also Cicely U. Wedgwood, *The Thirty Years War* (New Haven: Yale University Press, 1939), pp. 510–22.

[23]David Maland, *Europe in the Seventeenth Century* (New York: St. Martin's Press, 1966), pp. 300–306.

[24]Knittle, p. 4.

[25]Ibid., p. 5.

[26]Ibid., p. 11.

[27]Ibid., pp. 19–22.

[28]Ibid., pp. 12–17.

[29]Wolf, p. 89.

[30]Knittle, p. 28.

[31]Ibid., pp. 35–38.

[32]Ibid., p. 41.

[33]Ibid., p. 66.

[34]Ibid., p. 71.

[35]Ibid., pp. 65–66.

[36]Ibid., pp. 100–107.

[37]Ibid., p. 141.

[38]Ibid., pp. 155–56. The east bank acreage was called the Evans tract and was part of the so-called "extravagant land grants" in the Mohawk, Schoharie, and Hudson river valleys given in 1698 by Governor Fletcher to Nicholas Bayard, Godfrey Dellius, Captain Evans, and Caleb Heathcote. Lord Ballomont, who

succeeded Fletcher as Governor, favored another land owning group and, on March 2, 1699, persuaded the New York Assembly to void the Fletcher grant. This was upheld by London on June 26, 1708 and the grant reverted to the Crown. See Qualben, p. 183.

[39]Knittle, p. 159. See also the Palatine Society of the United Evangelical Lutheran Church of New York and New England, *The Palatines of New York State: A complete compilation of the history of the Palatines who first came to New York State in 1708–1722* (Johnstown, N.Y.: Palatine Society, Inc., 1953), pp. 23–40.

[40]Knittle, pp. 182–83.

[41]"The House of Commons passed two resolutions: first that the inviting and bringing over into this kingdom of the Palatines, of all religions, at the public expense, was an extravagant and unreasonable charge to the kingdom, and a scandalous misapplication of the public money, tending to the increase and oppression of the poor to this kingdom and of dangerous consequence to the Constitution in church and state; second, that whoever advised the bringing over the poor Palatines into this kingdom was an enemy to the Queen and kingdom." (Ibid., p. 183)

[42]Ibid., p. 184.

[43]Kreider, p. 35.

[44]By 1722 there were at least fourteen congregations under his charge: New York City, Albany, Loonenburg (Athens), "Pieter Lassens" (near New Hamburg), Quassaic (Newburgh), Queensbury (Camp, East Camp, later Germantown), New Town (West Camp), Rhinebeck, Schoharie, Gospelhoeck (Preuwenhoeck), and Tar Bush (Manorton) in New York. In New Jersey there was Hackensack, the Raritan, and Remaboeck (Mahwah). (Ibid., p. 37)

[45]Ibid., p. 39. Kreider does point out the possibility, however, based on the fact that Berkenmeyer, an Orthodox, seems to have accepted him. p. 39.

[46]Qualben, p. 136.

[47]Ibid., p. 138.

[48]Ibid.; see also Jacobs, p. 81.

[49]Qualben, p. 81.

[50]Among the instructions given to Printz by the Swedish Council of State were the following: "Above all things, shall the Governor see to it that a true and due worship, becoming honor, laud, and praise be paid to the Most High God in all things, and, to that end, all proper care shall be taken that divine service be zealously performed according to the Unaltered Augsburg Confession, the Council of Upsala, and the ceremonies of the Swedish Church; and all persons, but especially the young, shall be duly instructed in the articles of their Christian faith; and all good church discipline shall in like manner be duly exercised and received. But so far as relates to Holland colonists that live and settle under the government of Her Royal Majesty and the Swedish Crown, the Governor shall not disturb them in the indulgence granted them as to the exercise of the Reformed religion according to the aforesaid Royal Charter." (Quoted in Jacobs, p. 82) The charter referred to was granted by the Swedish government in January, 1640, to one Henrik Hooghkamer allowing him to settle a number of Dutch immigrants from Utrecht in New Sweden. They were granted freedom of

religion and self-government under the suzerainty of the Swedish crown. (Qualben, p. 139)

[51] Tinicum is no longer an island but now part of the Pennsylvania mainland.

[52] Theodore Emanuel Schmauk, *The Lutheran Church in Pennsylvania 1638–1800* (Lancaster: Pennsylvania German Society, 1902), vol. 11 of *Proceedings and Addresses*, p. 37.

[53] Jacobs, p. 85.

[54] Ibid., p. 85.

[55] Qualben, pp. 150–51.

[56] Edmund Jacob Wolf, *The Lutherans in America: A Story of Struggle, Progress, Influence, and Marvelous Growth* (New York: J. A. Hill & Co., 1889), pp. 158–59

[57] Jacobs, p. 95.

[58] Ibid., p. 94; Schmauk, p. 51.

[59] Jacobs, p. 94.

[60] Ibid., p. 99.

[61] Jacobs, p. 100.

[62] Ibid.

[63] Ibid., pp. 101–3.

[64] Qualben, p. 190.

[65] Abdel Ross Wentz, *A Basic History of Lutheranism in America* (Philadelphia: Muhlenberg Press, 1955), p. 18. For a history of Virginia Lutherans, see William E. Eisenberg, *The Lutheran Church in Virginia 1717–1962* (Roanoke, Virginia: Trustees of the Virginia Synod of the Lutheran Church in America, 1967).

[66] Eisenberg, p. 18–19.

[67] Jacobs, p. 184.

[68] Wentz, p. 19.

[69] Jacobs, p. 185.

[70] Wentz, p. 19.

[71] Qualben, pp. 148–49; 190.

[72] Wentz, pp. 19–20.

[73] Ibid., p. 20.

[74] Qualben, pp. 190–91.

[75] Wentz, p. 20.

[76] Ibid.

[77] Jacobs, pp. 151–52.

[78] Ibid., pp. 152–53.

[79] Jacobs, p. 158; Wentz, p. 21.

[80] Wentz, p. 21.

[81] Jacobs, p. 161.

[82] Ibid., pp. 164–65. See also George F. James, "In Memoriam: John Martin Boltzius, 1703–1765, Patriarch of the Georgia Lutherans," *Lutheran Quarterly* 17 (May 1965): 151–66.

[83] Wentz, pp. 21–22.

[84] Lucy Forney Bittinger, *The Germans in Colonial Times* (Philadelphia: J. B. Lippincott Co., 1901), pp. 28–29. See also Jacobs, pp. 110–11.

[85] Qualben, p. 153; Bittinger, p. 46.

[86]Qualben, p. 154.

[87]Wentz, p. 15.

[88]Qualben claims that Daniel Falckner was ordained in Germany either before coming to America in 1694, or on his subsequent visit to Europe. (P. 163) There is, however, no evidence at all to back this up and it is doubtful whether Falckner ever received ordination.

[89]Jacobs, p. 96.

[90]Ibid., p. 97.

[91]John Ludwig Schulze, *Reports of the United German Evangelical Lutheran Congregations in North America, Specially in Pennsylvania*, 1 (Reading: Pilger Book Store, 1882), p. 55, n. 26.

[92]Ibid., pp. 56–57; also p. 61, n. 28.

[93]Ibid., p. 62, n. 29.

[94]Ibid., p. 65.

[95]Roy L. Winters, "John Caspar Stoever, Lutheran Pioneer," *Lutheran Church Quarterly* 18 (July 1945): 287; see also Charles H. Glatfelter, "The Colonial Pennsylvania German Lutheran and Reformed Clergyman," Ph.D. dissertation, Johns Hopkins University, 1952, p. 15.

[96]Winters, p. 288; Schmauk, p. 248.

[97]Schmauk, p. 249; see also Julius Friedrich Sachse, *The German Pietists of Provincial Pennsylvania, 1694–1708* (Philadelphia: Printed by the author, 1895), p. 329.

[98]Schulze, notes on preface, p. 8; see also Ernst T. Kretschmann, *The Old Trappe Church: A Memorial of the Sesquicentennial Services of Augustus Evangelical Lutheran Church, Montgomery County, Pa.* (Philadelphia: Printed by the congregation, 1893), p. 4.

[99]Winters, pp. 288–89; Schmauk, p. 252.

[100]Schmauk, p. 256.

[101]Winters, p. 295.

[102]"Copie des von dener Vorstehern derer Evangelish-Lutherischen Gemeinden zu Philadelphia, Neu Hanover und Providence ihren abgeordneten mitgegebenen offenen Briefes," in Johann Ludwig Schulze, ed., *Nachrichten von den vereinigten Deutschen Evangelish-Lutherischen Gemeinen in Nord-America, absonderlich in Pennsylvanien*, 1 (Allentown: Brobst, Diehl & Co., 1886), pp. 52–53. Hereafter referred to as *1 Nachrichten*.

[103]Ziegenhagen to a preacher in Hanover, London, January 28, 1734, in ibid., pp. 51–52.

[104]"Weisiger's Kurtze Nachricht Aus America," May 3, 1734, Hildesheim, in ibid., pp. 50–51.

[105]"Formular der Vollmacht," Halle, May 31, 1734 in ibid., pp. 54–55.

[106]Weisiger to Francke, Rotterdam, August 21, 1734 in ibid., p. 55.

[107]Weisiger to Cellarius, London, September 3, 1734 in ibid., pp. 55–6.

[108]Weisiger to Francke, London, September 23, 1734 in ibid., p. 56.

[109]Francke to Weisiger, Halle, March 11, 1735 in ibid., pp. 56–57.

[110]United Congregations to Francke, Philadelphia, February 28, 1735, in ibid., pp. 57–58.

[111]Francke to Ziegenhagen, undated in ibid., pp. 58–59.

[112]Ziegenhagen to Francke, London, October 17, 1735 in ibid., pp. 59–60.

[113]Ziegenhagen to Francke, London, February 5, 1736 in ibid., p. 61.

[114]Francke to Ziegenhagen, Halle, March 14, 1736, in ibid., pp. 60–61.

[115]Vorstehers of the United Congregations to Francke, Philadelphia, December 6, 1736, in ibid., pp. 62–63.

[116]Vorstehers of the United Congregations to Ziegenhagen, Philadelphia, December 6, 1736, in ibid., pp. 63–64.

[117]Francke to the United Congregations, Halle, June 18, 1737, in ibid., pp. 65–66.

[118]United Congregations to Ziegenhagen, Philadelphia, October 15, 1739, in ibid., pp. 67–70.

[119]Schmauk, p. 385.

[120]Ibid.

[121]Glatfelter, p. 7.

3

The Threat from the Left:
Muhlenberg versus the Moravians

As Muhlenberg continually reiterated in his reports to Halle, Pennsylvania's religious situation presented difficulties which did not exist in Europe. Lutherans in English America had been so long without ecclesiastical supervisors and pastors that their faith had weakened, education lagged, and heterodox opinions flourished. Too often they turned for leadership to unscrupulous vagabonds, tailors, and schoolmasters who assumed ministerial powers, causing confusion and division among their charges through their theological ignorance and scandalous lives. At other times pulpits were given over to men of base character who, though validly ordained, had fled Europe after deposition from the ministry to seek their fortunes in America. While such men posed a distinct danger to American Lutheranism, and while they troubled Muhlenberg throughout his American ministry, they were but a minor irritant compared to the threat from the left wing of pietism which emerged in the Moravian church. So baneful and effective was its influence that for a time it appeared it would ultimately triumph, utterly eradicating any traces of genuine Lutheranism in Pennsylvania.

Historically the Moravians were the heirs of the Slavic reformer John Huss, burned for heresy by the Council of Constance in 1415. A Czech priest stationed at the Chapel of the Holy Innocents in Prague, Huss demanded, among other reforms, the reintroduction of Slavonic in place of Latin in the liturgy, communion under both species as was customary in the Eastern rite, and the abolition of clerical celibacy. To some extent, his was a movement of Czech nationalism against the far-reaching power of the Roman church.

Huss's death plunged Bohemia into civil war. Ultimately his followers split into two camps, the Calixtines, who demanded communion under both species, and the more radical Taborites, who held out for a general reformation of the church, including the abolition of all sacraments save baptism and the Lord's Supper, the dissolution of all monastic orders, and the repudiation of the doctrines of the Mass, purgatory, confession, relics, image worship, and the efficacy of good works.[1]

In 1432 when the Council of Basel granted the chalice to the Bohemians, the radical Taborites were isolated and repudiated. In 1457 they constituted themselves a separate church known as the *Unitas Fratrum,* or, more popularly, as the Moravian church.[2] Persecutions and expulsion followed until by 1670 only a remnant of the church was left under its bishop, Daniel Jablonsky.

The Moravians might have suffered complete extermination had it not been for the appearance of the somewhat enigmatic and idealistic Nicholas Lewis, Count of Zinzendorf. Through his efforts they rose, phoenix-like, from the ashes to achieve a degree of importance out of proportion to their numerical strength.

Count Zinzendorf was born at Dresden on May 26, 1700. As a young boy he showed a definite interest in the religious life, frequently gathering his fellow six year olds into a make-believe congregation so he could preach to them.[3] In 1706 Nicholas was sent to Halle to pursue his studies under August Hermann Francke who, along with Spener, was a close friend of the Zinzendorf family. Spener, indeed, had been godfather to Nicholas at his baptism. At Halle, the citadel of German pietism, Zinzendorf's spirituality deepened while traces of mystical-spiritual inclinations appeared at an early age. When he was but ten years of age, the count organized the Order of the Mustard Seed whose members pledged themselves to carry the gospel to pagan peoples. Each had a small gold ring bearing an inscription from Romans: "No man liveth unto himself."[4]

Zinzendorf remained at Halle until 1716. If left to his own devices, he would have preferred to continue theological studies for the ministry. His family, however, wished him to pursue a secular education which would better prepare him for his duties as a member of the German aristocracy. Consequently Zinzendorf transferred to the University of Wittenberg where he studied law in preparation for a Saxon civil service career. Still he did not abandon his theological propensities but engrossed himself in theology in his spare time, praying and fasting in private to the derision of his more worldly classmates.[5]

On completion of his studies in 1719, Zinzendorf undertook a grand tour of Europe, visiting churches and theological faculties throughout France and Holland.[6] After his return to Germany, he accepted an appointment as counsellor to the king of Saxony, though his heart was not in his work. He purchased a little estate at Bertholdsdorf, close to his ancestral home, and spent his leisure time transforming it into a model of Christianity.

Meanwhile the Moravians were still experiencing difficulties. About 1715 religious revivals broke out in Fulneck, Moravia, and Lititz, Bohemia. Some of the Moravian brethren who still lived there had been conducting secret worship in the home of Patriarch Martin Schneider.[7] Among the worshipers were the Neisser brothers and their neighbors, the Nitschmanns. A young carpenter named Christopher David who met the Neissers at one of these gatherings was urged by them to seek out an asylum for their persecuted church.[8] David ultimately came into contact with Zinzendorf who welcomed the Moravians to his estate in Upper Lusatia. In 1722 the first community arrived at Berthelsdorf (later Herrnhut) soon to become a haven for scattered Moravians. In accordance with the law of the land, however, the count insisted that they pose as a Lutheran community and conduct liturgical worship accordingly.

Eventually the Moravians began to agitate for an abandonment of their Lutheran practices and the reconstitution of their ancient church. Against the wishes of Zinzendorf, twelve elders were elected to supervise the little community in 1727.[9] It was at this time that Zinzendorf accidentally stumbled across a copy of John Amos Comenius's *Order and Discipline*.[10] So impressed was

80 MISSIONARY OF MODERATION

he that he now resolved to reconstitute the church, though never really intending to abandon his concept of *ecclesiolae in Ecclesia* previously in effect at Herrnhut.[11] These *ecclesiolae* probably sprang from the traditional pietistic conventicle system. Whereas, however, a conventicle was merely a group of awakened people meeting in private, usually with a minister as leader, to discuss religious matters and to provide mutual edification, an *ecclesiola* was more akin to monastic orders within the Roman Catholic church. Members of the *ecclesiolae* led communitarian lives in structured religious societies of so-called awakened souls. Though they lived in isolation under their own leaders, they supposedly conformed, at least in externals, to the doctrines and liturgical forms of the Lutheran church. Hence they were not a sect but merely an order within Lutheranism. Indeed only under these conditions could they continue to exist, for the Moravians were not a recognized church in Germany.

When Zinzendorf reconstituted the Moravian church in 1727, he seemingly abandoned the *ecclesiolae in Ecclesia* and produced yet another church.[12] In reality, however, the count was merely using the Moravian church as an ecclesiastical engine to produce an all-inclusive *Ecclesia,* termed by him "The Congregation of God in the Spirit." According to this scheme, all existing denominations, Lutheran, Reformed, Catholic, and so on became *ecclesiolae,* or *tropi,* in a far-reaching, all-inclusive spiritual union of professing Christians which alone was the true *Ecclesia* of Christ. Each *tropus* retained its denominational and doctrinal distinctiveness within the whole church. The Moravians were to function as a catalyst to spark this union. Consequently Zinzendorf conceived the idea of dispatching his men on extensive missionary ventures, especially in those areas of the world where lack of ministers had prevented a firm implantation of the European churches. Moravian brethren there offered their services to pastorless flocks, externally conforming to the dogma and liturgy of their particular denominations, but working all the while to effect an ecumenical union of all churches.

Such a visionary scheme, noble though it was in concept, was a direct outgrowth of Zinzendorf's personal theology. Spurning all dogmatic subtleties, Zinzendorf reduced religion to faith in the person of the God-man, Jesus Christ. So Christocentric was his theology that his Trinitarianism became highly suspect. He seems to have held, for example, that God the Father is not the Father of men until after Christ's mediation and reconciliation.[13]

With orthodox Lutherans, Zinzendorf believed that human nature had been corrupted by Adam's fall. Unlike them he reduced all sin responsible for this corruption to one, disbelief in the Lord Jesus.[14]

> Therefore the very Substance of Sin is to be found in Unbelief, manifesting itself either in a careless Indifference, Estrangement, and Negect towards the Lord, or in declared Enmity and Rebellion against him.[15]

The process of justification, for Zinzendorf, was simply the positing of an act of faith in the divinity of the suffering God-man who freely chose to die for humanity's sins. Faith became the individual's sole duty or obligation.[16] Christ himself would initiate justification and impart saving grace.[17] The individual, for his part, need only give passive acceptance[18] and "quietly attend the Voice of the Lord when he comes and approaches the Heart with his Power."[19] Unlike Muhlenberg, Zinzendorf did not require a conscious struggle with the sinful self before conversion was had. The process reached completion in an inspirational flash, in a twinkling of God's eye.[20]

For Zinzendorf, there was no one set pattern for the attainment of salvation for God deals with each individual soul in a unique, personal way.[21] Since Christ suffered death on the cross for all persons, every individual could be saved on the merits of His sacrificial act.[22] In Zinzendorfian theology there could be no such thing as a predestined body of the elect.

Salvation, then, resulted from knowledge of Christ which led to faith in his divinity. Such knowledge did not come from the Law, since the Law tempts people to pursue evil by stating what is forbidden: "The Strength of Sin is the Law"; whereas the gospel liberated people by destroying the legal machinery.[23] It did not come from education, for education merely impressed ideas in the head but could not implant them in the heart.[24] This knowledge, instead, resulted from an immediate illumination by Christ of the essential truths of his Incarnation, death, and Resurrection.[25]

Once Christ entered the soul, sin was cleansed away. Indeed, Zinzendorf seemed to hold that the justified were incapable of sinning any more.[26] Even a person who had lived all his or her life mired in the basest evil but received Christ on his death bed was saved. Moreover, since one did not know when and to whom Christ would present himself, one had no right to condemn the natural man for his failure to know God.[27]

Sanctification, in Zinzendorfian theology, was accompanied by a divinely inspired certitude of redemption.[28] As the faithful steward, one need only say "I believe" and rest assured in the certain knowledge of eternal reward. Christ had chosen me; he would not give me up. Contrary to the emphasis of Halle pietism, Herrnhut theology reached back to the Reformation in its strong emphasis on the inefficacy of good works, or even piety, to merit salvation. As Zinzendorf said:

> There is no need of our Piety and Godliness, to make us Partakers of the Death and Cross of Christ, but we obtain that as Sinners, without [any] concurrence of our Works, if we can but really believe it.[29]

In like manner, any business or recreational pursuit is permissible provided it not be in itself evil, that is, a denial of faith.[30] Holiness became the very nature of the human person, not the object of so-called moral activity.[31]

Given his extreme piety, interlaced as it was with strong mystical-spiritual elements, and his emphasis on the atoning merit of Christ's salvation, Zinzendorf evolved a blood and wounds theology with a maudlin and mawkish expression of pietistic sentimentality over Christ's death, which pictured people as poor maggot worms revelling in the bloody wounds of the slain lamb. Equally dangerous, in Muhlenberg's view, was the count's insistence on an instantaneous, once-for-all salvific conversion experience gained by a childlike faith. During the "Sifting Period" of Moravianism from 1743 to 1750, childish

replaced childlike qualities while licentious and orgiastic behavior at Moravian gatherings provided further ammunition for
the count's enemies.[32]

In 1732, after an investigation of Herrnhut heterodoxy by a
special board of inquiry, the Saxon court ordered Zinzendorf to
sell his estates.[33] The count now resigned all his official court
functions to occupy himself as a warden of the Moravian community. In 1734 Zinzendorf was ordained to the Lutheran
ministry by the Consistory of Tubingen, and together with the
Reverend Augustus Gottlieb Spangenberg, a Lutheran minister
who joined the Herrnhut community in 1732 after his dismissal
by Francke from his Halle posts as assistant professor of divinity
and inspector of the orphanage, began to lay plans for Moravian
ecumenism.[34] Distasteful as were these heterodox opinions of
Zinzendorf to Halle, the court's disdain for dogmatic and denominational differences along with his methods of evangelism
in behalf of his ecumenical "Congregation of God in the Spirit,"
caused the Reverend Fathers the greatest concern.

Zinzendorf had already dispatched a group of Moravian missioners to the West Indies in 1732 and in the following year to
Greenland. In part their function was to discover a suitable
haven for the removal of the church from European persecution
and a site where the religious and political climate would afford
an opportunity to realize Zinzendorf's plans. Spangenberg led
another band of missioners to Georgia in 1735, followed closely
by David Nitschmann, recently consecrated a bishop by Daniel
Jablonsky.[35] For a time Spangenberg and Nitschmann tried to
make a success of the Georgia mission field, but there were too
many obstacles in their way. Contact with native Indians, a
primary objective of the missionary work, proved impossible.
Moreover, impending war between the Georgia colony and
Spanish Florida prompted Oglethorpe to call all colonists to bear
arms, a practice anathema to the pacifist-minded Moravians.[36]

As early as 1736, Spangenberg had journeyed to Penn's colony in search of more fertile fields, his steps directed there by
the settlement of a group of Schwenckfelders who had sought
refuge in Pennsylvania after their banishment from Herrnhut in
1734. Spangenberg's interest in Pennsylvania was also aroused

by a series of meetings with Daniel Weisiger, the agent sent to Europe by the United Congregations. Though Weisiger denied the charge made by Halle, it is probable that he had considered seeking pastoral help from Moravian ministers, especially since they did not require any financial reimbursement for their labors. At least Spangenberg learned from Weisiger about the disordered and pastorless state of Pennsylvania Lutherans which would work to the advantage of the Moravians.[37]

Spangenberg's mission to Pennsylvania was to bring about a union between the Moravians and Schwenckfelders. He was also to test the climate to see whether it could support a transplanted Moravian church. While in Pennsylvania, he based his efforts at the home of Christopher Wiegner, a Schwenckfelder, in Skippack.[38] Also associated with him was Henry Antes, an unordained Reformed preacher working at Oley.[39] Soon these three men formed the "Associated Brethren of Skippack," which regularly met on Wiegner's farm to promote interdenominational union vis a vis Zinzendorf's *tropus* scheme.[40] Spangenberg's preliminary overtures to the Ephrata Society were rebuffed when he insisted they terminate their monastic existence if union occurred.[41]

Encouraged by Spangenberg's report, Zinzendorf sent Andrew Eschenbach to travel throughout Pennsylvania in 1739 preaching Christian union.[42] Meanwhile the great English evangelist George Whitefield persuaded the Georgia Moravians to build and supervise a school for Negroes on a plot of Pennsylvania land he owned, called Nazareth. The offer was accepted though financial reverses caused Whitefield to sell the land outright to the Moravians in 1743 before the school was established.[43] A second settlement of Moravians was begun on a site on the Lehigh River called by them, Bethlehem.

From these settlements, in particular Bethlehem, Moravianism spread at an alarming rate, owing, in part to the support lent it for a time by Whitefield, a personal friend of Peter Boehler, Moravian missioner and organizer of the New York branch of the church in 1741. Not until late 1740 did Whitefield finally break with the Moravians over a disagreement on election and reprobation. In the meantime, he had preached at Wiegner's farm and Antes's plantation (as well as in Georgia), had entrusted the site of his proposed Pennsylvania Negro school to the Brethren, and had thus lent them the respectability of his awesome reputation.[44]

In Europe, much to Halle's dismay, Count Zinzendorf was preparing for a move to America to promote his plans for church union. At a conference held in 1741, he resigned his office as a Moravian bishop, to which he had been consecrated four years earlier while still a Lutheran minister, and assumed his family name, Herr von Thurnstein, to dissociate himself from denominationalism.[45] On November 18, 1741, the count landed in New York City, setting out immediately for Philadelphia. Henry Antes, the Reformed itinerant, then issued a circular letter to all Pennsylvania denominations, inviting them to attend a conference at Germantown on January 1, 1742.[46] Supposedly the conference was to seek a common doctrinal ground, thus easing denominational tensions. In actuality, it intensified differences all the more. Seven conferences were held at various localities during the first six months of 1742, but all failed to establish the "Congregation of God in the Spirit." Part of the opposition to union stemmed from the heterodox peculiarities of Zinzendorfian theology; part came from fears of Moravian proselytizing.[47] Yet another reason for their failure could be laid to the dogmatic and overbearing personality of the count himself. When, for example, he announced to the Schwenckfelders that he had been appointed by Christ to reform their church and purge it of errors, they withdrew from the conference in a huff.[48] At the seventh meeting, held in Philadelphia June 13–14, 1742, only a few Moravians and Lutherans were present. Zinzendorf, accepting the inevitable, abandoned the idea of church union and devoted himself, instead, to staffing vacant Lutheran churches with Moravian pastors posing as Lutherans.[49]

After his arrival in the Philadelphia area, Zinzendorf had immediately begun to preach. On one occasion some German Lutherans from Philadelphia heard him in Germantown. So impressed were they that they invited the count to preach at the Philadelphia warehouse which they shared with the German

Reformed. The invitation was issued on December 26, 1741. Since the Reverend John Philip Boehm, the organizer of colonial Pennsylvania German Reformed church, was then present in Philadelphia, a disaffected group of Lutherans who opposed Zinzendorf brought the matter to the Reformed minister for his opinion. Though Boehm had previously warned German Reformed people against Zinzendorf's heresy, he refused to prescribe for the Lutherans, stating instead that his people would have nothing to do with the count. Because of Boehm's equivocal answer, Zinzendorf preached in his town house instead of using the church. Despite Boehm's opposition, Zinzendorf did receive a call to be pastor of the Philadelphia congregation. On January 19, 1742, he inquired whether Boehm would object if Zinzendorf preached in the jointly shared church building.[50] Boehm reiterated his answer of the previous December, so Zinzendorf began to minister in the church. During the summer of 1742, the count left Philadelphia to work in the Indian missions, appointing in his place John Christopher Pyrlaeus, then twenty-nine years old. Pyrlaeus, a native of Saxony, had joined the Moravians in Germany after studying theology at the University of Leipzig.[51] Nitschmann had ordained him at Oley in 1742. Immediately thereafter he replaced Zinzendorf in Philadelphia.

Unfortunately for Pyrlaeus, disaffection with the Moravians was rapidly growing in Philadelphia. A climax was reached on July 18, 1742, when a Lutheran deacon, Thomas Mayor, changed the lock on the church door to bar the Moravians from preaching. Though there is no evidence that Boehm was implicated in this, he certainly approved of the action. When Pyrlaeus and his followers reached the church, they broke the lock and entered to conduct divine services. Thereupon a Lutheran elder confronted Pyrlaeus in the pulpit ordering him to leave the church. On his refusal a crowd of both Lutherans and Reformed who had gathered outside the church doors rushed in, grabbed him, and unceremoniously threw him into the street. The resulting riot between the factions was quelled by the civil authorities.[52]

When Zinzendorf learned of the commotion, he returned to

the city to institute a civil suit against both Lutheran and Reformed. During the early part of August, 1742, while the Lutherans were gathered for services, Zinzendorf and his followers entered the church. Violence was avoided when he agreed to withdraw peacefully. Negotiations failed to settle the dispute and the court case dragged on until February, 1743, when the Lutherans were exonerated, though the Reformed were adjudged guilty of dragging Pyrlaeus from the pulpit and thus starting the riot.[53] Even before the decision was handed down, Zinzendorf had withdrawn his faction to a new church, including a Lutheran elder who took with him the church book and copper chalice, possession of which was subsequently disputed by the Lutherans.[54] When Muhlenberg finally reached Philadelphia, he discovered that though the city Lutherans had broken with the Moravians, those in most other localities had not. In particular serious difficulties between Moravians and Lutherans erupted at Tulpehocken and Lancaster.

The beginnings of the German Lutheran settlements in the Tulpehocken region began with Palatine land woes in Schoharie, New York. Pennsylvania's governor, George Keith, chanced to be present at an Indian conference in Albany while the Albany partners, supported by Governor Fletcher of New York, were attempting to eject the Palatine squatters from their grant. Seeking a population buffer on the Pennsylvania frontier, Keith invited the Germans to relocate in the Tulpehocken region. Many accepted this offer and between 1723 and 1729 made the trip from New York.[55] Conrad Weiser and his family, including his daughter Anna Maria Weiser, Muhlenberg's future wife, also migrated to Pennsylvania, settling near the present town of Womelsdorf. Once settled, the Germans petitioned the governor for permission to purchase the lands they had already occupied. Unfortunately, the Proprietors had not yet themselves purchased them from the Indians in accordance with Penn's policy, an oversight that was not corrected until 1732.[56]

Because the Palatines moved in a body from their New York homes, they brought with them a preexisting congregational structure. Once established in Tulpehocken, they were occasionally served by Bernhard von Dieren, an unordained tailor from Königsberg who had assumed ministerial duties for them in Schoharie, and by the Reverend Anthony Jacob Henkel who ministered to congregations in southeastern Pennsylvania. In 1727 it was Henkel who convinced them to erect their first log meeting house which they shared with the Tulpehocken Reformed.[57] Henkel and von Dieren made visits to Tulpehocken until 1729. For a time during the fall of 1729, John Caspar Stoever, Jr., also administered the sacraments there but did not remain. After Stoever's departure, Conrad Weiser, then thirty-three years old and but recently arrived in the area, took over the duties of a *Vorleser,* conducting services on Sundays and catechizing the children.[58]

Until 1730 John Philip Boehm had ministered to the Reformed element of the union church. In that year a twenty-year-old German Reformed minister, the Reverend Peter Miller, just ordained by the Presbyterians in Philadelphia, wrested away from Boehm Reformed congregations in Cocalico, Conestoga, and Tulpehocken.[59] Weiser formed a fast friendship with Miller which had deleterious consequences for Tulpehocken Lutheranism. Through Miller Weiser fell under the influence of the spiritual-mystic Conrad Beissel, the head of a monastically inclined Seventh Day Dunker sect which preached total separation from the world of flesh.

Weiser had already made provisions for the procurement of a permanent pastor. When Caspar Leutbecker, a tailor from Matescha, near Skippack, was engaged by the Tulpehocken congregation as school master, he indicated that he had connections with the Halle fathers and with the London court preacher. Accordingly, Weiser entrusted him with a call for a pastor. In due time Leutbecker informed the congregation that a pastor named Pagenkopf (Bagenkopf) was on the way and urged them to construct a suitable parsonage. No sooner had this edifice been completed than Leutbecker claimed that Pagenkopf had died at sea and since he, Leutbecker, had been ordained in London by Court Preacher Anton Boehme, he would serve as pastor.[60] In 1734 Leutbecker moved into the parsonage supported by one faction of the congregation, among them the Rieth (Reed) family which had donated the land for the church.[61] Convinced that Leutbecker had never sent the call, Weiser opposed his pastorate and finally withdrew from the Lutheran church.[62] With Miller, Weiser went to Ephrata where he was baptized by Conrad Beissel after he had publicly burned various devotional books, among them Luther's large and small catechisms, the Heidelberg catechism, and John Arndt's *Paradies Gärtlein*.[63] For a time he became teacher and head of the Tulpehocken Anabaptist congregation, until the winter of 1735 when he moved with his family and parishioners to Ephrata. The loss of Weiser, *Vorleser* and most influential member of the congregation, as well as a number of leading elders and deacons to Ephrata, further confused the already beleaguered Lutherans.

Leutbecker was only able to win over a small portion of the congregation. The majority in 1735 gave a call to the Reverend John Caspar Stoever, Jr., to be their pastor.[64] At first the Stoever faction conducted services in barns and houses. Then in 1736 it expelled the Leutbecker group from the church, forcing them to hold services in the parsonage whose possession they retained. Actually, nobody seemed quite sure of exactly who did own the church. Though the Rieth family had claimed the church lands which they donated to the congregation in 1727, they never possessed a valid title since the land legally still belonged to the Indians. After the Proprietors purchased the Tulpehocken tract from the natives in 1732, they sold the church lands on September 17, 1735, to an English gentleman, John Page, who in turn on February 17, 1736, commissioned attorneys William Allen, William Webb, and Samuel Powell to sell it for him.[65] Thus, legally, Page was the owner of both the land and the church erected on it.

On discovering this, Leonard Rieth and his party visited attorney William Webb at his Kennett Square home and obtained his recognition of Leutbecker as legal pastor with exclusive rights over the use of the church. To reinforce this, Webb visited Tulpehocken and personally presented the Leutbecker faction with a legal document to this effect. Still the issue remained unresolved. When Webb padlocked the church, Stoever's group broke in. Webb then tried to work out a compromise but Stoever would have no part of it. Meanwhile the hapless Leutbecker abandoned the parsonage to take refuge in private homes after several attempts were made on his life.[66] Broken in body and spirit, Leutbecker died in 1738, leaving his faction leaderless. Because they still would not reconcile themselves to Stoever, the feud continued.

Leonard Rieth then secretly purchased the church lands from Page on May 15, 1742, forcing the Stoever group to begin construction of another building which it called Christ Church. But Leutbecker's death had created a vacuum which the Moravians filled in the second phase of the Tulpehocken confusion.

During his stay in Pennsylvania, Bishop Spangenberg had been a frequent visitor to Tulpehocken where he allied himself with the Leutbecker faction and occasionally preached to them. It was he who delivered Leutbecker's funeral sermon and helped reconcile Conrad Weiser to Leutbecker shortly before the latter's death. Weiser had met Spangenberg in 1736 while visiting the Schwenkfelders at Towamensing.[67] A pietist himself, Weiser befriended the Moravian bishop who informed him of his Halle training and connections. After he left Ephrata and renounced Beissel in 1741 to assume the duties of a justice of the peace, Weiser once more interested himself in Tulpehocken Lutheran affairs, this time as an opponent of Stoever. Still determined to secure a Halle pastor, Weiser now turned to the Moravians, contact with whom continued through occasional visits of Andrew Eschenbach from Oley.

Weiser met Count Zinzendorf at the first of the synodical conferences in Germantown in 1742 which he attended as an observer. Since the count passed himself off as a pietistic Lutheran minister, Weiser invited him to Tulpehocken and entrusted him with a call to be transmitted to Halle. This task Zinzendorf readily accepted, offering to assign one of his own men, Gottlieb Büttner, whom he had recently ordained at Oley, to serve without pay until a Halle pastor could be secured.[68]

Once his pastorate began, Büttner gained the support of both Weiser and the Leutbecker faction. He then mounted an increasingly vicious attack upon Stoever, seeking to lure his followers over to the Moravian side by discrediting him. When he discovered that his tactics had failed, Büttner ostentatiously resigned his office on May 30, 1742. The following month, on June third, Zinzendorf, Büttner, Pyrlaeus, and Paul Brycelius, Moravians all, formed a "Consistory of the Lutheran Church" in Philadelphia. Their first official act was the deposition of Stoever from the ministry for invalidity of ordination and for scandalous and licentious conduct.[69] Büttner then returned to Tulpehocken and, armed with the recently acquired deed to the church, forced Stoever out. Stoever's group now worshiped in the Reformed church while planning the construction of a new Lutheran church building. Shortly thereafter, Zinzendorf withdrew Büttner, replacing him with John Philip Meurer, another of his recent *ordinandi*. Through these actions, the count was actually claiming the superintendency of the Lutheran church in Pennsylvania, a claim to which Weiser gave some semblance of legitimacy by his acquiescence in Zinzendorf's actions.

In November, 1742, Valentine Kraft, the pretender to the pastorage of the United Congregations, arrived in Tulpehocken, supposedly to lend Stoever his support in the struggle with the Moravians. In reality, Kraft tried to unite both factions around himself, for like Zinzendorf he cherished dreams of establishing himself as a Lutheran superintendent. Instead, Kraft managed to form a third party, thus greatly adding to the already confused religious situation.

Meanwhile, news of the count's American activities reached Francke at Halle. When it became evident that Zinzendorf was making deep inroads into Pennsylvania Lutheranism, Francke promptly resurrected the call entrusted to him by the United Congregations seven years previously. Because Halle had terminated negotiations with them in 1739, the only logical reason for Francke's turnabout was the emergency posed by the Moravian threat. He now abandoned all the preconditions and guarantees which he had previously demanded and upon which the negotiations had broken. It is also questionable whether Francke any longer had the right to issue a call in the name of the United Congregations since they had informed him in 1739 that they were now directing their appeal to the Darmstadt Consistory.

Nevertheless, the call was offered to Henry Melchior Muhlenberg on September 6, 1741, and after some deliberation was accepted. Muhlenberg hurriedly set out from Grosshennersdorf where he had, ironically, labored under the patronage of Zinzendorf's aunt and traveled to America by way of London. He finally reached Charleston, South Carolina, on September 23, 1742, then immediately set out for Ebenezer, Georgia, to confer with Boltzius and Gronau. Evidently Francke had decided that because the United Congregations had previously expressed their trust for Boltzius by repeatedly urging his dispatch on an investigatory visit, Boltzius should accompany Muhlenberg to Philadelphia, thus lending him his support in the difficult matter of establishing his authority. By October 20, 1742, the two clergymen were back in Charleston vainly searching for a ship that would sail before the winter freeze. When none was found, Boltzius returned to Georgia to be followed later by Muhlenberg should he be unable to arrange passage to Philadelphia. While in Charleston, Muhlenberg came across two reports, one describing Count Zinzendorf's Pennsylvania conferences, the other reporting the July clash between Lutherans and Moravians in Philadelphia.[70] Eager now to reach his parishes, Muhlenberg booked passage on a small sloop bound for Philadelphia on November 12, 1742, though Boltzius was unable to make the trip. Thirteen days later Muhlenberg arrived in the city of brotherly love ready to do battle with the Moravians.

His first task, however, was to gain control of the New Hanover and Providence congregations, as yet untainted by Moravianism, and to wrest the Philadelphia congregation from the hands of the pretender Kraft. The day after his arrival in Philadelphia, Muhlenberg set out for New Hanover in the company of Philip Brandt, one of its residents. From him he learned that the congregation was now served by a "quack salver" named John George Schmidt.[71] Muhlenberg quickly gathered together the elders of the church, read them his call from Ziegenhagen, and, on November 28, 1742, preached his inaugural sermon, unceremoniously dismissing Schmidt. It is evident from his journals that not everyone willingly accepted Muhlenberg. Some wished to retain Schmidt; others wanted him to assist Muhlenberg as a deacon; still others, who had broken away from the Lutheran church because of previous fraudulent pastors, refused to commit themselves to Muhlenberg until they were certain he was what he claimed. Finally there were those who balked at the mention of salary and refused to bind themselves to his support.[72] This was Muhlenberg's first experience with American voluntarism, a phenomenon strange to him.[73]

Muhlenberg then journeyed to Providence in the company of three New Hanover elders. Here his reception was more cordial. Once again he presented his call from Ziegenhagen to the senior deacon. Though his authority was not disputed, Muhlenberg was advised to split the congregations with Valentine Kraft.[74] This, however, he had no intentions of doing, so he went back to Philadelphia for a showdown with Kraft.

Kraft and Muhlenberg first met face to face in a German inn in Philadelphia on December 1, 1742. Kraft welcomed him but chided him for his independent actions. Finally he promised to place Muhlenberg in one of the congregations. Kraft had already concocted a general presbytery for Pennsylvania, a special presbytery for Philadelphia, and a consistory of which he was president and John Caspar Stoever, Jr., assessor. He informed Muhlenberg that these administrative arrangements had been reported to the Darmstadt Consistory from which he claimed his appointment. Muhlenberg, however, refused to recognize the authority of either Kraft or his consistory, insisting, instead, on the validity of his call from Ziegenhagen and the authority of the Halle fathers.[75]

Kraft then tried to persuade Muhlenberg to join his consistory and assist him in the ordination of a schoolmaster. This Muhlenberg flatly refused to do, disputing Kraft's right to ordain anyone.[76] Finally Kraft hit on the idea of isolating Muhlenberg in the back country by appointing him to serve Providence and New Hanover.[77] In reply Muhlenberg once again read his call from Ziegenhagen, denied that anyone but he was the legal pastor of all the United Congregations, and rejected any claim advanced by Kraft to jurisdiction in Pennsylvania.[78] In less than a month after his arrival, Muhlenberg had firmly installed himself as leader of the Lutherans in the

Philadelphia area. Kraft, abandoning the struggle, departed for Lancaster on December 15, 1742, while Muhlenberg set about consolidating his position. He presented all three congregations with a document which pledged their subscription to three points: (1) that Muhlenberg was the only rightfully called pastor in accord with the Unaltered Augsburg Confession, (2) that the congregation would support and obey him and his lawful successors, and (3) that it would shun the teachings and ministrations of those who violated the Unaltered Augsburg Confession.[79]

The next logical step was a meeting with the count himself. On December 30, 1742, Muhlenberg sent two of his deacons to Peter Boehler to demand that the Moravians surrender the church book and chalice which belonged to the Lutheran church.[80] Boehler replied that they were in the count's possession and that Zinzendorf desired to meet Muhlenberg. When Muhlenberg arrived at the count's home, he found himself confronted by a board of inquiry composed of Zinzendorf and his elders. They required Muhlenberg to stand throughout the conversation and the count addressed him in the familiar *du,* instead of the polite *Sie.* Zinzendorf then challenged the validity of Muhlenberg's call, claiming, instead, that he was the only legitimate pastor and demanding an apology from the renegades who followed Muhlenberg. For his part, Muhlenberg insisted on the derivation of his authority from Ziegenhagen and Francke (whom Zinzendorf dismissed as arch liars and hypocrites), refused any apology, and chided the count for his duplicity in masquerading under pseudonyms and for his unusual and irregular behavior in holding orders in both Lutheran and Moravian churches.[81] When Zinzendorf threatened to go to Germany to expose the machinations of the Hallensians, Muhlenberg could not resist throwing a well-aimed barb: "You certainly are full of suggestions; in fact you are just what your aunt [the Baroness von Gersdorf] told me you were."[82] To which Zinzendorf replied: "Hold your tongue as far as my aunt is concerned, or I shall be compelled to expose her."[83] At length the count offered to return the cup and book provided Muhlenberg signed a receipt, thus acknowledging Moravian ownership, and apologized. This he refused to do since, as he told Zinzendorf, he did not recognize the count as a genuine Lutheran, let alone as a Lutheran pastor and inspector.[84] Finally Muhlenberg reluctantly went to the courts causing the mayor of Philadelphia to order the Moravians to return the disputed items. After repeated evasive replies by the count, Muhlenberg let the matter drop since, all along, his purpose had merely been to expose Zinzendorf as a liar and hypocrite.[85] On January 1, 1743, Zinzendorf returned to London. The Moravian problem, however, still remained for Muhlenberg to solve.

Everywhere Moravian incursions assumed the same form. They would send a minister posing as a Lutheran pastor to a congregation which was either pastorless, or served by an untrained, itinerant preacher, or a specially hired schoolmaster. Soon, according to Muhlenberg, they attracted the allegiance of the better classes, the most wealthy and worldly Lutherans.[86] Ultimately their peculiar doctrines aroused suspicion, and the more orthodox members of the congregation would demand that they depart. Backed by their followers, the Moravians then denounced the orthodox as schismatics and attempted to seize the school and church buildings.[87] The congregation then splintered into factions, bitter strife broke out, and the matter wound up in court. There, according to Muhlenberg, the Lutherans were at a decided disadvantage because they were for the most part poor and uneducated, nor could they afford the legal fees involved. As a result, many Lutherans either went over to the Moravians or abandoned religion altogether. As Muhlenberg discovered, it was useless in America to appeal to a secular authority for a decree on doctrinal purity because of the separation of church and state. In matters of religion too, each person had full liberty of choice, and the pastor's tenure depended on the good will of the majority.[88]

Compounding Muhlenberg's difficulties was the scattered condition of his flock. German Evangelical Lutheran settlers were the most recent arrivals in Pennsylvania. By the time they came, the best lands had already been settled. The luckiest were able to scratch out a marginal existence on the less productive lands. Most first had to work off their indenture secured as payment for the voyage from Germany, then had to accept tenant status on the spare lands of their wealthier neighbors. When rents rose too high, they pushed farther into the wilderness, leaving Muhlenberg to follow them as best he could. By 1747 only one-half of all the parishioners in the United Congregations were members of the original flock that had greeted Muhlenberg four years previously.[89]

The Moravians, on the other hand, had had no lack of laborers who served without pay and preached in English to win over the colonial German youth already slipping away from the moorings of Germanic culture under the pervasive influence of the process of Americanization. Since their central authority was nearby, while Muhlenberg was bound to European ecclesiastical superiors, the Moravians were somewhat more mobile and adaptable to the changing American environment than were the Lutherans. Their willingness to conform, chameleon-like, to any and all denominational practices, made them yet more fluid and dangerous. Even the arrival of the Reverend Peter Brunnholtz and the two Halle catechists, John Nicholas Kurtz and John Schaum, in January, 1745, did not alleviate the situation, for by then Muhlenberg's ministerial obligations had expanded beyond Pennsylvania into Maryland, New York, and New Jersey. Brunnholtz and Muhlenberg could not preach in every church on each Sunday. And on the Sundays when they were absent, their congregations were wont to attend Moravian services.

Fortunately Muhlenberg was more a practical preacher than a speculative theologian. It was essential to the very survival of Pennsylvania Lutheranism that he was. A less gifted man might have been palsied by the will of his superiors in Europe. It is to Muhlenberg's credit, however, that he correctly grasped the situation and discovered the only solution to the Moravian threat, namely, organization of the church, improvized the means to achieve this, and adapted to the American environment. Muhlenberg's Americanization process was a compromise between democracy and authoritarianism, retaining European features without compromising American distinctiveness.

Distinctive features of American Lutheranism which he found harmful to the church, Muhlenberg did away with. In this way he countered Moravian pandenominationalism by emphasizing

Lutheran exclusivism in his opposition to union churches which fostered indifference to doctrinal distinctions, opened the door to teachers not in conformity with the Augsburg Confession, and led to interminable law suits over ownership. Instead he spurred his congregations on to erect churches of their own, forcing them at the same time to subscribe to articles legally excluding any preacher not in full accord with Lutheran teachings.

Because the European custom of collecting fees for the administration of the sacraments had fallen into disrepute through the abuses of grasping itinerant preachers, Muhlenberg abolished the practice, relying instead on an annually contracted salary supplemented by whatever generosity the people might care to show.[90] To combat ignorance in doctrinal matters, which left Lutherans susceptible to Moravian incursions, he instituted schools for youth in every parish, supervising them himself wherever possible. Liturgical practices were codified and made conformable to the diverse backgrounds of his flock.[91]

Most significant of all, however, was Muhlenberg's willingness to ignore instructions from Europe when they interfered with his work in America. In this vein he ultimately took upon himself the right of ordination and the erection of an American ministerium. Thus Muhlenberg met the Moravian threat through pragmatic improvisation and the extension of his own authority beyond the limits of his original call.

Gradually this authority came to be recognized outside the confines of the United Congregations, making Muhlenberg virtual superintendent of the Lutheran church in English America.

Congregations experiencing difficulties frequently sought Muhlenberg's assistance. For example, as the Tulpehocken confusion deepened, some Lutherans there turned to Muhlenberg for leadership. By 1743 three parties existed in Tulpehocken: the Moravians who held old Rieth's church; the Stoever faction which had possession of the new Christ Church; and a third faction leaderless since Kraft's departure for Lancaster, which held no church but claimed rights in Christ Church. In 1743 this third faction appealed to Muhlenberg for assistance. Since he was preoccupied with his own congregations, Muhlenberg was unable to accept its call but promised instead to find a suitable pastor.

In July, 1743, the Reverend Tobias Wagner arrived in Pennsylvania from his former pastorate at Waldoborough in the Maine region. Muhlenberg finally recommended Wagner to the Tulpehocken congregation which extended him a call on October 25, 1743.[92] Hostility soon developed between the two men. Wagner was an orthodox Lutheran, as was Stoever, and thus highly suspicious of Muhlenberg's pietism. Also because it did not receive Muhlenberg, its first choice, the congregation refused to give Wagner more than an *ad interim*, one year appointment. Finally, because Wagner had the poorest segment of Tulpehocken Lutherans, they were unable to provide him with a salary which he felt would be sufficient for his large family.[93] Somehow Wagner became convinced that Muhlenberg was supported by a stipend from the Anglican Society for the Propagation of the Gospel in Foreign Parts and demanded a like stipend for himself. Despite congregational dissatisfaction, Muhlenberg was able to get Wagner a second one-year appointment in 1744. But Wagner proved himself incapable of winning over either the Stoever or Moravian factions so the confusion continued unabated.

Meanwhile Muhlenberg had befriended Conrad Weiser who then supported the Moravian faction. On April 22, 1745, Tobias Wagner united Muhlenberg and Weiser's daughter, Anna Maria, in marriage. Thus Muhlenberg greatly strengthened his position among Germans in Pennsylvania by marrying into one of the province's most influential German families. After the wedding ceremony, during Wagner's absence, the elders informed Muhlenberg that if he provided them with a new pastor, all three factions would unite. Muhlenberg then submitted to them a written call, promising to get them a new pastor if all three groups subscribed and pledged sufficient financial support. When only Wagner's adherents subscribed, Muhlenberg informed them that they must stay with Wagner until he could be placed elsewhere. This incident sheds light on Muhlenberg's view of his own authority. Legally, Wagner was the pastor at

Tulpehocken, removable only by the congregation, not by a fellow pastor. In asserting his right to remove him, Muhlenberg was not only claiming the powers of a superintendent but undermining what little influence Wagner still retained. This administrative prerogative Muhlenberg based on the fact that the call had first been entrusted to him and given by him to Wagner. Hence he claimed that he had the right to withdraw it at his pleasure. Still Muhlenberg had not himself accepted the call so would not normally have had any authority to dispose of it once accepted by another.

Rightfully annoyed at this interference, Wagner allied with Stoever against Muhlenberg, resigned his Tulpehocken post on April 30, 1746, and moved to the Reading area.[94] Muhlenberg now appointed a catechist, John Nicholas Kurtz, to Tulpehocken, giving him emergency powers to administer the Lord's supper to the dying, again on his own authority.

During Wagner's time, the Moravians had erected a new stone church to replace the Rieth's old log church. Christ Church was still held by Wagner and Stoever's faction. With the accession of Conrad Weiser to Kurtz's side, the Halle faction gained strength from the other two parties. Eventually it built a church of its own.

During the winter of 1747, the deadlock between the three parties was finally broken when Leonard Rieth, the Moravian miller who had donated the land for Rieth church used by the Moravians, fell and was crushed to death in his mill's cog wheel. His sons, who were not themselves Moravians, asked the Moravian pastor to bury him in his cemetery. For some reason, he refused, so the sons turned to Kurtz who agreed to preach the funeral sermon in the Moravian-held church. Kurtz led the funeral procession from Rieth's home to the church, sending ahead for the key. Since the Moravians refused to surrender it, Kurtz was forced to conduct a graveside service in knee-deep snow. Dissension over this disgraceful conduct broke out among the Moravians, resulting in the recall of their pastor. Spangenberg himself went to Tulpehocken to reconcile the feud but was unable to do so. Finally Conrad Weiser seized both the church and school buildings, earning for himself an excommunication from

Bethlehem. In the autumn of 1747, Brunnholtz came to rededi-
cate the church as an Evangelical place of worship.[95] Eventually
all three parties came together, thus terminating the Moravian
threat in Tulpehocken.

In Lancaster there was even greater confusion than in Tul-
pehocken. After 1710 a wave of Scotch-Irish and German
Palatine settlers had moved into the area. By 1730 Lancaster was
a flourishing town. Lutherans organized a congregation, which
Stoever served until 1742. Toward the end of the following year,
Valentine Kraft, recently ejected from Philadelphia, began
ministrations there, with an occasional visit from the Reverend
John Dylander, Swedish provost and pastor of Gloria Dei
Church in Philadelphia. Because of the great distance involved,
Dylander suggested that Lancaster Lutherans apply to Upsala
for a permanent pastor, which they did.[96] After carefully
checking his qualifications, the archbishop of Upsala appointed
the Reverend Lawrence Thorstonsen Nyberg. Unknown to
church authorities, however, Nyberg had become involved with
the Moravians through a Swedish friend, Arvin Gradin. On his
way over to Lancaster, Nyberg had met with Spangenberg in
London but denied any connection with the Moravians when
questioned by Muhlenberg on his arrival in 1744.

Though Nyberg soon departed from pure doctrine, he stead-
fastly denied having any association with the Moravians. Secretly, however, he carried on a lengthy correspondence with
Bethlehem and attended various Moravian conferences. Gradually Nyberg moved into open opposition to Muhlenberg, denouncing him as a pietist and a Hallensian.[97] During Advent of
1745, the Moravians held a conference in Lancaster. Nyberg was
most helpful in securing for them lodgings and the use of the
town hall, and, despite protests from his congregation, he personally graced the meetings with his presence.

On the Sunday following the conference, Nyberg arrived at
the church only to find that the doors were locked and guarded
by orthodox Lutherans.[98] With his followers, he stormed the
church, took possession, and locked the others out. They in turn
appealed to the governor and Muhlenberg for assistance. When
the governor suggested that Nyberg submit the dispute to the

arbitration of the other German Lutheran pastors, including Muhlenberg, he replied that this was impossible because they were heretical pietists while he alone was orthodox.[99] He did agree, however, to have the archbishop of Upsala decide the case. Technically Nyberg was within his rights, for though he ministered to a German Lutheran congregation his call had come through Sweden. Thus Dylander, the Swedish provost in America, and not Muhlenberg had jurisdiction in the matter.

The governor worked out an interim compromise giving Nyberg the use of the church on Sunday mornings, the others on Sunday afternoons.[100] When the German Lutherans asked Nyberg if they could use the church on a weekday morning to celebrate a feast, he refused. Once again they seized the church and locked Nyberg out. Once more the matter wound up in court, this time with Nyberg charging his opponents with disturbing the peace. At the governor's request, Muhlenberg, Brunnholtz, and Wagner went to Lancaster on January 31, 1746, to try to work out a settlement. One week later they proposed that a German Lutheran pastor be appointed for Nyberg's opponents while he continued to serve his own followers. Both parties would share the church and cemetery, and each would have its own elders and treasury. The one condition was that Nyberg, when preaching in the church, had to stay in line with traditional Lutheran doctrine.[101] Conrad Weiser delivered these proposals to Nyberg who curtly rejected them. On February 6, 1746, the disturbance of the peace suit was decided against Nyberg who withdrew to build his own church.

Despite the subsequent condemnation of Nyberg's preaching by the archbishop of Upsala, the conflict did not end. Nyberg continued to attack Muhlenberg in the German papers and to make inroads on Lancaster Lutherans on the alternate Sundays when Kurtz, whom Muhlenberg had appointed to the town, was absent. Disreputable conduct on the part of both German Reformed and Lutheran ministers worked to his advantage. Caspar Schnorr, the Reformed preacher in Lancaster, was found guilty of rape, while John Caspar Stoever managed to get so drunk in a Lancaster tavern that he vomited in public. The German printer, Christopher Sauer, gleefully reported all the lurid details, causing some parishioners to forsake their church in disgust and join the Moravians. Not until the Reverend John Frederick Handschuh, a Halle missioner, was placed permanently at Lancaster by Muhlenberg in 1748 did some semblance of order return.

At the end of 1748, a relative calm prevailed in Pennsylvania leading Muhlenberg to report, somewhat cautiously, to Halle that "During this past year the Zinzendorfers . . . have been somewhat more quiet and peaceful than usual."[102] The explanation for this lull in battle can be found in the fact that the Moravians had finally abandoned their *tropus* scheme and decided to form themselves into a church. On June 6, 1749, England granted them recognition as a legal church within the Empire.[103] Henceforth Muhlenberg would be relatively free to turn his attention to other matters. The great Moravian threat was finally at an end.

Muhlenberg's opposition to Moravian incursions in colonial Lutheran churches cannot be considered simply as a struggle for supremacy between two somewhat divergent strains of Lutheran pietism. At the basis of the Pennsylvania controversies lay Muhlenberg's conviction that Moravianism was heresy rendered yet more dangerous for its Lutheran disguise. Curiously enough, Muhlenberg was able to establish a Lutheran church in English America in part at least because of Moravian inroads. The key to the stabilization of colonial Lutheranism lay in its ability to cast off its European shackles and adapt itself to the circumstances of the New World. Muhlenberg undertook the Americanization of Lutheranism partly to combat Moravianism. In a rather indirect way, therefore, Zinzendorf deserves some share of Muhlenberg's reputation as the founder and organizer of American Lutheranism.

NOTES

[1]Edward Langton, *History of the Moravian Church* (London: George Allen & Unwin, Ltd., 1956). p. 26.

[2]Ibid., pp. 29–30.

[3]Ibid., p. 64.

[4]Ibid., p. 65.

[5]Ibid., p. 66.

[6]Ibid., p. 67.

[7]Ibid., p. 68.

[8]Ibid., p. 57.

[9]Ibid., p. 73.

[10]John Amos Comenius (1592–1671) led the Moravians from Bohemia to exile in 1627. In 1632 a synod of the church was held at Lissa in Poland which consecrated Comenius as bishop. Cossak invasions of Lissa in 1656 scattered what was left of the church. Comenius departed for Amsterdam where he died in 1671. Before his death, however, at the Synod of Mielenczyn in 1662, he commissioned Daniel Vetter to act on his authority in consecrating Nicholas Gertichius and Peter Jablonsky as bishops, thus ensuring the apostolic succession.

[11]Langton, p. 74.

[12]Ibid., p. 80.

[13]Ronald A. Knox, *Enthusiasm: A Chapter in the History of Religion* (Oxford: Clarendon Press, 1950), p. 408.

[14]Lewis von Zinzendorf, *Sixteen Discourses on Jesus Christ Our Lord: Being an Exposition of the Second Part of the Creed Preached at Berlin by the Right Reverend, Lewis, Bishop of the Ancient Brethren's Churches,* trans. from the High Dutch, 2d ed. (London: William Bowyer, 1750), pp. 9, 16; hereafter referred to as *Discourses*.

[15]Ibid., p. 18.

[16]Ibid., pp. 8, 66.

[17]Ibid., p. 10

[18]Ibid., pp. 20–21.

[19]Ibid., pp. 20–21, 121–22.

[20]Ibid., p. 20; see also Knox, p. 410; and J. Taylor Hamilton, *A History of the Church Known as the Moravian Church, or the Unitas Fratrum, or the Unity of the Brethren, During the Eighteenth and Nineteenth Centuries* (Bethlehem, Pa.: Times Publishing Co., 1900), p. 190.

[21]*Discourses,* p. 21.

[22]Ibid., p. 10.

[23]*Discourses,* pp. 101–02.

[24]Ibid., p. 122.

[25]Ibid., pp. 123, 54–55.

[26]Ibid., pp. 6, 115, 126, 104.

[27]Ibid., p. 57.

[28]Ibid., p. 153.

[29]Ibid., p. 129.

[30]Ibid., p. 66.

[31]Ibid., p. 144.

[32]John R. Weinlick, *Count Zinzendorf* (New York: Abingdon Press, 1956), pp. 198–203.

[33]Langton, p. 83.

[34]Ibid., p. 84.

[35]E. De Schweinitz, *The Moravian Manual* (Philadelphia: Lindsay and Blakiston, 1859), p. 47.

[36]Lucy Forney Bittinger, *The Germans in Colonial Times* (Philadelphia: J. B. Lippincott, 1900), p. 171.

[37]Ibid., pp. 169–70; see also Henry Eyster Jacobs, *A History of the Evangelical Lutheran Church in the United States* (New York: Christian Literature Co., 1893), pp. 199–200.

[38]Levin Theodore Reichel, *The Early History of the Church of the United Brethren, Commonly called Moravians, in North America, A.D. 1734–1748* (Nazareth, Pa.:Moravian Historical Society, 1888), p. 70.

[39]Martin Ellsworth Lodge, "The Great Awakening in the Middle Colonies," Ph.D. dissertation, University of California at Berkeley, 1964, p. 236.

[40]Ibid.

[41]Ibid., p. 237.

[42]A. J. Lewis, *Zinzendorf the Ecumenical Pioneer: A Study in the Moravian Contribution to Christian Mission and Unity* (Philadelphia: Westminster Press, 1962), p. 142.

[43]Weinlick, pp. 151–52; Langton, pp. 113–14.

[44]Lodge, p. 239; Reichel, p. 86.

[45]Lewis, p. 143.

[46]Lodge, p. 241.

[47]For the text of Boehm's pamphlet, entitled *Getreuer Warnungs Brief an die Hochteutsche Evangelisch Reformierten Gemeinden und alle deren Glieder in Pensylvanien, zur getreuen Warschauung, vor denen Leuthen, welche unter dem nahmen von Herrn-Hüther bekandt seyn. Umb sich vor deren Seelverderblichen und Gewissenverwüstenden Lehre zu hüthen und wohl vorzusehen, damit sie nicht, durch den schein ihres euterlichen scheinheiligen Wesens, und selbst eingebildeten Gerechtigkeit und Heiligkeit, zu ihrer Seelen ewigen Schaden, mögen verführt werden. Nach dem Exempel eines Ehrwürdigen Kirchen Raths von Amsterdam in Holland*, see Johann Philip Fresenius, *Nachrichten von Herrnhutischen Sachen*, 3 (Frankfort: Heinrich Ludwig Bronner, 1748), pp. 562–677.

[48]Lodge, p. 423.

[49]Weinlick, pp. 166–67.

[50]Lodge, p. 249. Muhlenberg admits that the count did indeed obtain a written call but that no one had subscribed to it. See Henry Melchior Muhlenberg, *The Journals of Henry Melchior Muhlenberg in Three Volumes*, trans. Theodore G. Tappert and John W. Doberstein, vol. I (Philadelphia: Muhlenberg Press, 1942), p. 75. Hereafter referred to as *I Journals*.

[51]William J. Mann, *The Life and Times of Henry Melchior Muhlenberg* (Philadelphia: G. W. Frederick, 1887), p. 114.

⁵²For an account of the riot, see Fresenius, III, 205–7; *I Journals,* pp. 75–76; Mann, p. 115.

⁵³Lodge, p. 250. Secretary Richard Peters reported Boehm's feelings on this incident to the proprietors on January 15, 1743. It should be mentioned that Peters thought Boehm was a Lutheran minister and hence fails to mention the Reformed.

"There is a great quarrel between ye Lutherans and Moravians, chiefly on account of principles. The Count's party increasing considerably, the Lutheran minister, Philip Boehm, could not bear it. The Lutheran meeting house is on a lot of Mr. Allen's, and by contract with the Lutherans, as I understand, ye Moravians were to use it every third Sunday. Philip Boehm wanted to hinder them from this contract, and finding no other method would do, one Sunday morning, as Christopher Pyrlaeus was performing Divine service, a party of Lutherans appeared at ye door. He took no notice. . . . Ye Lutherans then came on with violence, and drove him and the Moravians out of the meeting house, and locked ye doors. The Count got the Lutherans indicted for a riot. . . . At the trial, ye Lutherans were acquitted. There is indeed a mortal aversion between Boehm's congregation and ye Count's people. . . . I tried to soften and accomodate ye differences between ye two parties, and thought I had some influence on Boehm; but ye moment I mentioned it his eyes perfectly struck fire, and he declared with great passion he would so soon agree with ye devil as with ye Count. He is a hot, indiscreet man; and after expatiating on the Christianity of his temper, I left him with abundance of contempt." Quoted in William J. Hinke, ed., *Life and Letters of the Rev. John Philip Boehm, Founder of the Reformed Church in Pennsylvania, 1683–1749* (Philadelphia: Publication and Sunday School Board of the Reformed Church in the United States, 1916), pp. 365–66.

⁵⁴*I Journals,* p. 75.

⁵⁵Theodore Emanual Schmauk, *The Lutheran Church in Pennsylvania, 1638–1800* (Lancaster: Pennsylvania German Society, 1902), vol. 12 of *Proceedings and Addresses,* pp. 438–39.

⁵⁶Ibid., p. 441.

⁵⁷Ibid., pp. 447, 468.

⁵⁸Ibid., pp. 469–70.

⁵⁹Ibid., p. 473.

⁶⁰*I Journals,* p. 170.

⁶¹Schmauk, p. 491.

⁶²Conrad Weiser to Peter Brunnholtz, undated, in Johann Ludwig Schulze, ed., *Nachrichten von dem vereinigten Deutschen Evangelish-Lutherischen Gemeinen in Nord-America, absonderlich in Pennsylvanien,* 1 (Allentown: Brobst, Diehl, & Co.), pp. 191–92. Hereafter referred to as *Nachrichten.*

⁶³Schmauk, pp. 488–89.

⁶⁴Ibid., p. 493.

⁶⁵Ibid., p. 496.

⁶⁶See Ibid., pp. 497–98, note 563, for the text of Webb's document, entitled "Power of Attorney in the Lithbecker and Stiever [*sic.*] Difficulties at the Reeds

Church, 1736." The more common spellings of these names are Leutbecker and Stoever. In colonial times spelling was inconsistent & varied.

⁶⁷Schmauk, p. 503.

⁶⁸*I Journals*, p. 170.

⁶⁹Schmauk, p. 510.

⁷⁰"In the evening [October 24, 1742] I accidently received a printed book in which were described seven conferences which Count Zinzendorf had held in Pennsylvania, particularly Germantown, Philadelphia, and New Hanover. Also received a document concerning a tumult which had taken place in an old house on July 18 in Philadelphia between the Reformed, the Moravian Brethren, and the Lutherans. The weak and immature actions which Mr. Zinzendorf exhibited in the conference and the tumult of July 18 grieved me very much." (*I Journals*, p. 63)

⁷¹Ibid., p. 67.

⁷²Ibid.

⁷³"The deacons and elders are unable to do anything about it [congregational intransigence], for in religious and church matters, each has the right to do what he pleases. The government has nothing to do with it and will not concern itself with such matters. Everything depends on the vote of the majority. A preacher must fight his way through with the sword of the Spirit alone and depend on faith in the living God and His promises, if he wants to be a preacher and proclaim the truth." (*I Journals*, p. 67)

⁷⁴Ibid., pp. 67–68.

⁷⁵Ibid., p. 68. Muhlenberg considered Kraft's consistory to be a vehicle for the validation of unworthy clergymen.

⁷⁶Ibid., p. 69.

⁷⁷Ibid., p. 71.

⁷⁸Ibid.

⁷⁹Ibid., pp. 73–74.

⁸⁰Ibid., p. 76.

⁸¹Ibid., p. 177.

⁸²Ibid., p. 79.

⁸³Ibid.

⁸⁴Ibid., p. 82.

⁸⁵Ibid.

⁸⁶Muhlenberg's journals were intended for publication to justify the actions of the author. Hence they tend to be somewhat vague on his controversial actions and highly self-justifying. On certain issues, such as his role in the American Revolution, Muhlenberg later deleted whole pages. The *Hallesche Nachrichten* consist mainly of reports by Muhlenberg to the reverend fathers in Europe, published to raise money for the Pennsylvania missions. Though they are based on the journals, Muhlenberg presents only those facts he desires them to read.

⁸⁷*I Journals*, p. 158.

⁸⁸Ibid., p. 67.

⁸⁹Ibid., p. 142.

⁹⁰Ibid., p. 84.

[91] Ibid., p. 193.
[92] Schmauk, p. 525.
[93] Ibid., p. 529; *I Journals*, p. 171.
[94] Schmauk, pp. 533–36; Mann, p. 148.
[95] *I Journals*, p. 172.
[96] Mann, p. 174.
[97] *I Journals*, p. 164.
[98] Ibid.
[99] Ibid., p. 165.
[100] Ibid.
[101] Ibid., pp. 113–14.
[102] Ibid., p. 211.
[103] Langton, p. 133.

4

The Threat from the Right: Muhlenberg versus New York Orthodoxy

Once Muhlenberg had blunted the thrust of left-wing Moravianism and eliminated Zinzendorf as a serious threat to the stability of a churchly brand of colonial pietism, he turned his attention to the provinces of New York and New Jersey, the last Lutheran outposts in English America still not under the influence of Halle. In those colonies there flourished an orthodox brand of Lutheranism dominated by the Reverend Wilhelm Christoph Berkenmeyer, a missioner from the Hamburg consistory.

Born in 1686 at Bodenteich in the Duchy of Luneburg, Berkenmeyer had studied theology at the University of Altdorf, where he thoroughly imbibed orthodox doctrine. As a subject of the Consistory of Hamburg, the scene of particularly violent clashes between the orthodox and pietistic wings of Lutheranism, Berkenmeyer developed a strong dislike for Spener and his Halle associates which profoundly influenced his actions in colonial affairs.

After the death of Justus Falckner in 1723, the New York Lutheran congregation sent a call for a pastor to the Hamburg Consistory which in turn presented it to Berkenmeyer after ordaining him on May 25, 1725.[1] Berkenmeyer arrived in New York City on the following September 11th, only to find that, as

108

in Muhlenberg's case, his pastorate was occupied by a pretender, a pietistically inclined tailor named Bernhard von Dieren who claimed ordination by the Reverend Gerhard Henkel.[2] Though Berkenmeyer disposed of von Dieren in short order, the incident only served to further intensify his dislike for and mistrust of pietists.[3]

Because of the immense geographical area covered by his call, Berkenmeyer, realizing that the congregations could not be adequately served by one man, divided them into five parishes, pastors for which he secured from the orthodox Hamburg Consistory and Old Hamburg Church in London. He then tried to unite the whole into some sort of supracongregational organization.[4] Since two of these parishes, the Raritan and the Central Hudson, existed before Hamburg began to send missioners on a regular basis, Berkenmeyer had first to move against their pastors, replacing them with Hamburg men who would be subject to his authority.

The Raritan was a region in New Jersey which embraced four congregations: "the Mountain," Racheway, Leslysland, and Hanover.[5] Since 1724 it had been served by Daniel Falckner, the brother of Justus, who immediately incurred Berkenmeyer's disdain. Because Falckner had been ordained by the same Gerhard Henkel who allegedly ordained von Dieren, this made him, in Berkenmeyer's eyes, both a vagabond and a pietist.[6] Equally offensive to Berkenmeyer were reports of Falckner's alleged immorality, which he deliberately broadcast in an attempt to undermine Falckner's authority and force him to resign.[7] Claiming that his brother Justus had warned against Daniel, Berkenmeyer finally secured his resignation in exchange for a cash settlement in 1731.[8] Warning Hamburg that the Raritan now lay exposed to "all the fanatics in Pennsylvania,"[9] he secured the parish for another Hamburg missioner, the Reverend Johann August Wolf, a native of Lebegin, who arrived in 1734.

The Central Hudson parish, centered at Rhinebeck, with other congregations at East Camp, Tar Bush, Ancram, and Staatsburg, was organized in 1731. On March 31, 1732, the congregants extended a call to the Reverend Johann Spaler.

Spaler had originally been given a call by Court Preacher Ziegenhagen to accompany a group of German immigrants who intended to settle in Virginia but changed their minds at sea and sailed for New York instead. His connections with the Hallensian Ziegenhagen as well as his continued refusal to recognize Berkenmeyer's authority, led Berkenmeyer to mount a public campaign of vituperation against him which culminated on August 8, 1736, in his issuance of a letter denying the validity of Spaler's call.[10] His reputation and authority seriously undermined by these charges, Spaler resigned his post in 1736. Ten years later the Hamburg consistory sent the Reverend John Christopher Hartwick to replace him.

When the Reverend Michael Christian Knoll, a native of Rendsburg in Schleswig-Holstein, who had studied at the University of Kiel, was sent to New York by the Hamburg Consistory in 1732, Berkenmeyer created two more parishes. Knoll assumed the pastorate of the Lower Hudson parish which included New York City, "Pieter Lassens," Hackensack, and Ramapo. Berkenmeyer established himself in an Upper Hudson parish centered at Loonenburg, with additional congregations at Albany, New Town, Kiskatemensy, Claverack, and Hosek. A fifth parish, the Schoharie-Mohawk, was established in 1743, with the arrival of the Reverend Peter Nicholas Sommer, also sent from Hamburg. Sommer established his headquarters at Schoharie, serving other congregations in Stone Arabia, the Falls, and Cani-Schoharie.[11] An orthodox Lutheran himself, as well as Berkenmeyer's son-in-law, Sommer gave Berkenmeyer unquestioned support in his claims to ecclesiastical authority.

Similar to Muhlenberg, Berkenmeyer realized the grave necessity of a supracongregational authority to maintain order and uniformity among New York Lutherans. Unlike his Pennsylvania counterpart, however, he never did achieve a lasting, effective synodical structure. There were several reasons for this failure, which in the long run was caused by an inability to adapt to the new American environment.

Part of the explanation of why he failed where Muhlenberg succeeded can be found in Berkenmeyer's orthodoxy. Hamburg, his European theater of operations, had been a principal battleground between pietism and orthodoxy. Under attack as it was, Hamburg Lutheran orthodoxy drew in upon itself, emphasizing its doctrinal, liturgical, and denominational distinctiveness. Such traits were deeply imbedded in Berkenmeyer and proved a great hindrance to his long-range effectiveness in colonial New York and New Jersey. Berkenmeyer's ecclesiastical vision, in contrast to that of Muhlenberg, was that of an alien immigrant church surrounded by heretical religious sects hostile to it. The long history of Dutch Reformed persecutions of Hew York Lutheranism only served to reinforce his tendency toward isolationism. Berkenmeyer was not ecumenical in any sense of the word, nor did he enter into contact with neighboring ministers of other religious denominations as did Muhlenberg. Though he did make some effort to adapt to his new environment, his excessive conservatism, which was too eager to preserve both form and substance of the European church, prevented him from going far enough in this direction, thus rendering nugatory what few concessions he did make.

Thus in the matter of the liturgy Berkenmeyer, as Muhlenberg, insisted upon continuity and order in the schema used by all the congregations, for this was necessary if any cohesive union were to bind them into a collective body. But, unlike Muhlenberg, he went beyond continuity in insisting on a rigid conformity to a church agenda which was mainly European in spirit and content. In his General Church Order of 1735, Berkenmeyer laid down a minutely detailed liturgical schema which insisted on an exact following of the Amsterdam Church Agenda of 1689. His only novel contribution was his outlawing of conventicles to discourage the intrusion of any pietistic elements.[12]

Berkenmeyer's frame of ecclesiastical government, which, with few exceptions, closely followed that of the Amsterdam Lutheran church, was explained in the second part of the constitution. The consistory, or church council, composed of pastor, elders, and deacons, was designated as the ruling body of the congregation. Provisions were included for regular as well as emergency sessions of the council. While the elders controlled church funds, in important matters they were to seek the advice of their retired members as well as of the deacons. No provision was made for obtaining full congregational approval on any issue, including the calling of a pastor, nor did the congregation elect the members of the church council.[13]

In the matter of pastoral calls, Berkenmeyer's constitution bound the congregations to seek ministerial aid only from orthodox ministeriums or universities. Any pastor thus obtained was prohibited from performing his official duties until he had subscribed in writing to the church constitution and had satisfied his fellow New York pastors of his doctrinal purity.[14] Moreover, the constitution made it clear that innovations on the part of the pastor in the liturgical, ritual, or doctrinal life of the church would be considered grounds for removal or censure.

One provision was inserted into the constitution which provided for staggered, annual elections of church council members to ensure a complete turnover of personnel every two or three years.[15] In actuality this stipulation cut both ways for it also guaranteed that a lay power-bloc, opposed to the pastor, would be incapable of entrenching itself in power for long. It should be recalled, too, that the congregation itself had no role in the elective process, nor was the council responsible to anyone but the pastor and the consistory. Thus, unlike Muhlenberg's later congregational constitutions, the Berkenmeyer constitution represented a failure to adapt to American political and elective realities.

What few innovative ideas the constitution did contain were confined to two articles which provided for a limited form of quasi-synodical government and for American ordination. From the beginning of his colonial ministry, Berkenmeyer had seen the need for a central governing body. He was, however, unlike Muhlenberg, incapable of viewing this authority in other than European terms. In 1730 he had proposed a plan to the Reverend John Lidman, Swedish provost at Gloria Dei Church, and to Bishop Svedberg of Sweden, whereby the king of Sweden would assume spiritual authority over the New York and New Jersey congregations, to be exercised either by his colonial representative, the provost, or by a Swedish bishop dispatched to America to assume control over all colonial Lutheranism.[16] Since

Swedish Lutheranism was of the orthodox variety, such a plan would be acceptable to both Berkenmeyer and Hamburg. When Swedish authorities turned him down, Berkenmeyer gradually assumed the powers of a superintendent. Still, his inability to cut himself off from his European ecclesiastical superiors, or to exercise any degree of independent action, guaranteed the impermanence and impotence of any governmental structure he devised.

A case in point was the limited synodical organization legislated by the constitution of 1735.[17] Indeed, the use of the word 'synodical' is misleading, for Berkenmeyer's synod was not a permanent governing body, as was that devised by Muhlenberg, but merely an *ad hoc* assembly called as needed to settle congregational disputes. It could be convened only when the congregations could not themselves reach a decision and when they promised to obey its decisions. At any rate, the congregation retained its right to appeal its decisions to a European consistory.[18]

In the second point, the matter of native ordination, Berkenmeyer exhibited more daring and adaptability. Any congregation which desired the ordination of a candidate first informed the pastor and church council at New York as well as neighboring pastors and councils. These then examined the candidate's life, doctrinal orthodoxy, and preaching ability. Having passed this test, the candidate received a temporary one-year license to preach without compensation while the New York council investigated his European background and training. Should this information prove the man acceptable, and if he had exhibited ministerial competence during his probationary period, the sponsoring congregation might then extend him a formal call. The candidate was then reexamined, ordained, and inducted into his pastorate. Ordination had to be conferred by the Pennsylvania Swedish consistory if there was only one regularly called Lutheran pastor in the New York–New Jersey area. If three such were present, they were empowered to ordain the candidate themselves, without prior permission of European authorities. Thus Berkenmeyer did adopt a pragmatic solution to the question of ordination. But this was not so much because of a desire to adapt to the American environment by providing a native clergy, as it was to forestall the conferring of ordination by the "fanatics" in Pennsylvania. At best it was a compromise which would allow Berkenmeyer to guarantee the orthodoxy of those pastors who labored in his vineyard, a theoretical compromise which Berkenmeyer, unlike Muhlenberg, never found occasion to use.

Despite his hesitant steps toward some independence of action, Berkenmeyer remained, at heart, thoroughly oriented toward Europe. He was reluctant to make independent judgments on even the most basic of doctrinal issues without prior sanction from either the Hamburg or Amsterdam authorities.[19] This inability to adapt pragmatically to ecclesiastical conditions which differed radically from those in Europe ultimately meant that his influence would be supplanted by that of his more flexible counterpart, Muhlenberg. These two giants of colonial Lutheranism came into direct conflict in three major controversies: the Wolf affair in the Raritan, the Hartwick controversy in the Central Hudson parish, and the English language schism in New York City. In each instance Muhlenberg emerged victorious.

Johann August Wolf, who had first been sent to the Raritan by the Hamburg Consistory in 1734 to succeed Daniel Falckner, fell into a bitter dispute with his congregation shortly after his arrival. As early as February 21, 1735, Pastor Knoll reported this dissension to Berkenmeyer in a tone which indicated his support of the congregation.[20] Knoll accused Wolf of reading his sermon and of improvising liturgical rituals.[21] In answer to demands that he correct these deficiencies, Wolf offered his resignation upon payment of six months back pay still due him.[22] In fact, his disaffection stemmed from his contention that the parish had not fulfilled the terms of his call by failing to meet the salary promised or to build a parsonage. Knoll indicated that circumstances beyond its control had prevented the congregation from living up to its responsibilities and that Wolf's intransigence showed a lack of desire on his part to remain at his post.

Berkenmeyer answered Knoll the following month, admitting that his first reaction to the news had been "Let them give the old

Magister [Wolf] half his salary and throw him to the dogs."[23] Upon reflection, however, Berkenmeyer attributed Wolf's conduct to a melancholy disposition which had to be treated through gentle means. Instead Berkenmeyer ordered Knoll to support Wolf against the congregation, to order it to dispel thoughts of dismissing him, and to bolster his spirits. To Berkenmeyer the affair involved the authority of the ministry and the ministerium against the will of the congregation and he viewed with alarm the prospect that Wolf's dismissal under fire would set a dangerous precedent for New York Lutheranism. Indeed he described the relationship of pastor and people as "a bond of marriage, where the slightest thought of separation is sinful and dangerous."[24] As for Wolf's dismissal, Berkenmeyer would only agree to his vacating his call if (1) it was a voluntary act on Wolf's part, not a forced release by the congregation, and (2) if the whole matter was finally submitted to the Hamburg Ministerium which had extended the call in the first place. Indeed, the only condition under which he would consent to artibrary dismissal was Wolf's refusal to subscribe to the church constitution of 1735, for, as he said, "if that fails, then our brotherly unity fails, and I will acknowledge no one, whether he stands or falls, comes, remains or runs, or is a magister or a doctor of doctors or anything else."[25]

Acting on Berkenmeyer's orders, Knoll dutifully wrote to the Raritan congregations charging them to have patience with Wolf in his mental and emotional illness.[26] He pointed out Berkenmeyer's contention that a congregation lacks the power to dismiss a minister since that prerogative belonged only to the ministerium which had appointed him. Implicit in this was the assumption that the power of removal did not rest in Berkenmeyer's synod either.[27] As for Wolf's failure to preach from memory, Knoll declared that this was not essential to the office of a pastor whose sole obligation was to impart the word of God by whatever means best suited him.[28] This would be consonant with Berkenmeyer's orthodoxy which placed much less emphasis on the effectiveness of the manner of preaching than did advocates of pietism. Finally Knoll counseled the parish to erect the parsonage and then see if Wolf's attitude changed, since hasty and rash actions on its part would leave it pastorless, for no replacement for Wolf could be had.

Difficulties continued to mount at Raritan. Overeager to marry, Wolf paid excessive and unwelcome attention to the single maidens of the area.[29] As his social activities increased, his conscientious execution of ministerial duties diminished. For his part, Knoll felt that the congregation was justified in its discontent and that Wolf's refusal to perform his duties or to take any advice made a reconciliation all but impossible.[30] Still Berkenmeyer refused to abandon Wolf, prompting Knoll to demand that he take a personal hand in the affair and cease to use him as a go-between.

Meanwhile, Wolf responded to congregational threats to leave the church unless he preached from memory by refusing to preach at all. Assuming that this meant that Wolf had vacated his call, the Raritan congregations sought out the Reverend Johann Albert Langerfeld, then preaching to the Lutherans in Philadelphia.[31] Langerfeld had been born in Halberstadt, had studied at Halle, and had finally been driven from Europe by French invasions. This man the Raritan congregations presented to Knoll as their candidate for ordination, who in turn referred them to Berkenmeyer at Loonenberg.[32] The entry onto the scene of Langerfeld forced Berkenmeyer's hand. Under the provisions of the constitution of 1735, he summoned an assembly to settle the dispute. This meeting began on August 20, 1735, in the Raritan, the only such synodical meeting called by Berkenmeyer.

At the outset of discussions, Berkenmeyer demanded that both Wolf and the Raritan church council first subscribe to the constitution, thus giving him jurisdiction in the matter. This Wolf did immediately, as did some of the lay delegates. The majority, however, viewed this suspicious procedure with alarm as a trap laid by Berkenmeyer. Consequently they then stalked out of the meeting, returning only when they were assured that the matter of constitutional subscription would be deferred to the close of deliberations. Acting in his capacity as chairman, Berkenmeyer then presented eight points for consideration which he insisted be the sole basis for deliberation. These points in reality represented a complete vindication of Wolf. In them Berkenmeyer denied that a pastor had the power to resign his office or the congregation the power to dismiss him, regardless of any wrongdoing. Such a right belonged only to the local consistory, subject to approval by and appeal to Europe. Inability to preach from memory was excluded as valid grounds for violation of a pastoral call. Finally Berkenmeyer suggested that the congregation reinstate Wolf and complete and cede to him the parsonage provided he promised to preach from memory. But no time limit was placed on this save "within such a time as it pleases him [Wolf] to stipulate."[33] To further this reconciliation, both sides were to sign an amnesty. Failing this, the whole matter would be referred to Hamburg.

By insisting on the adoption of these preconceived points, Berkenmeyer negated the purpose of the entire meeting, revealing his real concept of the function of the consistory. It was to be not a deliberative body, but a rubber stamp for his own decisions. Despite an abortive attempt at a walkout by some lay delegates, Berkenmeyer had his way except that the congregations refused to pay Wolf the salary in arrears. The agreement as finally signed, entitled the 'Act of Submission,' failed miserably to resolve the matter. The congregations were obligated both to pay Wolf back salary, despite their previous refusal, and to complete and turn over to him the parsonage. On his part, he only promised to preach from memory within four weeks after occupying the parsonage. If this did not resolve differences, the Wolf case was to be turned over to the Hamburg Ministerium.[34]

Shortly after Berkenmeyer returned to Loonenberg, trouble flared up once again on the Raritan. By October, 1735, the congregations were reporting to Berkenmeyer that Wolf remained adamant in his refusal to perform his duties.[35] To make matters worse, Wolf finally married a farmer's daughter shortly after the August meeting but proceeded to brutalize her terribly. After the girl had borne him two children, Wolf cast her out claiming that the last child was sired by a Negro.[36] This was too much for the long-suffering congregation, which not only repudiated the settlement of August, 1735, but indicated its desire to separate completely from Berkenmeyer and Hamburg.[37]

Again Berkenmeyer backed Wolf against the congregations, going so far as to claim that "as far as we can look into the matter we have not found the pastor guilty of any offense which would deserve punishment."[38] Finally, with the blessings of both Berkenmeyer and Knoll, the matter was brought to court by Wolf. In a letter to Governor Lewis Morris of New Jersey, Berkenmeyer urged him to heed Wolf and take action against the congregations which he accused of "unfair dealings" and "uncharitable deportment."[39] Confronted by this solid array of New York pastors, the Raritan congregations appealed directly to the Hamburg Ministerium, relating the sorry tale of Wolf from the beginning and complaining bitterly that Berkenmeyer had forced the matter into court.[40] Claiming that the point of reconciliation had long since passed, the congregations requested that the ministerium recall Wolf.

In the meantime Wolf won his suit against the congregations which were now ordered to pay his salary and surrender to him the church. As a result many members moved out of the congregation to avoid payment as stipulated by the court order, while the church stood empty.[41] On September 21, 1740, the Hamburg Ministerium answered the Raritan congregations that, although they did not desire to impose an unfit minister upon them, they could make no final disposition in the case until they received more information from Berkenmeyer and them. While Wolf's alleged conduct was not excused, the congregations were chastened for withholding his salary and not completing the parsonage.[42] When Berkenmeyer was then questioned about the Wolf affair by the Hamburg Consistory, he wrote a lengthy reply completely supportive of Wolf.[43] Dismissing the Raritan complaints as "depraved" and "conceited," Berkenmeyer launched into a detailed summary of the dispute as he saw it. And while he still placed most of the blame for the unfortunate situation on the congregations, Berkenmeyer did not completely exonerate Wolf. Among other charges, he claimed that Wolf was a disciple of the rationalist, Christian Wolf, that his inability to speak from memory came from his indifferent attitude toward his ministerial obligations, that he suffered from a melancholic and despondent nature, that he was suspicious and overly sensitive and, finally, that his temperament was unsuited to the American mission field.[44] In short, Berkenmeyer admitted that fault existed on both sides and that reconciliation was, indeed, impossible. He did recommend that the Hamburg ministerium take matters into its own hands but stated that he himself could do no more. Berkenmeyer felt he lacked the authority, as well as the inclination, to remove Wolf under fire, for such an action would serve to strengthen the American Lutheran tendency toward voluntarism.[45]

That this interpretation was taken by the ministerium as well is evident from a summary made by the Reverend Adolph F. Meyer of Hamburg who urged that the body should "consider ways and means to save Pastor Wolf's office."[46] Finally, on September 10, 1744, the ministerium drew up three letters in an attempt to resolve the situation. To the lay leaders of the Raritan, the Hamburg Consistory directed an admonition against the uncharity they had shown toward their pastor and suggested Christian understanding, repentance, and reconciliation.[47] In a letter directed to Wolf, the ministerium berated him for his inexcusable behavior and unwillingness to explain himself to Hamburg. He was then ordered to reconcile himself to his wife as well as to the parish and warned that, unless he did so, the ministerium felt it "right and fair that his parish, with the assistance of the two other pastors [Knoll and Berkenmeyer] and by appealing to the civil authorities, separate itself completely from him and pay him no further salary, but call another orthodox and pious pastor and avail itself of his ministry."[48] On October 16, 1744, the ministerium informed Knoll and Berkenmeyer of its final disposition of the Wolf matter.[49] The consistorial agreement of 1735 was to be the basis of any reconciliation and a general amnesty was to be demanded from both parties. Should the parish be willing but should Wolf refuse and not agree to resume his ministerial duties within a stated time, his dismissal should be sought through the civil authorities so that the parish would be free to call another pastor. Should, however, Wolf accede to the Hamburg Consistory's demands but the parish refuse, the civil authorities were to be asked to impose Wolf on them. Should both parties remain obstinate,

then Wolf should resign, the parish should repudiate Langerfeld, and a call should be extended to an orthodox substitute.

The end result of the decade-long controversy then was that
neither Hamburg nor Berkenmeyer was willing to intervene
decisively in the Raritan situation but preferred instead in European fashion to rely on a decision by secular authorities. Sensing
this, the Raritan congregations looked for help to Henry Melchior Muhlenberg.

From 1743 on, delegates from the Raritan periodically journeyed to Philadelphia to request Muhlenberg's intervention.
This he refused on the grounds that his responsibilities to his
own flock were too great and that the Raritan was under the
jurisdiction of Berkenmeyer and Hamburg. Finally, in 1745
both Wolf and the congregations agreed in the presence of
magistrates to submit their disagreements to a board of arbitration. To guarantee that both sides would accept the board's final
decision, bond was posted in conformity to colonial English law.
Each party had the right to nominate two of the board's four
members. Wolf chose Berkenmeyer and Knoll while the congregations requested Muhlenberg and his Philadelphia assistant,
the Reverend Peter Brunnholtz. Because of the latter's illness,
however, he was replaced by the Rev. Tobias Wagner of Tulpehocken.[50]

Despite his reluctance to condone civil interference in religious affairs, Muhlenberg finally agreed to participate because of
the scandal and spiritual harm the Raritan situation was causing
for him in Pennsylvania.[51] Before giving his consent, however,
Muhlenberg wrote to Berkenmeyer about the proposed arbitration.[52] He stated in appropriately diffident and flattering terms
that he had no wish to take precedence over Berkenmeyer and
hence would not himself participate without his "presence and
instruction."[53] He further suggested that Berkenmeyer dispose
of the matter himself by simply packing Wolf off to Europe and
providing for a replacement. And, though Muhlenberg offered
to affix his signature to any reasonable opinion written by
Berkenmeyer, he made it clear that any such decision would
have to "save these poor scattered sheep [the Raritan con-
gregations] and free them from Pastor Wolf."[54]

Berkenmeyer sent a restrained and cool answer to Muhlenberg on May 20, 1745.[55] While he welcomed Muhlenberg's participation in the proposed arbitration, Berkenmeyer denied he had any knowledge of it. As for Muhlenberg's suggestion that he settle the issue himself, Berkenmeyer stated that this was impossible, nor would he consent to appear at the Raritan conference. While admitting that reconciliation between Wolf and the parish could not be achieved, he refused to send Wolf back to Europe for that would be to accuse Hamburg "of having sent a raving lunatic to the parish, and that it [the ministerium] would now have to take back the lunatic and support him."[56] Muhlenberg's criticism of Wolf's actions in taking the case to court was curtly dismissed by the New Yorker.[57] All Muhlenberg's attempts to get Berkenmeyer to commit himself in the matter were rejected for, as Berkenmeyer flatly stated, he felt they were intended to shift responsibility and blame for an unpleasant situation on his shoulders. To this the wily Berkenmeyer would not consent.[58] He had already reported the affair to Hamburg and, since the ministerium had failed to take definite action, Berkenmeyer claimed the matter was now a civil not an ecclesiastical concern.[59] In conclusion, Berkenmeyer asked to be excluded from the deliberations since neither the parish nor Wolf had any confidence in him. He did, however, give his consent to Knoll's participation. He also demanded that both sides bind themselves beforehand to accept whatever decision the arbitrators reached and, if Wolf were proven incapable of performing his duties, then the ministerium's reply of September 12, 1740, should be applied. In this letter the ministerium had only requested that additional information be furnished to it for a decision and that the parish support Wolf until one was reached. If Wolf declared himself incapable, then Berkenmeyer suggested that the congregation petition Hamburg for his removal. Finally he agreed to countersign, if necessary, whatever agreement was reached.[60]

On August 1, 1745, Wagner, Knoll, and Muhlenberg assembled at the Raritan. Because Berkenmeyer was absent, a new bond was drawn up providing for three arbiters instead of the original four. Deliberations continued until August 5, though it was quickly ascertained that reconciliation was impossible, for neither party would budge an inch. Further investigations led the arbiters to conclude that Wolf had broken the agreement of 1735, whereupon the three pastors suggested this information be forwarded to Hamburg and a final decision left to the ministerium. To this the congregation agreed, but Wolf, fearful at the prospect of further protracted litigation, refused.[61]

Muhlenberg and Wagner then drew up a final judgment suspending Wolf from office but to this Knoll would not agree, for he feared Berkenmeyer's wrath should he do so. Thus the document was discarded.[62] A way was finally found out of the impasse by a private agreement between Wolf and the congregation whereby Wolf resigned his office for a payment of £90, New Jersey currency, from which sum he would pay the legal expenses incurred.[63] This agreement was merely witnessed by the arbiters thus avoiding the necessity of having themselves assumed the authority of removing a pastor appointed by the Hamburg Consistory. Wolf then surrendered his call to the lay leaders who promptly ripped their names off the document and entrusted both call and seal to Muhlenberg who was to return them to Hamburg.[64]

Here the matter might have rested save for Wilhelm C. Berkenmeyer. He had cleverly managed to steer clear of a sticky situation while Muhlenberg and the others straightened out the affair in the only way possible, the removal of Wolf. With the thorny problem resolved for him, Berkenmeyer proceeded to make capital out of the Raritan arbitration. Shortly after the termination of the proceedings, he wrote to Knoll denouncing them as a "Council of blood."[65] Deploring the fate of Wolf who, he said, "was turned into a beggar and a spectacle for the 'pastor slanderers'," Berkenmeyer rejected the proceedings as being in violation of the New York Lutheran constitution because, among other reasons given, there were not four arbiters present, a situation created by Berkenmeyer's refusal to serve on the board.[66] While most of the blame was placed on Muhlenberg, Knoll was chided for signing the agreement. Berkenmeyer's main contention was that Muhlenberg had illegally mutilated the

Hamburg call and seal, thus usurping the right to remove a pastor which properly belonged only to the ministerium.[67]

Muhlenberg, Berkenmeyer claimed, had tried to implicate him in this illegal action by misquoting his letter of May 20, 1745, and by emphasizing that Wolf had chosen him, Berkenmeyer, as an arbiter.[68] Condemning Muhlenberg for his duplicity, Berkenmeyer declared his intentions of bringing the whole case to Hamburg's attention[69] The reasons he gave Knoll for his absence from the conference were: (1) that the civil courts had already reached a decision while the ministerium of Hamburg was still debating the matter; (2) "the proposed conference . . . involved a group of outside church leaders, and . . . was announced orally and in writing in an underhanded way, with trickery and falsehood"; and (3) the situation in Loonenberg had prevented his absence at that time.[70]

Knoll responded to Berkenmeyer in an angry letter dated October 16, 1745, defending Muhlenberg's actions.[71] All the preconditions demanded by Berkenmeyer, claimed Knoll, had been scrupulously followed. He dismissed as impractical the advice given by Hamburg in 1740 and pointed out that the courts had entrusted a final solution to the arbiters. He further stated that Berkenmeyer had himself suggested that Wolf resign with compensation if no reconciliation could be reached. Chiding Berkenmeyer for reneging on his solemn promise to endorse the Raritan settlement, he emphasized that Wolf had voluntarily resigned and had not been deposed. The mutilation of the call was done by Wolf and the laymen, an action in which the pastors present did not participate.

Berkenmeyer replied to Knoll on November 25, 1745, informing him that he had just received the Hamburg letters of October 16, 1744.[72] He now proposed that Knoll prevail upon Muhlenberg to reopen the question, request the parish to reconcile itself to Wolf, reinstate him, and restore his call.[73] This, of course, was impossible as Berkenmeyer well knew.

Informed by Knoll of Berkenmeyer's intention of denouncing him to Hamburg, Muhlenberg hurriedly dispatched his own account of the incident to his Halle superiors, together with a detailed report signed by the three arbiters.[74] Emphasizing the care he had taken to avoid intruding on Berkenmeyer's domain or the authority of Hamburg, Muhlenberg nonetheless claimed that he had acted as an agent of the New Jersey court, with the approval of both the congregations and Wolf, and that the latter had resigned of his own free will without the pastors deposing him. He also informed the Reverend Fathers that the Raritan congregations had entrusted him with a call to be directed to Halle, requesting in the interim the services of the Pennsylvania catechist, Nicholas N. Kurtz.

It is in Muhlenberg's reaction to this request for help that the vast difference between Berkenmeyer and himself became even more obvious. Berkenmeyer's slavish dependence on a far-distant European authority prevented him from undertaking bold and decisive actions. He seemed afraid to assume a public stand in a controversial matter for fear that he would be found in error by his superiors. Instead he insisted upon supporting an intolerable status quo until some higher-up should assume the onus of decision. In contrast, Muhlenberg was quite willing to take an independent course of action when he believed that necessity demanded it. Uppermost in his mind was the welfare of the church as he envisioned it, and for its sake Muhlenberg willingly strayed far beyond the limits of his authority.

The Raritan, for example, lay beyond his call, was in fact an integral part of the rival New York consistory under the supervision of a ministerium other than that from which his own authority derived. Muhlenberg realized full well that a decision on his part to assume oversight of the Raritan was beyond his authority and would surely arouse the resentment of the Hamburg Ministerium, already hostile to pietism. As he phrased his dilemma: "Now what should be done? If we act too promptly we may deserve to be reprimanded. If we delay to act, conscience might reprove us."[75] Conscience prevailed over the fear of reprimand for Muhlenberg did dispatch Kurtz to the Raritan, pleading the danger of a Moravian takeover of the now pastorless congregations.

There was, moreover, an ulterior motive which Muhlenberg aptly summed up: "if the door be once open for us here, we can extend our operations in the surrounding regions."[76] This he did, and the next five years witnessed a steady encroachment by Muhlenberg on the New York congregations under Berkenmeyer's care. By abandoning effective leadership of his consistory, Berkenmeyer created a vacuum into which Muhlenberg rapidly moved. Eventually the Muhlenberg brand of pietism—pragmatic, moderate, opportunistic, and dynamic—totally supplanted Berkenmeyer's timid and stagnant orthodoxy, and New York fell under the dominion of the much-feared fanatics of Pennsylvania.

Muhlenberg's next opportunity for expansion came in the Central Hudson parish which had been vacant since Spaler's resignation in 1736. In its search for a successor, the Hamburg Consistory, curiously enough, turned to Halle for want of a candidate of its own. In 1744 the Reverend Doctor Friedrich Wagner, Senior of the Lutheran Ministerium at Hamburg, informed the Reverend Doctor Philipp D. Krauter, pastor of London's Holy Trinity Lutheran Church (Old Hamburg Church), of the ministerium's intentions in this regard, asking if he had any objections.[77] Krauter replied that he had none and that a Halle man would be quite acceptable.[78] Accordingly, in March, 1746 the Central Hudson call was extended to John Christopher Hartwick, a native of Thuringia in Saxe-Gotha. Hartwick had attended Halle, indeed, had been there while Muhlenberg was teaching at the institution. Thus when Hartwick arrived in America, he proceeded to Philadelphia to visit Muhlenberg in July, 1747, and assisted in Germantown and Philadelphia during Brunnholtz's illness.[79] Upon learning of this, Berkenmeyer, still enraged over the Wolf affair, became deeply suspicious of his young colleague, regarding him as a trojan horse for the undercover infiltration of the despised pietists into his citadel of orthodoxy.[80] When in 1748 Hartwick attended Muhlenberg's synod, even taking part in its official proceedings, Berkenmeyer openly broke with him, accusing him of *Crypto-Herrnhuthianismus,* a secret affinity with the Moravians.[81]

In all, Berkenmeyer published four treatises against Hartwick in addition to a formal denunciation and list of charges which he forwarded to London to the Reverend David Krauter who had ordained Hartwick. Though neither Krauter nor the Hamburg authorities took any action against Hartwick, Berkenmeyer's savage attacks made his position in Rhinebeck virtually untenable.

In January, 1750, Berkenmeyer, Knoll, and Sommer gathered in East Camp to depose Hartwick from his office, an action foiled only by their failure to win over his still sizable following in the parish.[82] To complicate matters even more, a vagabond preacher named Carl Rudolph, the self-styled "Prince of Württemberg," took advantage of the confusion to invade Hartwick's parish and minister to the Berkenmeyer-inspired malcontents at East Camp.[83] Hartwick promptly resigned as pastor of that congregation.

Informed of this state of affairs, the Pennsylvania ministerium delegated Muhlenberg to accompany his father-in-law, Conrad Weiser (who was traveling to Canada to attend an Indian conference), as far as Rhinebeck to give Hartwick its support.[84] They set out on August 18, 1750, arriving at Rhinebeck five days later. Muhlenberg immediately began a visitation of the various congregations within the parish to size up the situation. On September 2, he summoned a conference at Rhinebeck to which the elders of the four congregations, as well as the parishioners, were invited. After hearing the charges brought against Hartwick by Berkenmeyer and the malcontents, as well as Hartwick's defense, Muhlenberg concluded that though Hartwick had erred in several matters because of his youthful zeal and indiscretion, "the complaints had been brought in and magnified by hostile persons, that they were false, perverted, unjust and contrary to the truth, and that they had been set in motion through reasoning *a particulari ad universale* by unfriendly persons and used as a weapon."[85] He then presented the congregations with a choice: either Hartwick should resign his call and move to Pennsylvania, or he should take a six-month leave of absence to work in Pennsylvania while passions cooled. The congregations chose the latter alternative, provided Muhlenberg would supply them with a temporary substitute pastor.[86] This he did, sending the catechist Lucas Rauss in November, 1750.

Muhlenberg's actions at Rhinebeck went far beyond his conduct in the Raritan. Here he entered into the heartland of the New York Consistory as the official representative of an alien ministerium without any invitation from the congregations, had denounced Berkenmeyer—the head of the consistory—as a liar, and had assumed control of a congregation which was a member of a Lutheran synod that already existed, at least nominally. This he did in the name of expediency to heal a split within the congregations which threatened great harm to the church. Though Berkenmeyer was immediately informed of Muhlenberg's coup, he did nothing to prevent it.[87]

On his return journey Muhlenberg stopped in New York City where, despite his reluctance, he soon found himself snared in yet another controversy, the origins of which dated back to 1742. In the fall of that year, German-speaking members of the New York parish had petitioned Pastor Knoll to preach in German, as well as in Dutch which they did not fully understand. They did this, they asserted, to prevent their members from defecting to the Anglican church. Knoll and the church council agreed to only three German preparatory services a year, which the Germans found unacceptable.[88] In April of 1743 another petition for linguistic parity resulted in a concession that one-sixth of the services were to be conducted in German. This was rescinded when Knoll later claimed that the German language services were poorly attended.[89]

Again in June, 1745, four German lay leaders renewed the demand, this time obtaining a concession that one-third of the services would be given in German provided the parishioners attended the Dutch services as well. Meanwhile, during the winter of 1745, a German Lutheran preacher, the Reverend Johannes Ludwig Hofgut, appeared in the city. He had been deposed from the ministry in Württemberg, as Muhlenberg claimed, on charges of adultery.[90] During Knoll's absence in Hackensack, the German lay leaders petitioned Governor George Clinton to license Hofgut and, by a ruse, secured the New York pulpit for him. Knoll hurried back to the city, met with the church council, and had Hofgut banned from preaching until he could produce the proper testimonials. Nonetheless,

Hofgut continued to preach in private homes until Knoll secured an order from the governor forbidding him to perform pastoral acts until his qualifications could be ascertained. Eventually a response from Europe confirmed that he was an imposter.[91]

In May, 1749, the Germans once again petitioned for services in their own language. Because the church council was now hopelessly deadlocked on the issue, it sought the advice of Berkenmeyer and Sommer. Berkenmeyer eventually answered that the two languages should be placed on a parity, but his letter did not reach New York City until early 1750, after a schism had already taken place.[92]

The Reverend Johann Friedrich Ries had arrived in Philadelphia in September, 1749. When the New York German Lutherans learned of this, they extended a call to Ries which he accepted despite Muhlenberg's advice that he refuse since Knoll was still the legal pastor.[93] A congregation was soon organized in an old brewery purchased by the Germans as a temporary church. Ries then petitioned Governor Clinton for permission to collect funds for a permanent church, which request was granted. Though Knoll's congregation immediately voted linguistic parity on receipt of Berkenmeyer's letter, the schism was not healed. Completely disillusioned, Knoll resigned his office in the summer of 1750 to open up a school.[94] In desperation the church council requested Berkenmeyer's assistance. He set out at once for New York but was preceded there by Muhlenberg who arrived from Rhinebeck on September 23, 1750.

Muhlenberg's sympathies in the controversy lay with Knoll and the orginal congregation whose church order and liturgy he found "suitably and edifyingly adapted to American conditions."[95] In his opinion Knoll alone was the legal pastor of the congregation, while Ries and his party:

> had no other purpose and desire except to gain legal half-rights and *possession* of the old Lutheran church so that they would be the masters, set up their own laws in the church, introduce any vagabond as preacher, and use one-half of the contributions and church property to their own will and pleasure.[96]

Muhlenberg visited Ries who asked him to preach in his church and lend his support to the German cause. He declined, blaming Ries for causing the schism by his opposition to the lawful pastor.[97] Instead, Muhlenberg accepted an invitation to preach in Knoll's parish, thus indicating his support for its position.

When Berkenmeyer arrived in the city on September 29, Muhlenberg was placed in an awkward situation. That evening he visited Berkenmeyer to seek his permission to preach which he graciously gave, though he could not bring himself to attend the service.[98] This is the only occasion on which these two Lutheran pastors met each other face to face.

Muhlenberg left New York on October 1 out of deference to Berkenmeyer, now engaged in the delicate task of reuniting the congregation. Once more, however, Berkenmeyer's unimaginative insistence on the maintenance of the status quo and the following of European leadership proved his undoing. His solution to the crisis was that the congregations either reinstate Knoll or apply to Hamburg for a successor. Neither was acceptable. Since Knoll, though innocent of any wrongdoing, had been the occasion for the schism and had discredited himself by his resignation, he was incapable of reuniting the warring factions. Neither could the congregation face the uncertain arrival of an unknown European successor who might prove himself unsuited to the task. Decisive action was needed immediately, but this was beyond Berkenmeyer's capabilities. Sensing that the congregation would turn to Pennsylvania and his archrival Muhlenberg, Berkenmeyer sadly departed for Loonenberg after giving one final warning "that after his departure the ravenous wolves would come and would not spare the flock."[99]

On February 1, 1751, the New York congregation formally issued a call to Muhlenberg which he accepted on May 17. Upon his arrival in the city, on leave from his Pennsylvania congregations, Muhlenberg immediately set about to mold New York Lutheranism in his image. To end the ghetto isolationism fostered by Berkenmeyer, he established contacts with Episcopal, Dutch Reformed, and Presbyterian ministers. He preached regularly in both Dutch and German, as well as in English to retain the allegiance of Anglicized German youth. Though he could not reunite the dissident Germans, they were left isolated and leaderless by Ries's resignation in the summer of 1751.

In October, 1751, Berkenmeyer died, a tired and broken man, to be succeeded by Knoll in Loonenberg. Sommer still held sway in the Mohawk parish, but Muhlenberg's influence rapidly penetrated there as well. Before relinquishing his post with the New York German faction, Johann Ries had reconciled himself to Muhlenberg, requesting permission to join the Pennsylvania Ministerium which he did in 1763.[100] Sommer then assigned Ries to serve some congregations in the Mohawk Valley. In 1760 Ries was called by Claverack and New Town in Berkenmeyer's old Upper Hudson parish and nine years later succeeded Knoll at Loonenberg as temporary pastor. Ries then entrusted a permanent call to Muhlenberg who extended it to the Reverend John Christian Leps. The Loonenberg congregation now entered the Pennsylvania Ministerium to be followed by Albany, entrusted to another Pennsylvanian, the Reverend J. W. Samuel Schwerdfeger.[101] Sommer now remained the last representative of Berkenmeyer orthodoxy. On his retirement in 1789, the Schoharie parish too passed under Pennsylvania's influence. Indeed after 1751, the year of Berkenmeyer's death, all new New York and New Jersey pastors came from the Pennsylvania Ministerium.

With the appointment of Muhlenberg's son-in-law, the Reverend John Christopher Kunze, to the New York parish in 1784, the pietistic victory was complete. Kunze finally reunited the dissidents with the main congregation and in 1786 organized the Synod of New York, closely patterned on the Pennsylvania model. Muhlenberg's pragmatism triumphed in the end in New York precisely because it proved both flexible and resilient enough to accommodate itself to a foreign environment while retaining essential features from its European heritage.

NOTES

[1]Harry Julius Kreider, *Lutheranism in Colonial New York* (New York: Privately printed, 1942), p. 39.

[2]Theodore Emanual Schmauk, *The Lutheran Church in Pennsylvania, 1638–1800* (Lancaster: Pennsylvania German Society, 1902), vol. 2 of *Proceedings and Addresses*, p. 448; see also Report of Reverend Wilhelm C. Berkenmeyer to the Amsterdam Consistory, Oct. 21/Nov. 1, 1725 in Arnold J. H. Van Laer, trans., *The Lutheran Church in New York, 1649–1772: Records in the Lutheran Church Archives at Amsterdam, Holland* (New York: New York Public Library, 1946), p. 142. Hereafter referred to as *LCNY*.

[3]It should be noted that the conflict dragged on for several more years. Around August, 1735, the Reverend Michael Christian Knoll addressed a letter to von Dieren "defunct member and stray sheep of the Lutheran Congregation, seducer of the ignorant, shunner of the light of day and servant of darkness, who in all dumbness causes schisms in the congregations and evades proof by all sorts of deceit, lies, denials and slanders in opposition to public testimony, letters and writings; first born of the devil and on account of such qualities a rogue and arch-rogue before all men, for the following reasons:" Knoll goes on to repeat the charges levied by Berkenmeyer of unorthodoxy, moral turpitude, nonvalidity of ordination, and religious indifferentism. See *LCNY*, pp. 205–8. Knoll was answered on August 5, 1735, by the elders of the congregations at Schoharie, Kinderhook, and Canijoharie in a vitriolic attack which labeled him, among others, as a "false scribe," "hypocrite," "a drunken false pharisee," a "simple minded Achitophle," and an "unmitigated liar, who has a shameless whore's forehead and is an advisor of the same." See *LCNY*, pp. 208–10.

[4]Kreider, p. 43.

[5]Ibid., pp. 43–44.

[6]"Letter from the Rev. Wilhelm C. Berkenmeyer to the Very Rev. Johann Friedrich Winckler, Senior of the Lutheran Ministerium of Hamburg," September 24, 1731 in Simon Hart and Harry J. Kreider, trans., *Lutheran Church in New York and New Jersey, 1722–1760* (New York: United Lutheran Synod of New York and New England, 1962), p. 17. Hereafter referred to as *LCNY-NJ*.

[7]Thus Berkenmeyer wrote to Hamburg that Falckner "also has the habit of forcing people to bring him an abundance of intoxicating beverages and abuses and threatens to beat up those who try to talk him out of it. He even annoys women on the street, and is sometimes found sleeping on the side of the road with the brandy keg on his back. Among other excesses of this kind he threatened to cut the throat of a man in whose house he slept, because the wife of this man refused to do as he told her." (Ibid., p. 17)

[8]"Already at that time his offensive life was so abominable to his own sainted brother [Justus Falckner] that even on his death bed the latter warned his whole parish not to have anything to do with this drunkard. But although the late Falckner said this because he was urged by his conscience, I still must admit that he made out the call to his brother, which the latter is showing off." (*LCNY-NJ*, p. 17)

[9]Ibid., p. 16.

[10]"Declaration of the Pastors and Church Councils of the Lutheran Congregations in New York and New Jersey That they do not Recognize the Rev. Johannes Spahler as a Lutheran Pastor," August 8 seq., 1736, in *LCNY-NJ*, pp. 115–16.

[11]Kreider, pp. 44–48.

[12]"All private conventicles and secret meetings, . . . which might be planned without the positive knowledge and approval of the Church Council, shall be denounced as very dangerous, and are hereby forbidden [and] to be prevented as much as possible, in order that thereby neither disturbance nor offense may be caused." (chap. 2, art. 3 of the Constitution of 1735, cited in Kreider, p. 88)

[13]Ibid., pp. 88–89.

[14]Ibid., p. 89.

[15]Ibid.

[16]Ibid., pp. 99–100.

[17]For the text of this article, see Ibid., pp. 92–93.

[18]Ibid., p. 93.

[19]Thus in a letter of Brekenmeyer to the Amsterdam consistory dated Oct. 21/Nov. 1, 1725, he asks advice on his decision to baptize privately an illegitimate child in the absence of the father who had abandoned both mother and infant. (*LCNY*, pp. 145–48) Other examples of Berkenmeyer's hesitancy to take independent action abound.

[20]The Reverend Michael C. Knoll to the Reverend Wilhelm C. Berkenmeyer, Hackensack, February 21, 1735 in *LCNY-NJ*, p. 67.

[21]Ibid., p. 65.

[22]Ibid.

[23]Letter from the Reverend Wilhelm C. Berkenmeyer to the Reverend Michael Christian Knoll, Loonenberg, March 12, 1735, in *LCNY-NJ*, p. 67.

[24]Ibid.

[25]Ibid., p. 68.

[26]Letter from the Reverend Michael C. Knoll to the lay leaders of the Lutheran parish at Raritan, New Jersey, April 12–13, in *LCNY-NJ*, p. 70.

[27]Said Knoll: "You know quite well, my very dear brethren, that even in the old countries a king or a prince would hardly dare to dismiss an ordained pastor, even though there were a hundred there to our one here, and we here in this wilderness do not want to take the matter into our hands so brazenly." (Ibid)

[28]Ibid., p. 71.

[29]Henry Melchior Muhlenberg, *The Journals of Henry Melchior Muhlenberg in Three Volumes,* trans. Theodore G. Tappert and John W. Doberstein, I (Philadelphia: Muhlenberg Press, 1942), 108. Hereafter referred to as *I Journals.*

[30]Letter from the Reverend Michael C. Knoll to the Reverend Wilhelm C. Berkenmeyer, Hackensack, April 13, 1735, in *LCNY-NJ*, pp. 72–73.

[31]Letter from the Reverend Wilhelm C. Berkenmeyer to the Reverend Johann C. Wolf, Loonenberg, June 20, 1735, in *LCNY-NJ*, p. 90.

[32]As can be supposed, Berkenmeyer thoroughly opposed Langerfeld not only

because he was unable to produce any testimonials from Europe but because of his pietistic background. Said Berkenmeyer: "He appears to be very untrustworthy because he associated with and knows so many Quakers." (Ibid., p. 91)

[33]"Preliminary articles or Points for Consideration, by the Rev. Wilhelm C. Berkenmeyer for the Lutheran Classical Assembly to be held in New York City on August 4–10, 1735," in *LCNY-NJ*, pp. 103–4.

[34]The text of the agreement accepted on August 24, 1735 is found in *LCNY-NJ*, pp. 106–7.

[35]"Letter from the lay leaders of the Lutheran congregation in the Mountain (Raritan), New Jersey to the Rev. Wilhelm C. Berkenmeyer," Raritan, October 13, 1735, in *LCNY-NJ*, p. 110.

[36]*I Journals*, p. 108; see also letter of the Reverend Michael C. Knoll to the Reverend Wilhelm C. Berkenmeyer, November 20, 1738, in *LCNY-NJ*, p. 137.

[37]"Letter from the Rev. Wilhelm C. Berkenmeyer to the Very Rev. Johann Friedrich Winckler, Senior of the Lutheran ministerium of Hamburg," Loonenberg, August 19, 1736, in *LCNY-NJ*, p. 116.

[38]"Certificates signed by the Revs. Wilhelm C. Berkenmeyer and Michael C. Knoll, concerning the Classical Assembly of August 20–24, 1736, Certificate dated September 11, 1736," in *LCNY-NJ*, p. 121.

[39]"Petition of the Revs. Wilhelm C. Berkenmeyer and Michael C. Knoll to Gov. Lewis Morris of New Jersey, on behalf of the Ref. Johann A. Wolf." ca. July, 1739, in *LCNY-NJ*, pp. 145–46. See also the draft of June, 1739, in ibid. pp. 144–45.

[40]"Letter of Complaint from the Lay Leaders of the Lutheran Parish at Raritan, New Jersey, to the Lutheran Ministerium of Hamburg," Raritan, August 1, 1739, in *LCNY-NJ*, p. 151.

[41]Letter from the Reverend Johann A. Wolf to the Reverend Michael C. Knoll, Raritan, January 4, 1740, in *LCNY-NJ*, p. 154.

[42]"Letter from the Ministerium of Hamburg to the Lay Leaders of the Lutheran Parish at Rareton, New Jersey," Hamburg, September 12, 1740, in *LCNY-NJ*, pp. 164–67.

[43]"Report from the Rev. Wilhelm C. Berkenmeyer to the Lutheran Ministerium of Hamburg, Concerning the Controversy in the Lutheran Parish at Rareton, New Jersey," Loonenburg, November 14, 1741, in *LCNY-NJ*, pp. 173–204.

[44]Ibid., pp. 193–95.

[45]"Our congregations in this country are like a runaway horse, which can make those run which do not know how to run, to say nothing of those of the same stripe, so that they respect neither bridle nor reins, nor anything in the world, until saddle and harness, carriage and conveyance are broken and splintered to pieces. They are not to be stopped, neither will they stop themselves until the frenzy has passed, or until they run into something which they cannot overcome, break through or evade." (Ibid., p. 201)

[46]"Summary Made by the Rev. Adolph F. Meyer of the Report dated

November 14, 1741 from the Rev. Wilhelm C. Berkenmeyer to the Lutheran Ministerium of Hamburg." Summary dated ca. November 1, 1742, in *LCNY-NJ*, p. 213.

[47]"Letters proposed to the Lutheran Ministerium of Hamburg by the Rev. Johann W. Fischer, in Connection with his summary dated August 27, 1744," Hamburg, September 10, 1744, in *LCNY-NJ*, p. 234.

[48]Ibid., p. 235.

[49]"Letter from the Very Rev. Dr. Friedrich Wagner, Senior of the Lutheran Ministerium of Hamburg, to the Revs. Wilhelm C. Berkenmeyer and Michael C. Knoll," Hamburg, October 16, 1744, in *LCNY-NJ*, pp. 244–45.

[50]*Journals*, p. 106; see also Muhlenberg to Halle, December 12, 1745, in John Ludwig Schulze, ed., *Reports of the United German Evangelical Lutheran Congregations in North America, Especially in Pennsylvania*, 1, trans. C. W. Schaeffer (Reading: Pilger Book Store, 1882), 182.

[51]"Report of the Arbitrators on the affairs of Wolf," wirtten to Halle by Muhlenberg and countersigned by Knoll and Wagner, in Schulze, p. 190.

[52]Letter from the Reverend Henry M. Muhlenberg to the Reverend Wilhelm C. Berkenmeyer, Philadelphia, May 1, 1745, in *LCNY-NJ*, pp. 248–49.

[53]Ibid., p. 249.

[54]Ibid.

[55]Letter from the Reverend Wilhelm C. Berkenmeyer to the Reverend Henry M. Muhlenberg, Loonenberg, May 20, 1745. Berkenmeyer's annoyance can be seen in the following: "Concerning the altogether exaggerated compliments: while I have so much respect for you my brother that I believe you wrote sincerely and not ironically, I must perforce disapprove of it and protest against it most vigorously. My horse is not fed on that, so that he would dare to leap higher or run faster when given the spurs. Nor are such overly polite excuses necessary if nothing else is kept in mind than the work of the Lord to which your reverence was chosen and which demands everything a man has." (In *LCNY-NJ*, p. 250)

[56]Ibid., p. 251.

[57]"I have never approved of Pastor Wolf's way of acting in the present situation, but in general I thank God that He permitted him to find protection behind this earthly shield." (Ibid)

[58]Ibid.

[59]Ibid., p. 252.

[60]Ibid., p. 253.

[61]Schulze, p. 194.

[62]"Declaration of the Revs. Henry M. Muhlenberg, Tobias Wagner and Michael C. Knoll, Suspending the Rev. Johann A. Wolf from the Ministerial Office," August 5, 1745, in *LCNY-NJ*, pp. 261–62.

[63]"Resignation of the Rev. Johann A. Wolf and the Settlement of the Rareton Controversy," August 5, 1745, in *LCNY-NJ*, p. 262.

[64]"Report of the Arbiters," in Schulze, p. 196.

[65]Letter from the Rev. Wilhelm C. Berkenmeyer to the Rev. Michael C. Knoll, Loonenberg, September 18, 1745, in *LCNY-NJ*, p. 266.

[66]Ibid., p. 267.

[67]"What do you think, my brother? To destroy, to tear up and to abuse the call, is that not to remove a pastor from his office? Who gave the pastors the authority to do that?" (Ibid., p. 267)

[68]Ibid., p. 268.

[69]"I have decided, out of due respect for the very reverend Ministerium of Hamburg, to send all these documents [on the Raritan affair] to Hamburg, so much more since Pastor Muhlenberg's impure motives in dealing with me and Pastor Wolf are clearly apparent from the unforgivable way in which he misquoted and mutilated my letter. If Pastor Muhlenberg had presented my entire letter to you my brother or to the conference, or had used the parts quoted in their right context and without mutilating them, then I would say that he had acted as an honest and upright man. But I cannot say so now, when I cannot help notice the deceitful changes in the contents and abridgements of such a nature that they imply an entirely contrary meaning. In short, I cannot help seeing that he took extracts from my letter to make a ladder to the gallows to which I am supposed to have sentenced Pastor Wolf even before an investigation. This act by Pastor Muhlenberg amazed me; I had believed him capable of better things." (Ibid., p. 269)

[70]Ibid.

[71]Letter from the Reverend Michael C. Knoll to the Reverend Wilhelm C. Berkenmeyer, New York City, October 16, 1745, in *LCNY-NJ,* pp. 270–72.

[72]Letter from the Reverend Wilhelm C. Berkenmeyer to the Reverend Michael C. Knoll, Loonenberg, November 25, 1745, in *LCNY-NJ,* pp. 278–81.

[73]Ibid., p. 279.

[74]Muhlenberg to Halle, Providence, December 12, 1745, in Schulze, pp. 180–200.

[75]Ibid., p. 185.

[76]Ibid.

[77]"Letter from the Very Rev. Dr. Friedrich Wagner, Senior of the Lutheran Ministerium of Hamburg, to the Rev. Dr. Philip D. Krauter, Pastor of Holy Trinity Lutheran Church in London," Hamburg, October 25, 1744, in *LCNY-NJ,* p. 246:

> I sincerely beg your reverence to let me know whether you would agree to consider someone straight from Halle for the post? I know that nowhere as at Halle do excellent students decide to accept such calls. Up to this time, however, I have hesitated proposing someone from there, for I have seen from some writings which Pastor Berkenmeyer sent here that persons who have studied at Halle are regarded on that account alone as under suspicion and objectionable in America. Therefore I must first be assured whether the laudable consistory in London is of a different opinion."

[78]"Letter from the Rev. Philip D. Krauter to the Rev. Friedrich Wagner," London, January 22, 1745, in *LCNY-NJ,* pp. 247–48:

> I sincerely assure your reverence that for my part I have no objection whatever to Halle. In fact, at the very beginning it was mentioned in the

consistory here that if your reverence could not find a suitable person to recommend, we might find one readily at Halle. I did not notice any unwillingness to this idea in the entire consistory. . . . Indeed, it seems to me, from letters received from America, that the local prejudice there causes unnecessary misgivings. . . . Hitherto I have always had the hope that this might be only a leftover from the time when these people were still in Germany and the distressing controversies were perhaps (alas indeed!) flaming high.

[79]Kreider, p. 108.

[80]"Pastor Berkenmeyer, as an old guardian and champion of liturgical forms and opponent of the power of godliness, had been angry from the very beginning when he learned that the preacher assigned to him had come to Pennsylvania first and was acquainted with us. His premises were fixed beforehand: whoever has acquaintanceship with the Pietists is a Pietist: therefore Mr. Hartwick is a Pietist," in *I Journals*, pp. 248–49.

[81]Kreider, pp. 108–9.

[82]Ibid., p. 109.

[83]*I Journals*, p. 249.

[84]Ibid., pp. 246–47.

[85]Ibid., p. 251.

[86]Ibid.

[87]Ibid., p. 252.

[88]Kreider, p. 59.

[89]Ibid.

[90]*I Journals*, pp. 254–55.

[91]Ibid., p. 255; Kreider, p. 61.

[92]Kreider, p. 63.

[93]Ibid., p. 62.

[94]*I Journals*, p. 256.

[95]Ibid., p. 154.

[96]Ibid., p. 255.

[97]Ibid., p. 256.

[98]Ibid., p. 257.

[99]Ibid., p. 260.

[100]Kreider, pp. 117–18.

[101]Ibid., pp. 118–19.

[5]
The Theology of Henry Melchior Muhlenberg

Before his death in 1787, Muhlenberg's influence extended from the northern tip of New York State to Maryland and Virginia, and the brand of pietism which he represented emerged as the dominant characteristic of American Lutheranism. His pragmatic and innovative approach to ecclesiastical crises had enabled him to stave off the Moravian threat and supplant Berkenmeyer orthodoxy. More important still, his willingness to adapt and accommodate himself to a new environment had resulted in the creation of a distinctively stable American Lutheran church.

Still, Muhlenberg was more than just an organizer; he was a theologian as well, and the flexibility of his actions in concrete situations sprang from the peculiar resiliency of the theological concepts which permeated his whole life.

Surprisingly, this side of Muhlenberg has been virtually ignored by church historians who have concentrated the vast bulk of their research on New England puritanism, to the neglect of Middle Colony religious history. Those brief biographical sketches which do mention him dismiss him as intellectually "clear and vigorous, though not original," and summarize his biblical and theological scholarship as "sound" but unimaginative.[1] Part of the reason for this state of affairs is that, unlike his great New England contemporary, Jonathan Edwards, Henry Melchior Muhlenberg has left us no systematic or lengthy exposition of his beliefs, which may be classified as a theology in the strict sense. This omission was the result of several factors.

In the first place colonial Lutheranism, unlike Congregationalism, was still largely an immigrant church, beset with all the organizational, linguistic, ethnic, and cultural-economic disabilities suffered by newcomers. In addition, a dearth of trained ministers caused German-speaking colonials to turn to itinerant preachers whose incompetence further fragmented a Lutheran polity already torn between orthodox and pietistic poles. As a result many Germans joined the various German sectarians, went over to English-speaking congregations, or adopted a posture of outright religious indifferentism. After 1736 the activities of Moravian missioners posing as Lutheran ministers confused even more an already bewilderingly complex religious picture.

Into this unrest came Muhlenberg in 1742, to plant firmly a native Lutheran church and to secure it from its own internal divisions and external threats. So serious were these threats that it is possible that Lutheranism might have been exterminated in the province of Pennsylvania had Muhlenberg not appeared on the scene. Throughout the forty-five years of his colonial ministry, he was wholly engaged in these disputes.

Unlike Edwards, then, Muhlenberg did not have the leisure or opportunity to develop a systematic theology. Only if an organization is firmly established and somewhat defined can it afford the luxury of reflecting on the nature of its definition. Congregationalism is English America had reached this stage; Lutheranism had not.

An equally important factor contributing to Muhlenberg's failure to systematize or organize his thought was the nature of his personality. He was, above all, an activist, a missionary, and a pastor. From his earliest days, he had envisioned a ministry to the Indies. His transportation to England's American colonies caused no abatement of this missionary zeal, for here too he encountered a church in its infancy. Combined with his activism and concern for the pastoral problems of individual souls, not theological systems, was a genius for accommodation and moderate adaptation. Muhlenberg's mind functioned in categories of concrete problems and specific responses. As he himself was the first to admit, his mind "had never been sharpened and polished to comprehend abstract ideas."[2] Thus circumstances and personality combined to prevent Muhlenberg from bequeathing to posterity a systematically organized treatise of his theological speculations.

It is one thing, however, to admit that Muhlenberg was not a systematic theologian but quite another to deny that he had any personal theology at all, or, if he did, that it was sound but dull and unimaginative. A patient gleaning of his journals reveals a body of religious thought which is both comprehensive and, in certain respects, unique. While, therefore, it can be conceded that Muhlenberg left no formulated theology as such, he did leave a body of religious thought which sets him apart as a theologian of some importance.

Muhlenberg represents a subtle combination of both orthodox and pietistic elements, softened and shaped by his experience in English America. He was a revivalist, but in an entirely different sense than is usually understood by that term. For Muhlenberg insisted that awakenings occur within and through a liturgical framework and, unlike his contemporaries of other religious denominations, he succeeded in this synthesis. This accomplishment is, perhaps, Muhlenberg's greatest claim to recognition as one of colonial America's outstanding theologians.

Similar to New England Puritans, Muhlenberg held a form of covenantal or federal theology, though not in the same sense as did they. God, whom he defines in Johannine terms as love, created Adam and Eve in His own image and likeness, perfectly good in both body and soul.[3] God then made a pact with them, the Covenant of Works, whereby He gave to Adam and Eve dominion over all lower creation, immortality, and a host of other preternatural gifts if they, in return, would love their Creator and their fellow men with all their heart and obey His precepts. To keep before people's eyes a reminder of their creaturely dependence, God gave them a *lex positiva,* which Muhlenberg seems to equate with the natural law, allegorized in the metaphor of the Tree of the Knowledge of Good and Evil.[4]

This positive law, moreover, was not extrinsic to humans but imbedded in their very heart.[5] To keep the terms of the covenant, it was necessary merely to render *obedientia activa* to the law.[6] Though human beings had ample glory and happiness under the covenantal terms, and though they had sufficient moral and natural law to indicate to them God's will, as well as the grace needed to follow it, they chose instead to disobey their creator. In this act of disobedience, they violated the terms of the covenant, lost salvation, and brought death into the world, for Adam, acting as the federal head of all mankind, imparted to all of his descendants, the stain of original sin. Hereafter, no person would be born justified but would enter the world as an enemy of God.

Despite man's ingratitude and disobedience, God did not turn his back on him, but made a new covenant, the Covenant of Grace, which manifests his incomprehensible love, wisdom, and mercy toward his fallen creatures.[7] In his concept of the Covenant of Grace, Muhlenberg parts company with Puritan theologians. Whereas the New Englanders viewed the *proto-evangelium*, Genesis 3:15, as a promise of a covenant to come with Abraham, Muhlenberg interpreted the passage as the actual Covenant of Grace made, not with Abraham, but with the first man and woman. For his part, God promised to unite a divine person with human seed to accomplish the redemption of humanity. On the other hand, the individual had only to be convinced of God's promise, to give consent to the covenant, and to render obedience to its terms through the sufficient means of grace which were offered to him.[8] Once more, however, people were unfaithful to their covenant-God. God then destroyed the wicked by flood but still did not abrogate his covenant. Instead he renewed it, first with Noah, later with Abraham.[9]

Muhlenberg gives no indication of why he chose to deviate from the norm regarding the Covenant of Grace. To be sure, pietists never concentrated on covenantal theology as did the Puritans. One might, therefore, speculate that because the whole concept was peripheral to his theological heritage, Muhlenberg merely added it as window dressing, and in so doing, erred. This, however, would be at variance with his usual painstaking exactitude in exegesis. Neither would it make sense to suppose that he was incorrectly transcribing some bit of Puritan theology which he did not fully understand for, in this case, it would seem illogical for him to record it at all. Rather it seems that there was a reason for this change. Certainly by locating both covenants with Adam and Eve, Muhlenberg downplayed the historic role of the Jewish people as special mediators of salvation, thereby striking at the whole concept of an elect or chosen people. Salvation, in his mind, was promised to all mankind, to be mediated directly between creator and creature, without the need of a vessel of election.

This Covenant of Grace could only be cemented and made efficacious through the Son of Man, the Second Adam, who made reparation for Adam's sin by a perfect obedience to the positive law.[10] Since flesh had conquered spirit in humans, had indeed become the starting point of their moral guilt and helplessness, the Son of Man had to assume flesh to redeem fallen flesh so that redemption and reconciliation could take place.[11]

For Muhlenberg, the Incarnation is a wondrous vindication of the faithfulness of the Covenant God, since it was fulfilled in the bloody sacrifice on the cross whereby humanity was redeemed and the Saviour implanted the fruits of his redemption.[12] Jesus Christ conquered death, overcame evil and so laid the foundations for a rebirth, a new life, a second creation. Through baptism, which Muhlenberg calls "the seal and covenant of Grace,"[13] the individual enters into the covenant relationship with the Father by becoming a partaker in the meritorious sufferings of his Son. He or she is buried with Christ, dies to this world, and rises again to a new life of grace. Through the waters of baptism, then, the individual receives forgiveness of sin, the imputed righteousness of the Father to whom he or she is reconciled, life, and salvation. To serve as a seal and pledge of this new inheritance of grace, the Holy Spirit enters into the person's soul.[14]

Baptism then is the beginning of the process of salvation. It is a rebirth which, since it is purely an *actio passiva,* should not be confused with conversion.[15] Through it we are cut off from the

corrupt seed of Adam and "translated, ingrafted, or incorpo-
rated" into the Kingdom of Grace.[16] Though on the individual's
part, baptismal rebirth is a passive action, for God it is a
gratuitous *actus judicalis,* an act of "imputative righteousness."[17]
Thus people have no active role in the process of rebirth, nor do
they effect it through any merit or works of their own. All
persons then have an equal right to the grace and righteousness
merited by Christ.[18] Since, moreover, an act of God is by its very
nature absolutely perfect, baptism, once conferred, is sufficient
and need never be repeated, in contradistinction to Anabaptist
teachings.[19] Since, too, individuals can only enter into the Covenant of Grace through baptism, and only thereby receive salvation through a passive reception of grace, Muhlenberg defended
infant baptism.

This new life of grace given gratuitously in baptism can be lost
through neglect in daily resisting the onslaughts of the devil or
in fostering its renewal. Satan was a very real presence to
Muhlenberg who saw his hand clearly in the confused religious
situation in Pennsylvania.[20] In his attacks on the godly life, Satan
first strikes at the means of grace, the word and the sacraments,
so that they cannot effect their intrinsic efficacy in souls.[21]
Failing in this, he stirs up hatred against the proponents of
godliness.[22] The result is that the old man, once more, rises to
the surface, pursues a life of sinful pleasure, fractures his
baptismal covenant vows, and rejects his covenant God for the
wiles of the devil, hardening his heart to both word and Spirit.[23]

Such a person, once fallen from baptismal grace, must become
aware of the misery of his lapsed state and the natural condemnation under which he stands as a descendant of the first
Adam.[24] Like Luther, Muhlenberg believed that it was the
function of the Law to convict one of his sins and that such a
conviction was the essential first step in the process of conversion. Like Luther, too, Muhlenberg retained a tension between
Law and Gospel; both are necessary for salvation, both must be
heeded. Since Gospel must always accompany Law, no Christian
should confine the joy of the Gospel to a so-called elect or apply
the censure of the Law to those supposedly damned.[25]

In a sense, the Gospel, too, convicts of sin for the sinner sees in the sufferings and death of Christ the heinousness of sin in God's eyes, as well as the role his or her sinful life played on Calvary.[26] Once the sinner comprehends the effect of his or her sins on the innocent Christ, he is left with a stricken conscience which, under the grace of the Holy Spirit, "reaches out and seeks to inwrap itself in the Surety and atonement."[27] To inwrap oneself in Christ's wounds means "to appropriate and assume Christ's merit and righteousness in faith" as if the sinner had, in his own person, made payment and satisfaction for his or her transgressions.[28] The more powerful one's feelings of repentance and conviction of sin, the stronger grace becomes in the sinner's soul.[29]

Grace follows upon repentance, for in repentance sinners once more open their hearts to the workings of the Holy Spirit and return to their baptismal covenant. Because it is the presence of the Spirit in the converted soul, grace is the touchstone of conversion. From the moment when persons lose their baptismal innocence and turn to sin, the Lord pursues them with his grace.[30] Individuals have but to agree to draw from this all-sufficient fountain of salvation to be saved.[31] Thus Muhlenberg categorically rejects the concept of irresistible grace. While admitting that the process of salvation depends solely on Christ who leads the wayward soul to conversion, he feels that unlike baptism, which is a purely passive act, conversion demands some active appropriation on the part of the individual.[32] Grace is offered, but it must be accepted or daily renewed else it will die. Its mere presence is no guarantee of its permanence. So Muhlenberg warns: "Let no man sin in reliance upon grace."[33]

Once individuals have become aware of their corruption and stand convicted of sin, they turn, in faith, to the gospel promises of salvation, accepting God's grace. This process is conversion, essentially an act of pure faith in the word of God. As such, it neither is dependent upon, nor can be initiated by, the individuals' purely natural powers, for the natural persons, utterly corrupt as they are, are incapable of positing such a supranatural act since, in their post-Eden state, all their natural faculties were weakened.[34] But, for Muhlenberg, man's natural powers, though seriously debilitated, were not completely destroyed. There yet remained in him a blurred outline of the divine image in which he had been created. Thus man can in some way know of God through nature which reflects a faint glimmer of the now lost *imago Dei*.[35] Moreover, because humans remain rational creatures, the process of conversion, in which they accept in faith the truths of revelation, must also be a rational act. Though the unaided reason and intellect can never achieve reconciliation with God, reason, enlightened by grace, is capable of grasping salvation.[36] Faith, then, is a rational act posited by a rational being. Muhlenberg therefore warned against the pitfalls of seeking a purely sensible feeling of salvation.[37] Rational assurance need not culminate in religious emotion.

A second characteristic of conversion is that it is for Muhlenberg a gradual process, not the result of a sudden and unexpected illumination.[38] Because grace builds upon nature, the natural person must first be prepared in his or her natural powers before grace can enter his or her soul. This presupposes that sinners have already despaired of their own powers and are willing to trust completely in God. Usually this despair occurred through material misfortunes and bodily illnesses through which the Lord prepared the sinners to receive and correctly employ the means of grace.[39] Indeed Muhlenberg held a decidedly biblical view of sickness, which he saw as the direct consequence of sin. "Sin is *causa*, sickness *effectus. Cessante causa, cessat effectus.*"[40] The more the body—the instrument of sin—is assailed, the more room there is in the soul for the Holy Spirit to effect repentance and faith, and through the word, to lead the soul to Christ's righteousness.[41] The chastened and usually desperately ill sinners now turn back in their search for salvation to the saving evangelical truths they had learned in their youth. If they are sincere in their quest, the Spirit will lead them to salvation.[42] As a result, the sinners see themselves through the eyes of faith as washed clean from sin.[43]

A third characteristic of conversion is that, for Muhlenberg, it is experiential.[44] Experience and certainty, however, do not come "through a voice from heaven, through a vision or in a dream, or through sensual feelings," though sinners must truly experience repentance and an assurance of the forgiveness of all their sins.[45] Rather it comes through the mediation of the Word in scripture and the sacraments. This conversion experience, moreover, produces in the converted sinners a true poverty of spirit and genuine, unostentatious humility which alone can provide the foundation for a godly life.[46]

Muhlenberg, therefore, always demanded that his converts be able to give testimony to a conversion experience and the presence of grace before he would give them the Lord's Supper in their final illness. But this experience need not be sensible and need not, indeed, should not, free the sinner from all doubts about his or her worthiness and eventual salvation. It was the minister's function to guarantee, as best he could, that the conversion experience was genuine, that grace was truly present. But, for Muhlenberg, there were no certain norms or standards by which one could judge such a conversion. Not even a well-lived life was sufficient proof that a person was in the state of grace.[47] Instead, the pastor had to hope for the best until theologians developed a spiritual litmus paper which would testify to the workings of the Spirit in the human soul.[48]

Faith, the means to converting grace, was of two kinds, the sensible, which Muhlenberg rejected, and that based on word and Spirit, which he advocated.[49] True saving faith, in Muhlenberg's opinion, must consist in *cognoscere* (knowledge), *velle* (desire), and *accipere* (submission and acceptance).[50] The intellect must first be enlightened concerning the truths of salvation, must then sincerely desire to adhere to these truths, and finally the will must actively choose and accept salvation. Thus, saving faith is "the heartfelt desire for that means which the enlightened understanding recognizes as the most necessary, best, and most perfect of all means to be tried."[51] Faith, then, is a rational act.

Sanctification follows upon conversion. Individuals become sanctified in the sight of God through their repentance of sins, their conversion to Christ, and their acceptance of grace. Conversely, they are now justified through the imputation of the merits of Christ.[52] They receive Christ's righteousness, not from any merit on their part but as a free will gift of God.[53]

Justification and sanctification are "inevitably followed by true Christian living and striving toward heaven."[54] Like Luther, Muhlenberg held that good works, though not essential to salvation, must inevitably be performed by one who is saved, for they are the genuine fruits of conversion. The infallible sign of a true Christian is active love culminating in works of charity.[55]

This whole process of repentance, conversion, sanctification, and justification culminates in regeneration or rebirth of sinners in which they are restored to their baptismal innocence.[56] The old man is subdued as grace conquers nature. Regeneration, however, is not a static state but a dynamic process, for grace can be lost. Though the old man dies, his death is slow and lingering, not instantaneous. Indeed, so long as an individual has within him the breath of life, the old man remains, albeit weakly, unceasing in his efforts to dominate the newly sanctified soul.[57] The reborn must daily renew and strengthen grace by crucifying anew the flesh in an ever more perfect imitation of Christ.[58]

Saving grace, for Muhlenberg, ordinarily comes through only two channels, the sacraments and the word of God in its oral and scriptural form. Nor can one be considered apart from the other, for it is the function of the preached word to induce people to frequent the sacraments as fountain heads of grace. "Where the Word is, there must also be the Sacraments."[59] Indeed Muhlenberg defines the church in terms of word and sacrament. For him, as for Luther, the church is where the word is rightly preached and the sacraments correctly administered.[60]

Like all pietists, Muhlenberg sought to exclude from the sacraments those who were living grossly immoral lives. So before giving communion, he read a list of the communicants and demanded that the congregation declare whether it knew of anyone on the list who was living in "intentional and deliberate" sin.[61] Because, however, he felt that the sacraments were also themselves a means of conversion, he did not demand an absolute conversion testimony, nor did he seek to inquire into the inner state of the soul.[62] It was up to the minister to dispense the sacraments to those who sought them. But it was the concern of the sinner and his God to be sure the sacraments were worthily received. Unlike other pietists, therefore, Muhlenberg did not restrict the sacraments to the converted or godly. He thus denied that the church had the power to place under interdict even congregations where grave abuses and disorders existed.[63]

While the sacraments do not operate *ex opere operato,* and do, to some degree depend on the state of soul of the recipient, this point, Muhlenberg felt, should not be over-emphasized.[64] The orthodox had erred in so stressing faith without works that they relied solely on the outward reception of the means of grace, divorced from godly living, for justification. Pietists as Arndt, Spener, Müller, and Francke, in their reaction to this, had so over-emphasized works and godly living that, in Muhlenberg's view, they "ran into the other extreme and rejected the proper use of the means of grace."[65] In his sacramental theology, Muhlenberg steers a decidedly middle course between orthodoxy and pietism.

In line with orthodox Lutheranism, Muhlenberg admitted of only two sacraments, baptism and the Lord's Supper. However, he lays so much stress on confirmation that he practically elevates it to sacramental status. Baptism is the seal of the covenant whereby original sin is forgiven, grace enters into the soul, making a person a child of God, a member of the church, and a partaker in the Covenant of Grace. It is to be administered to infants because it is a passive act on the person's part. Confirmation is needed to strengthen this original baptismal grace. It should be received between the ages of seven, the attainment of the use of reason, and fourteen, for this is the time when the child's conscience develops and learns to distinguish between good and evil. Hence this is also the stage of life most exposed to temptations.[66] Thus the purpose of confirmation is to strengthen the baptismal covenant and increase the grace needed to overcome temptation.[67]

The Eucharist is both "a means by which the Church was to bear uninterrupted, public witness to Christ's suffering, death, and atonement . . ." as well as a means to "sanctification and growth."[68] Muhlenberg holds to a quite literal interpretation of the words of consecration, insisting on a real, corporeal presence.[69] While he rejects Catholic transubstantiation and the Reformed mystical presence, he nowhere explains his philosophical basis for the doctrine.[70] It would be safe to assume, however, that he here follows the scholastic Lutheran concept of corporeal ubiquity as a foundation for the real presence.

The sacraments were not to be administered in a loose or haphazard manner, for Muhlenberg insisted upon the observance of a strict liturgical framework, created by synod and adhered to by each congregation. Even before his first synod had met, Muhlenberg had already drawn up a common liturgical schema which received synodical ratification in 1748.[71] Liturgical conformity was intended to prevent enthusiastic outbursts, for Muhlenberg believed that grace was distributed in a structured church according to institutional forms. For this reason, the sacraments must be issued in a regular and consistent manner.

As essential to salvation as the sacraments was the word of God, through which the sinner is awakened and in which the Spirit of God is mediated to people.[72] In his scriptural word, God has revealed his whole plan for humanity's salvation. It is in accordance with their acceptance of and conformity to this plan that persons will be judged.[73] To hardened sinners, however, the word functions as a condemnation unto death; but for those who are convinced of the truths of salvation, it spurs on to inquiry and concern for their spiritual welfare.[74]

Though the word of God contains all that is necessary for salvation, it must be communicated to sinners through ministerial preaching before it can become efficacious in their souls. But to be communicated, it must be delivered in a properly fitting fashion. Muhlenberg then insisted upon a regular form of preaching adapted to the needs and abilities of the people.

He was himself a revivalist preacher in the sense that he believed the preached word had the power to awaken souls, carefully noting in his journals any such signs of awakening elicited in his auditors by his sermons.[75] Unlike other revivalist preachers, however, Muhlenberg frowned upon manifestations of hysteria. Awakening a soul meant, for him, inducing a humble and repentant heart which would turn the sinner toward God through a holy and sacramental life while bringing peace to his soul.

In his preaching style, Muhlenberg again adopted a middle ground between enthusiasm and scholastic aridity. He believed carefully drawn expositions of biblical texts made no impression on the common Christian untrained in theological subtlety. They smacked of the seminary classroom.[76] On the other hand, bombastic threats of hell fire and brimstone were equally ineffective for they either paralysed the sinner with fear or made the preacher an object of ridicule.[77] Sermons, therefore, were to be delivered "in a lively and appealing manner, *plane et plene.*"[78] The preacher was to speak with a reserved dignity appropriate to his subject matter and at moderate length to avoid losing his audience.[79] In short everything had to be done to focus attention on the saving truths preached, not on the person of the preacher.[80]

What was to be spoken of was of far greater importance than the manner in which it was presented. In this vein Muhlenberg warned against two extremes, of preaching either damnation or the salvific mercy of Christ in isolation from each other.[81] If only God's wrath were preached, sinners would become discouraged in their efforts to improve. If only God's mercy were presented, they would be lulled into a false sense of security which also discouraged genuine effort on their part.[82]

Finally, the truths of salvation had to be presented in digestible form through copious use of illustrations and edifying examples, for the teacher was like a nurse who first prepares the food so it can be assimilated by her children.[83] For this reason, too, the preacher had to be himself a converted man, else he could never present in a meaningful way truths which he himself had not experienced.

It is particularly in his concepts of word and sacraments that Muhlenberg distinguished himself from enthusiastic revivalists and set himself off as a liturgical revivalist. He was a close friend of George Whitefield as well as the Tennents, and agreed with them that effective preaching can and should produce awakenings. Much as he liked Whitefield, Muhlenberg remained highly critical and suspicious of his penchant for producing emotional, enthusiastic, irrational outbursts in his auditors. He relates an incident when Whitefield was late for a speaking engagement and another preacher filled in. Shortly thereafter, the great evangelist appeared and began to preach on the same text in much the same manner as had his stand-in. Almost instantaneously, the audience, which previously had been calmly and quietly attentive, "could be seen to be deeply moved, to be in tears, and to be wringing hands, and the sighing, weeping, and shouting of the people could be heard."[84] Obviously skeptical that such manifestations were signs of grace, Muhlenberg wondered whether "name and fame, preconception and fancies play a part in the synergism?"[85]

More essentially, Muhlenberg opposed Whitefield's claim that it was an error to hold that regeneration takes place in baptism.[86] To Muhlenberg, this was tantamount to confusing erroneously regeneration with conversion.[87] For Whitefield, the process of regeneration could occur outside the sacramental and liturgical life of the church. Muhlenberg viewed this as an impossibility. That is not to say that he rejected revivalistic practices. He merely opposed them if they departed from a liturgical framework. So to separate grace from the sacraments was to open the door to chaos and a religion based solely on feeling with the result that "we shall be tossed to and fro and carried about with every wind of doctrine if nothing but blind, sensual feelings is taken as the standard of religion."[88] It is, unfortunately, human nature to go to extremes in either direction for, as Muhlenberg noted, "we either imagine ourselves to be wholly spirit and forget that there is a body connected with it, or we claim to be entirely body and sensuality without an immortal soul."[89] Awakenings and revival meetings were beneficial provided they did not over-emphasize the spirit, divorcing the person from his existential, incarnational existence. Should this occur, then revivalism degenerates into enthusiasm. A preacher conducting an awakening should, therefore, take care that "violent birththroes should be reduced by the proper remedies and a spiritual rebirth be promoted."[90] Such remedies included, above all, a channeling of awakened enthusiasm into a sacramental life, for only then will awakenings produce the desired fruits of the spirit.[91] Persons must conduct their religious life according to the plan of salvation presented in historical, scriptural revelation.[92]

Obviously, then, Muhlenberg rejected the concept of "an immediate revelation which God has not promised."[93] God manifests himself to individuals not in a blinding flash but by degrees, through institutionalized means.[94] The road to perfection is essentially an orderly progression.[95] While Muhlenberg does not deny the possibility of extra-biblical revelation, he considers it highly unlikely.[96] Rather, individuals should look for God's will in his word and sacraments.[97] At any rate, such immediate inspirations must be rejected as fallacious snares of Satan if they contradict God's revealed word.[98] Indeed Muhlenberg bases his condemnation of the sectarians—among them Quakers, Moravians, and Anabaptists—precisely on this: that they have sought "to be independent from God and His revealed Word and will."[99]

Adherence to historical revelation, then, is the hallmark of any true church. For Muhlenberg, the visible church is divided into many parts, Catholic, Lutheran, Reformed, and Anglican.[100] Salvation did not depend on membership in any particular church.[101] Within this church, there were three distinct offices: clergy, civil magistrates, and the laity, each with its own responsibilities. The clergy had been appointed by Christ to be "faithful stewards of the mysteries of God."[102] As such they were to be honored and obeyed. It should be noted that a true minister was distinguished not by his orthodoxy and living faith alone but also by his regular call and ordination. This it is which sets him off from unconverted, itinerant preachers, and this, too, is in keeping with Muhlenberg's insistence that all aspects of the religious life had to be ecclesiastically structured and ordered.

Muhlenberg viewed the state as a coordinate, supportive partner of the church. Its function was to provide for the person's temporal needs and only if the church utterly neglected its duty for his or her spiritual welfare as well. Since they were copartners, with different functions in the economy of salvation, Muhlenberg opposed interference in each other's spheres of activity.

The laity, of course, Muhlenberg saw as the people of God. Since he tended to elevate the ministry to a somewhat superior level, he did not emphasize as did Francke and Spener, the doctrine of the priesthood of all believers. Still he assigned to the laity an important, though subordinate, voice in church government as is evidenced by the various church constitutions which issued from his pen. The prime concern of the laity was the leading of a godly life within marriage whose primary end was "the procreation of the human race and the training of children in the nurture and admonition of the Lord,"[103] and whose secondary end was the mutual help and comfort of the marriage partners in their quest for salvation.[104] In his conception of the godly life, we can see clearly his capacity for growth. The puritanical young Muhlenberg denounced Philadelphia's wayward youth for skinny-dipping in the Schuylkill[105] and bemoaned his son Peter's "evil bent . . . toward hunting and fishing."[106] He also condemned the Reverend John Philip Boehm for condoning music, laughter, and dancing. As the years passed by, Muhlenberg mellowed considerably. Thus he could warn Pastor Hartwick not to denounce shooting, horse-racing, boozing, and dancing, for a good minister

> should first lay a foundation of true Christianity in the hearts of the people and then build from the inside to the outside; in this way the gross scales on their eyes would fall away of themselves.[107]

Even music and poetry, if "rescued from shameful abuse and employed for [their] rightful purpose and use . . . could well produce much blessing and fruit."[108] Ultimately Muhlenberg admitted that there were legitimate sensual pleasures in life, even one as innocent as his addiction to sauerkraut, for we find in Christ "the most acute, keen, and pure feelings and tastes, though they are subordinated to the anointed, superior faculties of the soul."[109] This, then, is the test of the legitimacy of pleasure; that it will help and not hinder an individual's quest for salvation. The Christ of Muhlenberg's youth could not laugh because he suffered so greatly. In old age, Muhlenberg at least admitted He might smile a bit.

It is possible to conclude that, though Henry Melchior Muhlenberg was not a systematic theologian, he did possess a developed and in some ways unique theology. Certainly his training at Göttingen and Halle exposed him to a first-rate theological education, and he continued his studies on leaving the seminary. Throughout the journals he refers to his readings in Luther, Melanchthon, the pietistic and scholastic Lutheran theologians, and others. He had an effective command of Latin, Greek, and Hebrew and painstakingly applied this knowledge to textual criticism to arrive at the precise meaning of scripture. His concept of biblical exegesis, which eschewed the outmoded allegorical approach, was in the vanguard of the critical thought of his day.[110]

Though he has been classified as a pietist, a charge, incidentally, which Muhlenberg consistently denied, he avoided the extremes of the Halle school. The heritage he left to American Lutheranism was a blending of both pietistic and orthodox elements. With the pietists, Muhlenberg believed that individuals must undergo a conversion experience which would convict and forgive them of sin, sanctify them through grace, and issue in a life of good works. This, however, he tempered through orthodox thought, for the conversion experience had to be rational, not sensible; conviction and forgiveness of sin had to avoid the tendency toward pharisaical feelings of election; grace must issue only through the means entrusted to the church; and good works must not negate the need for a sacramental life.

He was a revivalist, but a liturgical revivalist. By placing revivalistic practices within a strict liturgical framework, Muhlenberg tempered enthusiastic extremes and so spared American Lutheranism from the excesses which splintered other denominations into Old Side and New Side, Old Light and New Light. It is in this ability to incorporate revivalism within the liturgical framework of a structured, institutional church, an accomplishment which eluded most colonial clergymen, that Muhlenberg's theological importance lies. He was, then, more than an organizer of churches. He was a theologian as well whose vision of God and His Church grounded every action of his ministry.

NOTES

[1]Joseph G. Hopkins, ed., *Concise Dictionary of American Biography* (New York: Charles Scribner's Sons, 1964), p. 712.

[2]Henry Melchior Muhlenberg, *The Journals of Henry Melchior Muhlenberg in Three Volumes,* III, trans. Theodore G. Tappert and John W. Doberstein (Philadelphia: Muhlenberg Press, 1958), p. 131. Hereafter referred to as *III Journals.*

[3]Henry Melchior Muhlenberg, *The Journals of Henry Melchior Muhlenberg in Three Volumes,* II, trans. Theodore G. Tappert and John W. Doberstein (Philadelphia: Muhlenberg Press, 1945), p. 228. Hereafter referred to as *II Journals.*

[4]Ibid., pp. 44, 228.

[5]Ibid., p. 44.

[6]Ibid.

[7]Ibid., p. 228.

[8]Ibid.

[9]Ibid.

[10]Ibid., p. 44.

[11]Ibid., p. 42.

[12]Ibid., p. 41.

[13]Henry Melchior Muhlenberg, *The Journals of Henry Melchior Muhlenberg in Three Volumes,* I, trans. Theodore G. Tappert and John W. Doberstein (Philadelphia: Muhlenberg Press, 1942), p. 311. Hereafter referred to as *I Journals.*

[14]Ibid., p. 123.

[15]*II Journals,* p. 162.

[16]Ibid.

[17]Ibid.

[18]Ibid.

[19]Ibid.

[20]In July of 1742, while on board a ship bound from England to Charleston, Muhlenberg overheard a conversation centering on a denial of Satan's existence. He joined the group as an uninvited guest, stating "first, that there is a devil; second, how he is described according to God's Word; third, that he does his work in the children of unbelief. This last I illustrated by their cursing, swearing, and improper life. (*I Journals,* p. 131)

[21]*II Journals,* p. 49.

[22]As Muhlenberg phrased it, "he sows tares among the wheat, stands on guard against godliness, becomes an orthodoxist, and seeks to keep his house swept clean of Pietism and garnished with his own tapestries." (Ibid)

[23]*I Journals,* pp. 147, 42–43, 3.

[24]Ibid., p. 124.

[25]Ibid., p. 359. "Law" here refers to the corpus of the Old Testament of the Jewish dispensation, while Gospel refers to the New Testament evangelia.

[26]Ibid., p. 124.

[27]Ibid.

[28]Ibid., p. 123.

[29]Ibid., p. 124.

[30]Ibid., p. 134.

[31]Ibid., p. 315.

[32]Ibid., pp. 35, 124.

[33]Ibid., p. 370. This in contradistinction to the Moravian doctrine that the saved can no longer sin and the Calvinist theory of divine election.

[34]Ibid., pp. 353, 285.

[35]*II Journals*, p. 204.

[36]Ibid.

[37]*I Journals*, p. 325.

[38]Ibid., pp. 218, 382.

[39]Ibid., p. 355.

[40]*II Journals*, p. 188.

[41]*I Journals*, p. 242.

[42]Ibid., p. 383. Given his correlation between sin and sickness, Muhlenberg, as all Halle men, practiced medicine as an integral part of his pastoral work. Cf. John N. Ritter, "Muhlenberg's Anticipation of Psychosomatic Medicine," *Lutheran Church Quarterly* 19 (April 1946): 181–88.

[43]*I Journals*, p. 383.

[44]Ibid., p. 332.

[45]Ibid., p. 305.

[46]Said Muhlenberg: "High-flown words, artistic expressions, outward forms, and seemingly holy gestures, speaking with the tongues of men and angels— none of these effects anything whatsoever unless edification by the Word of God begins in the bottom of the heart." (Ibid., p. 273)

[47]Ibid., p. 381.

[48]"One must charitably hope for the best and be very careful in judging such matters until such time as our higher theologians have more clearly discovered the axis around which nature and grace turn and enlighten us concerning it." (Ibid., p. 298)

[49]Muhlenberg's distinctions between the two kinds of faith were: "(1) That which comes through the senses. (2) That which comes through the testimony of the Apostles and prophets connected with the Holy Ghost. The first kind has not been ordained by God as the way of salvation; the second is the surer, more blessed." (*II Journals*, p. 538)

[50]*I Journals*, p. 303.

[51]Ibid.

[52]Ibid., p. 216.

[53]Ibid., pp. 133, 227.

[54]Ibid., p. 123.

[55]*II Journals*, p. 39.

[56]Ibid.

[57]*I Journals*, p. 383.

[58]Ibid.; *II Journals*, p. 53.

[59]*I Journals*, p. 415.

[60]"Where the Word of God and the Holy Sacraments are used according to Christ's institution, there is the visible Church; and where the Church is, there the Word of God and the Holy Sacraments must also be used." (Ibid., pp. 118–19)

[61]Ibid., p. 119.

[62]*III Journals*, p. 615.

[63]"One would still have no authority to abolish the institution [the Lord's Supper]. One would seek rather to get rid of the abuses and disorders. *Abusus enim non tollit usum.*" (*I Journals*, p. 119)

[64]*Ex opere operato* is a scholastic term defining the Roman Catholic position that the efficacy of the sacraments stems solely from their own intrinsic power and in no way depends on the state of soul of either the minister or the recipient. However, it should be noted that the church has always held that if the recipient is in a state of sin, the sacrament of the Eucharist does not act as a means of grace but rather as an agent of condemnation.

[65]*I Journals*, p. 415.

[66]*II Journals*, p. 92.

[67]Ibid.

[68]Ibid., p. 216.

[69]"Delivered a sermon on the words of institution of the Lord's Supper. . . . I refrained from all scholastic and unnecessary fancies and adhered simply and sincerely to the clear testimentary words of our Lord Jesus Christ, and acted therein like Queen Elizabeth . . . who, when she was sharply questioned by the Roman Catholics about this article of faith, answered, *'It was the Word that spake it; He took the Bread and brake it: and what the Word did make it, that I believe and take it.'* " (*I Journals*, pp. 306–7)

[70]*II Journals*, p. 118.

[71]*I Journals*, p. 193.

[72]*II Journals*, p. 173; *I Journals*, p. 356.

[73]*I Journals*, p. 39.

[74]Ibid., p. 38.

[75]Ibid., p. 417.

[76]Ibid., p. 249.

[77]*III Journals*, p. 337.

[78]*I Journals*, P. 442.

[79]*III Journals*, p. 337; *I Journals*, p. 379. As Muhlenberg put it, "The blessed Melanchthon advised that one should preach not *multa* but *multum,* and *Beatus Lutherus* said that the preacher should stop when the hearers still had their best appetite and desired to hear more." (*III Journals*, p. 177)

[80]*II Journals*, p. 696.

[81]"If only the Law is taught, if one does nothing but demand and threaten and terrify, and does not apply the Gospel at the proper time, all one's trouble and labor will be in vain." (Ibid., p. 187)

[82]Ibid.

[83]*I Journals*, p. 660. Muhlenberg compares the preacher to a nurse who must first "crack open the nuts and chew them and then put them into the mouths of

children so that they can assimilate the nuts and turn them into chyle." (*II Journals*, p. 88)

[84]*II Journals*, p. 545.

[85]Ibid. He continued: "weeping, laughing, yawning, sneezing, etc. are all contagious and they seem to have something in common with electricity." (Ibid.)

[86]Ibid., p. 231.

[87]Ibid.

[88]Ibid., p. 683.

[89]Ibid., p. 592.

[90]Ibid., p. 53.

[91]As Muhlenberg phrased it, awakenings will be fruitful if they "are conducted in orderly fashion, in the presence of experienced pastors, for the glory of God, in the interest of the community, for the welfare of one's fellow man, and for the edification of awakened souls." (*I Journals*, p. 325)

[92]*II Journals*, p. 592.

[93]*I Journals*, p. 235.

[94]*II Journals*, p. 186.

[95]Ibid.

[96]*I Journals*, p. 140.

[97]*II Journals*, p. 530.

[98]*I Journals*, p. 349.

[99]*III Journals*, p. 707.

[100]Ibid., p. 502.

[101]"God's goodness provides the ingredients [of salvation] as a whole and the children of men must work upon them and make use of them according to the wisdom and strength bestowed upon them." (*III Journals*, p. 557)

[102]*III Journals*, p. 132. Muhlenberg continues to describe them as men "learned in divinity, immediately and mediately called by Christ to His service in the Church, and regularly ordained to teach God's Holy Word of the Old and New Testaments in Law and Gospel, rightly administer the Holy Sacraments, and be examples to the flock." (Ibid.)

[103]*III Journals*, p. 614.

[104]Ibid.

[105]*II Journals*, p. 89.

[106]*I Journals*, p. 699.

[107]Ibid., p. 268.

[108]*III Journals*, p. 147.

[109]*II Journals*, p. 591.

[110]"There are depths of riches in Holy Scripture still hidden and undeveloped, which are made more obscure by wretched allegories, superficially touched upon, it is true, by the scholarly world, but not yet discovered according to the true sense of the Spirit of God. We are all too prone to read our own ideas and notions into Holy Scripture, and it applies in this also that 'our thoughts are not God's thoughts.' *Exegesis vera* and allegory are *opposita*." (*III Journals*, p. 385)

[6]
Muhlenberg's Ecclesiastical Polity

From Henry Melchior Muhlenberg's theological orientation and his realization that adaptation to a new American environment was essential if Lutheranism was ever to become a true *ecclesia plantata,* emerged his ecclesiastical polity. His emphasis on the dignity and authority of the ministerial office stemmed from his concept of the preacher as the steward of God's mysteries, to whom Christ had entrusted both word and sacraments. The minister, in Muhlenberg's view, was both an exemplar of Christian life and a bridge between creature and Creator. In his hands lay the instruments of converting grace and, for this reason, he was owed respect and obedience by the people of God. To a great degree, Muhlenberg's theological basis for sacerdotal preeminence was European rooted. His formative years had been spent in a stratified, hierarchical society in which both church and state worked together for the salvation of people's souls. European Lutheranism was bound by distinct authoritarian lines, with synod and superintendent overseeing individual pastors who, in turn, managed congregational affairs. Though the European layman had a voice in matters ecclesial, it was definitely subordinate to that of the pastor.

No such hierarchical order existed among colonial American Lutherans. Unlike European governments, the magistrates of the province of Pennsylvania failed to establish any church, nor would they willingly intervene in purely religious matters. Hence there was no over-all governmental authority to which recourse could be had by a troubled pastor. Then, too, the laity as a whole had preceded the Lutheran clergy throughout the middle colonies. Congregations were organized and religious edifices erected by the laymen who then sought ministerial help from Europe. As a result, there arose the phenomenon known as voluntarism, in which the layman assumed the dominant role in church matters. Finally, American Lutheranism, isolated as it was and influenced by sectarian and denominational practices around it, developed a congregational form of government in which each congregation existed as an absolutely independent and separate entity.

Such was the situation into which Muhlenberg entered on his arrival in the colonies. He soon realized that if the Lutheran church was to flourish, order and unity would have to be imposed on the unruly congregational units. His first step in this direction was the assumption of virtual superintendency powers over the colonial church, basing his authority on the primacy of his call which, he claimed, superseded and preceded that of all successive preachers. Gradually he extended his influence by accepting calls in congregations scattered throughout the middle and southern colonies, then entrusting them to assistants sent over from Halle. Eventually he came to realize that further organizational progress could be made only if he was willing to exercise his authority independently of European superiors. To buttress this assumption of power, European synodical authority had to be replaced by an American central governing body which would not only exercise collective control over the hitherto independent congregations and bind individual pastors to recognize its spiritual and temporal supremacy but would also take into its own hands the matter of ordination, thus assuring the supply of a trained native clergy. Muhlenberg was to solve these problems in 1748, using as his *raison d'être*, the necessity of ordaining catechist John Nicholas Kurtz, recently assigned by him to the troubled Tulpehocken congregation to blunt Moravian incursions in that area. The occasion for a general meeting of all Halle-oriented pastors was provided by the impending formal dedication of St. Michael's Church in Philadelphia, which event would assure their collective presence.

Before these actions could be taken, however, Muhlenberg first had to slip loose from his European moorings. His gradual drift in this direction can clearly be seen in the evolution of his views on ordination.

From the beginning of his ministry in English America, Muhlenberg refused to claim the right of ordination without prior authorization from Europe. When Valentine Kraft requested his assistance in ordaining a schoolmaster in 1742, Muhlenberg refused absolutely.[1] Part of his condemnation of Kraft's so-called consistory was based on its unwarranted assumption of the power of ordination.[2] Again, on January 25, 1743, Muhlenberg was approached by another schoolmaster seeking ordination. Once more he refused declaring that he lacked the authority to ordain and that it "was contrary to our Lutheran Church order."[3] Thus instead of fostering the growth of a native clergy, Muhlenberg was at first content to await missionary help sent from Halle. A partial answer to his repeated pleas for such help came in January of 1745 with the arrival of the Reverend Peter Brunnholtz and two catechists, John Nicholas Kurtz and John Helfrich Schaum. Still it was inadequate. Brunnholtz Muhlenberg stationed in Philadelphia and Germantown while retaining Providence and New Hanover for himself. The catechists Kurtz and Schaum, however, posed a special difficulty. Halle had specifically limited their call to that of school teaching and catechization.[4] Such an arrangement Muhlenberg found impracticable and undesirable. One reason for his discontent was the possible occasion for misunderstanding among the American congregations since they "know nothing about such catechists, and every servant can play the part of a schoolmaster, who makes his living by schoolteaching in the winter and by farm work in the summer."[5] Moreover, Muhlenberg claimed, he faced a dilemma regarding the catechists. If he introduced them as schoolmasters, they would be unable to win the respect of the congregations. If, however, he referred to them as students of theology, it would be demanded that they preach since, in America, even theologically ignorant itinerants preached.[6] Besides, the more preachers Muhlenberg could station in the various congregations, the fewer fraudulent pastors could find their way in. In the final analysis, expediency won out over strict obedience to Halle for, as Muhlenberg informed Francke, "while we dutifully respected the instructions of our Fathers forbidding the catechists to preach, we had to consider very carefully what was best to be done under the circumstances."[7]

Muhlenberg stationed Kurtz at New Hanover and Schaum in Philadelphia. Though their chief duties were those of schoolmasters, Muhlenberg took it upon himself, in direct violation of Halle's specific injunction, to authorize them to preach as well as to administer the sacrament of baptism when necessity demanded. This latter step he justified by noting that in Pennsylvania, even midwives performed this service.[8]

When Muhlenberg transferred Kurtz to Tulpehocken in December, 1746, the question of his ordination moved to the foreground. On August 2, 1747, Muhlenberg's father-in-law, Conrad Weiser, wrote to him requesting that he ordain Kurtz since only a valid, canonical ordination would confer on him the prestige and authority necessary to unite the warring factions. Muhlenberg replied four days later indicating his willingness but only on the condition that three pastors were available to confer on the candidate's qualifications and to ordain him. He noted that pastor John Christopher Hartwick of Rhinebeck had been in Philadelphia a few days earlier and that, should he be able to reach him, he would then consider the matter of ordination.[9] In addition to synodical ordination Muhlenberg also insisted that valid ordination required a previous call from a definite congregation, which Kurtz had not as yet received from Tulpehocken. In conclusion, he informed Weiser that he expected the imminent arrival of two more ordained preachers from Halle and preferred to delay action until they came.[10]

Muhlenberg's views on the validity of one-man ordination are ambiguous. He repeatedly stated that he lacked the authority to ordain in this manner. In each instance, however, this was coupled with the fact that the candidates who presented themselves were, in his opinion, unqualified and unworthy of ordination. He had, in actuality, recognized the validity of the orders of men ordained by a single preacher.[11] In practice, however, one-man ordination had been, in Pennsylvania, the hallmark of the vagabond itinerants who so infuriated him, so his reluctance to initiate such a practice might well have been based on prudence than on any canonical scruples.[12]

As he mentioned to Conrad Weiser, Muhlenberg expected the arrival of two more Halle pastors. The Reverend John Frederick Handschuh had, indeed, accepted a call to Pennsylvania in July, 1746, but was forced to wait in Germany almost one full year while Francke sought another missioner. A Herr Thomson first accepted, then rejected such a call. Another man named Pezold, proposed by Ziegenhagen, failed to win Francke's approval.[13] In the end only Handschuh actually came, arriving in Philadelphia on April 5, 1748. From his later actions, it is evident that Muhlenberg felt that the presence of three validly ordained ministers gave him sufficient canonical authority to organize an American synod which would assume the power of ordination.

Just over three weeks after Handschuh's arrival, he, Brunnholtz, and Muhlenberg met at Providence to draw up a uniform liturgical schema which would be introduced in all the congregations under their jurisdiction. Muhlenberg gave as his reasons for delaying this act of uniformity until six years into his ministry, the need to await another pastor, in addition to himself and Brunnholtz, and the necessity of better learning the nature of conditions in America.[14] Since a uniform agenda could only be imposed by a supra-congregational ministerium, the presence of a third pastor was, in Muhlenberg's mind, necessary for the validity of the act.

In addition to an ordained ministry, Muhlenberg believed that the church in English America needed a common liturgical framework to serve as a compromise between various local customs and usages. In the end, he adopted the liturgical schema of London's Savoy Church, adding to or deleting from it as conditions warranted and necessity dictated.

Chapter one of the agenda provides detailed instructions for the order of public services. An entrance hymn preceded the penitential service which was immediately followed by another designated hymn. After this, the preacher read the collect to be taken from the *Marburg Hymnal for Sundays and Feast Days*, followed by a hymn from the same book to announce the gospel. The reading of the gospel was then followed by the confession of faith, an assigned hymn, and the sermon which was to average forty-five minutes or less but never to exceed one hour. Next came the universal prayer for the church, prayers for the sick, the Our Father, and dismissal. Chapters 2 to 5 gave detailed instructions and set prayers and ceremonies for baptism, the publication of banns and marriage, confession, the Lord's Supper, and burial services.[15] Given his strong views on the need to channel religious enthusiasm into a liturgical framework, it is understandable that Muhlenberg's first synodical action would be the framing of a uniform liturgy.

On August 8–9, 1748, Muhlenberg invited the Reverends Peter Brunnholtz and John C. Hartwick to Providence to discuss the possibility of ordaining Kurtz at the request of the Tulpehocken congregation, which had finally given him a formal call.[16] Since the impending formal consecration of the new St. Michael's Church in Philadelphia would serve to bring together all the Halle missioners, Muhlenberg decided to use it as the occasion for the ordination as well as for an organizational meeting of a Pennsylvania synod or ministerium.[17]

John Nicholas Kurtz was, on August 12, 1748, presented with a set of nine questions, answers to which he was to present at an oral examination the next day. Foremost among them was a *curriculum vitae* in which Kurtz was to give a brief autobiographical account of his life, including the nature and circumstances of his conversion experience, the signs of God's grace in his soul, his reasons for entering the ministry, and his academic background and theological training.[18] In this way Muhlenberg hoped to discover whether the candidate possessed two characteristics he felt necessary in a preacher: conversion and orthodoxy. Other questions dealt with the nature and divisions of theology, the justification of evangelical doctrine, and Kurtz's concept of the duties and characteristics of the ministry. In addition, the catechist was required to execute an exegesis of a gospel text, prepare a trial sermon, and answer a case of conscience. Finally, and most significantly in the light of Muhlenberg's plan for synodical union, Kurtz was asked whether "ministers of the Gospel [should] be subordinate to one another; and if so, how far should this subordination be maintained?"[19]

The following day, August 13, 1748, Kurtz was questioned by Brunnholtz, Handschuh, Hartwick, and Muhlenberg. To the question on his submission to a higher ministerial authority, Kurtz responded in words greatly pleasing to Muhlenberg:

> God is a God of Order, and it is His will that everything should be done decently and in order; Consequently, that order should be maintained in the office of the Ministry of the Word. . . .
> Whoever has been endowed with the wisdom that comes from Above understands this well, and feels nothing oppressive in the weight of superior authority. As occupying a subordinate position himself, he is respectful, humble and dutiful, never regarding the authority under which he stands as a burden or an oppression or a reproach.[20]

Having satisfactorily passed his examination, Kurtz then signed a *revers,* or pledge taken by an *ordinandi.* In it he acknowledged that the external call to Tulpehocken was invested in him by the pastors of the United Congregations to whom he pledged his fealty and reverence. He further pledged to recognize his parish as an integral part of the United Congregations, to conform to the Lutheran symbolical books and the Church Agenda of 1748, to undertake nothing of import without the advice and consent of the ministerium, to present to that body a verbal or written report of his official acts which were to be recorded in a diary, and to move to another congregation should the ministerium so desire.[21]

Finally Muhlenberg summoned the deacons and elders of Tulpehocken to sign a declaration which served as an important model for the future relationships between the individual congregations and the ministerium as envisioned by Muhlenberg. Acknowledging that they had requested aid from the United Congregations on July 8, 1745, of their own free will, and that they had presented Kurtz with a call requesting his ordination, they promised to recognize that their congregation and all others served by the Halle men "constitute one entire Evangelical Lutheran Congregation" under the authority and direction of the "College of Pastors."[22]

The reasons why the Tulpehocken elders should bind themselves to the ministerium were then listed. Among them were their legitimacy of call and ordination, the testimonials of the European fathers, their devotion to the Unaltered Augsburg Confession, and their zeal of office.[23] In view of this, the elders bound themselves to

> recognize and acknowledge, the reverend pastors of the united congregations in Pennsylvania as our spiritual guides and shepherds, investing them with full authority to watch over our souls in whatever manner they see fit, and by whatever agency, and for as long [a] time as may be agreeable to them.[24]

They also promised to recognize the ministerium "as a legitimate and regular presbytery and ministerium" with full authority over them, to take no action in important church matters without its consent, and to obey whatever decisions it should make.[25] Finally, they pledged to welcome and honor Kurtz, renounced their right to dismiss him or any other pastor, promised to offer no resistance should he be transferred by the ministerium, and to submit all disputes which arose within the congregation to ministerial arbitration. In addition, they agreed to bind themselves in writing to a fixed salary which would be adequate for pastoral needs.[26]

As was to be expected, the Tulpehocken council balked at signing what amounted to a complete abdication of lay control over congregational affairs. Muhlenberg, however, remained firm, threatening to send Kurtz to the Raritan instead. Faced with a possibility of a renewal of confusion and chaos should Kurtz depart, the elders reluctantly affixed their signatures to the document, the importance of which can scarcely be overestimated. In one sweeping gesture, Muhlenberg had dealt a crippling blow—at least in theory—to the whole concept of American voluntarism, had returned control over congregational affairs to pastoral hands, and had greatly consolidated his own authority. This document served as a model for all future congregational applications for membership in the ministerium.

On August 14, 1748, the pastors, elders, and deacons of the United Congregations gathered in St. Michael's Church to solemnly consecrate the new building. In attendance, too, were the Swedish provost, the Reverend John Sandin, the Reverend John C. Hartwick of Rhinebeck, Muhlenberg (with the church councils of New Hanover, Providence, Upper Milford, and Saccum), Brunnholtz (with the councils of Philadelphia and Germantown), Handschuh and lay delegates from Lancaster and Earltown, and Kurtz (with representatives from Tulpehocken and Nordkill). Schaum, now stationed at far distant York, failed to arrive in time.[27] In the afternoon the six pastors present, along with three Reformed preachers who attended as witnesses, ordained John N. Kurtz to the ministry.[28]

The following day, August 15, 1748, the first meeting of the Ministerium of Pennsylvania took place, though, in Muhlenberg's words, it was concerned with "only the external scaffolding of the spiritual edifice."[29] Present at the meeting were the six Lutheran pastors who had ordained Kurtz. Muhlenberg opened the conference with a reference to the ill-fated attempt at union between Swedish and German Lutherans in 1744, an effort aborted by the Moravians.[30] This synodical meeting was, he felt, the long awaited culmination of Lutheran desires for order and unity.

> We are assembled for this purpose, and, if God will, we shall assemble yearly; this is only a trial and a test. We preachers who are here present, not having wandered hither of our own will, but called and necessitated, are bound to give an account to God and our conscience. We stand in connection with our Fathers in Europe.[31]

The ministerium quickly showed its determination to assert its supremacy over both pastors and congregations in its first item of business, an inquiry into the relationships between pastors and their flocks. In turn the lay delegates were summoned in and asked how they stood with their pastors. All expressed satisfaction.[32] It is important to note here that although

Muhlenberg made provision for lay representation at ministerium meetings, the laymen's role was strictly limited to the
presentation of grievances for synodical arbitration. Laymen
possessed no voice in ministerium deliberations and had no vote
in its decisions. In this sense Muhlenberg refused to compromise
with American tendencies toward voluntarism which, he felt,
had no place in the ecclesiastical structure.

Education was the next concern of the pastors and here the
picture was not bright. Philadelphia, Saccum, Upper Milford,
Tulpehocken, Earltown, and Nordkill entirely lacked schools
while Providence and New Hanover possessed only inadequate
facilities. Germantown and Lancaster alone could boast of a
flourishing school system.[33] A decision was ultimately reached
that each congregation had to provide a school, either alone or in
union with a neighboring congregation, and that progress
should be made by the next synodical meeting.

When Muhlenberg next submitted the agenda or uniform
liturgical schema of 1748, it was quickly approved by the ministerium, though the elders requested that services be shortened
somewhat because of the severity of Pennsylvania winters.[34]
With this reservation in mind, each congregation bound itself,
henceforth, to employ only the approved ritual in its services.

Evidently one of the congregations then objected to the absence of pastors John Caspar Stoever, Streiter, John Andreae,
and Tobias Wagner and requested an explanation. Muhlenberg
replied that he had not invited them because:

> 1. They decry us as Pietists, without reason; 2. They have not
> been sent hither, have neither an inner nor external call; 3.
> They are not willing to observe the same Church Order that
> we do; each wants to conform to the ceremonies of his home;
> 4. Six years' experience has taught M. Muhlenberg that they
> care for nothing but their bread; 5. They are under no
> Consistorium, and give no account of their official doings.[35]

Muhlenberg had indeed nursed a deep grudge against Stoever
from the day he first arrived in Philadelphia and discovered
that he was a member of Valentine Kraft's so-called consistory.
His objections to Stoever, however, went beyond his adherence

to his erstwhile rival in the pastorate of the United Congregations. To Muhlenberg, Stoever was both unconverted and an orthodox who led a scandalous life. In January, 1747, Muhlenberg wrote an insufferably self-righteous and condescending letter to Stoever offering him his friendship should he "acknowledge the countless mass of sins which you have heaped up," experience a genuine conversion of heart, and amend his life-style.[36] Muhlenberg also recommended that Stoever read certain theological works, reform his preaching techniques, and bow out of the Tulpehocken controversy. Should he accede to these demands, Stoever would then receive an invitation to a ministerial conference which Muhlenberg planned to hold as soon as the new preachers arrived from Halle.[37] The fact that Stoever was not invited to this meeting which took place in 1748 suggests that he refused to accept Muhlenberg's fraternal advice.

After Muhlenberg's explanation for the exclusion of the four irregular pastors, the ministerium took up consideration of charges brought against him by Tobias Wagner to the effect that Muhlenberg had illegally driven him from his Tulpehocken call.[38] This the congregation elders denied, asserting that Muhlenberg did not force himself on them but had been their original choice for the call and that Wagner, after causing dissension within the congregation, had voluntarily resigned.[39]

Finally, the whole question of Moravianism was debated when Pastor Handschuh asked whether evangelical Lutherans who had joined Moravian churches but now sought reinstatement in their old congregations should be forced to sign a statement acknowledging themselves as members of that congregation, in effect, a loyalty oath.[40] Lancaster, which had suffered greatly through the Nyberg troubles, was adamant in demanding public recantation and some form of oath. The ministerium, however, decided on a course of leniency and ordered the Lancaster council to submit.[41] This it promised to do for one year. Thus in the first test of synodical authority over against that of a dissenting congregation, the principle was established that the ministerium was supreme.

After agreeing to hold meetings alternately in Philadelphia and Lancaster every year, the first meeting of the ministerium adjourned. Muhlenberg quickly wrote Francke news of the organization, including texts of Kurtz's *revers* and his answers to the theological questions given him. Francke answered Muhlenberg on March 26, 1749, approving of both the synodical and ordination acts with two exceptions—exceptions which suggest Francke had assumed a much more daring and liberal position than had Muhlenberg. The answers given by Kurtz were, Francke claimed, somewhat deficient, but the blame he placed on Muhlenberg, not Kurtz. Noting that the questions submitted to the candidate were vague and overly comprehensive, Francke suggested that Kurtz had still answered them better than could but one in ten European candidates for ordination.[42] Muhlenberg was advised to lower the standards he held for ordination, at least in so far as theological knowledge was concerned. The second objection raised by Francke concerned Schaum administering the sacraments while still a catechist despite his expressed orders to the contrary. Though Francke admitted that there was a precedent for this in the practices of Wurttemberg, he still felt it could occasion slander in the New World and thus ordered Muhlenberg to ordain Schaum without further delay. Evidently Francke remembered well the cautious conservatism of his former student, for he conjectured that Muhlenberg had failed to ordain Schaum since he lacked one of the traditional ordination prerequisites—a call from a specific congregation. Should York refuse to extend such a call, Francke suggested that Muhlenberg ordain him as his assistant, as a deacon, an adjunct of the ministerium, or by whatever other title he chose to call him, but ordain him he must.[43]

It is doubtful that Muhlenberg would ever have consented to this suggestion that he sidestep time honored practice. At any rate, conflict with Halle was avoided for before Francke's letter had arrived in Philadelphia, the York congregation had presented Schaum with a call. He was ordained June 3, 1749, at the second meeting of the ministerium in Lancaster and assigned to York by the college of pastors.[44] At this second meeting, additional steps were taken to consolidate power in the hands of the ministerium. First the pastors voted that the licensing of theological students to preach would henceforth be the sole prerogative of the ministerium.[45] Steps were then taken to dispose of disorderly congregation members living in gross sins. Such persons were first to be admonished by the preacher privately, then before the church council, then before the entire congregation, and should they still prove recalcitrant, finally publicly excommunicated from the pulpit.[46]

During the third convention, held June 17, 1750, in Providence, it was evident that synodical organization had spurred the growth of those congregations which allied with the Halle men. In addition to the five Halle pastors, two new catechists, Johann Albert Weygand and Ludolph Heinrich Schrenck, were present. Delegates from the old congregations were joined by new arrivals from the Forks (Easton), Birkensee (Perkasie), Goshenhoppen and Indianfield, Cohansey and Mackunshy (Macungie).[47] Muhlenberg now proposed the election of a superintendent or president of the ministerium who would preside over all the congregations. To this office Peter Brunnholtz was elected. In fact, except during those times when Muhlenberg himself held the office, the presidency was a figurehead position. As senior of the ministerium and superior of the Halle mission, Muhlenberg retained final authority. Several more firsts were recorded at this meeting. For the first time the ministerium investigated the conduct of one of its pastors on a charge levied by a congregation, in this case Lancaster against Handschuh. Macungie became the first new congregation admitted to the union, while the ministerium further extended its authority over congregation members by uniting Perkasie, Old Indianfield, and Goshenhoppen into one congregation.[48]

Ministerium growth continued unabated until 1754. New members of the college of pastors were added through synodical ordinations of Schrenck, Weygand, and Lucas Rauss.[49] By 1754, indeed, the seventh convention was attended by the Swedish provost, a Swedish pastor, and fourteen German pastors.[50] This was the last meeting of the ministerium until 1760. Muhlenberg did not explain the discontinuation of what had become a flourishing organization. It seems likely, however, that a combination of circumstances led to the six-year interruption.

Chief among these was the internal division in the United

Congregations caused by the troubles of John Frederick Hand-schuh. Shortly after his arrival in 1748, Handschuh had been stationed in Lancaster in the wake of the difficulties with Nyberg and, at first, found ready acceptance from the congregation. Handschuh then employed as a servant in his home the sister-in-law of a deacon in the congregation. The two eventually decided to marry, but opposition to the proposed union developed because of the girl's low social and economic standing and Handschuh's failure to consult the church council.[51]

When informed of Handschuh's decision to wed the girl, Muhlenberg recorded that he was alarmed and torn by doubts since he realized the possible consequences which could follow.[52] Moreover, he was rapidly developing an antipathy toward the volatile and ever complaining Handschuh whom he suspected suffered from *malum hypochondriacum*.[53] Still both Muhlenberg and Brunnholtz attended the wedding in Lancaster on May 1, 1750, but the congregation boycotted the ceremony. Trouble followed as Muhlenberg had foreseen. First the church council cut off Handschuh's salary, then withdrew the congregation from the ministerium. Faced with this defection of a major congregation, Muhlenberg decided to transfer Handschuh as soon as possible, placing him in Germantown in 1751.[54] The Lancaster congregation then extended a call to the Consistory of Wurttemberg which dispatched the Reverend Johann Siegfried Gerock.[55] Handschuh, however, met with no more success in Germantown than he had in Lancaster.

By 1752 a tempest was brewing in the Germantown congregation over the question of attaching bells to the collection baskets. The intention had been to wake up the potential donor during collection time, but one of the elders, smarting from sectarian ridicule, cut them off. Interpreting this as an unwarranted assumption of power by a church officer, a dissident element emerged, splitting both council and congregation. This faction demanded that Handschuh publicly condemn the church council which, as was to be expected, he refused to do.[56]

When, stung by the malcontents' revolt, the church council adopted a set of resolutions to be subscribed to by all faithful members, the split deepened. Among the resolutions were two provisions, one of which pledged recognition of Muhlenberg and his followers as lawful pastors and denied the use of the Germantown church to any preacher not of their company, the other promised recognition of the Halle fathers as legitimate superiors.[57] Although Muhlenberg advised against this action, warning that dogmatic statements could only add more fuel to an already seething unrest, his advice went unheeded.[58] As Muhlenberg feared, the articles only strengthened the hands of the malcontents. So organized and vicious became their attacks on the Halle men that Muhlenberg became convinced that they were part of a plot directed by some unknown but highly intelligent adversary bent on wrecking his ecclesiastical organization.[59]

By February 11, 1753, it was evident that the split was irreparable. At first those who remained loyal to Handschuh wished to seek a settlement in the English courts on the charges of heresy and financial wrongdoing brought against the pietists by the malcontents. Muhlenberg thought differently, aware as he was that the civil authorities would not interfere in a purely religious affair. Moreover, he saw a dilemma posed by the dissidents. Either they would expel the Halle faction, which was legally bound for the church debt, and take over the church debt free, or they would leave to form a church of their own. In either case, Muhlenberg's followers would be stuck with the debt.[60] He also realized that the vast majority of the congregation had gone over to the opposition and that, unless the issue was quickly settled, the contagion would spread to other congregations.

The following day, February 12, 1753, Muhlenberg met with the leaders of the opposition party. Their demands were uncompromising. They wished to sever all connections with the Halle pastors and the authorities in Halle and London, and demanded the expulsion of the church council, and possession of the church. To this Muhlenberg agreed, provided the opposition assumed the church debt, gave the Halle pastors a testimonial of good conduct, and permitted a public audit of the church books in the presence of the civil authorities. When this was done, Muhlenberg surrendered the church. Handschuh moved into a private home purchased by the faction favorable to him as a combination parsonage and meeting house. The dissidents declared their intention of seeking a pastor from the *Reich,* Brandenburg-Prussia.

It is difficult to assess the real reason for the Germantown schism. Certainly the cutting of bells from the collection baskets was only an excuse. Instead, the conflict seemed to revolve around the pastor, the Reverend John Frederick Handschuh. To a far greater degree than Muhlenberg, Handschuh was a revivalist. His reports to Halle during his Lancaster ministry are filled with references to emotional awakenings occasioned by his preaching.[61] Another report of the rump Germantown congregation, dated June 18, 1754, bears out this revivalist bent. Handschuh stated that:

> during the first eight weeks after our eviction no sermon went off without emotion and abundant tears from the majority so that it seemed that they wished with true earnestness to bring about their salvation with fear and trembling in divine order. Especially on Good Friday and Easter day, 1753, an almost universal awakening occurred among us. The deep sighs, copious tears and the extraordinary devotion of all present brought forth in me eager desires for the salvation of their souls to the depths of my capabilities. . . . There were seventy communicants most of whom communed with God in heartfelt bowing and almost none of whom were dry eyed.[62]

This emphasis on the physical, emotional manifestations seems to have offended the majority of the Germantown congregation. Handschuh's personality also presented a problem. He was a rigid, uncompromising, vain dogmatician who would brook no interference in his actions and who always suspected the motives of others.

It is also possible that the Germantown difficulties stemmed, to some degree, from events in Germany. From 1740 on, Prussia and Austria had been at odds over Silesia and Saxony. In 1744 and again in 1756, Prussian armies invaded Saxony. Thus, in a sense, the Hallensians who came from Saxony would be associated with Austria against German Prussia. It is possible that the Germantown dissident references to obtaining ministers from the *Reich* (Prussia) reflected their sympathies in the Prussia-

Austria-Saxony conflict overseas. Indeed, the American phase of this conflict, the French and Indian War, had already begun in 1754 with Pennsylvania a primary battleground.

Several other factors could explain the hiatus in ministerium meetings and also deserve consideration. Indian attacks on the frontier areas during the French and Indian War made travel impossible for many of the pastors. Then, too, the loss of two major congregations, Germantown and Lancaster, along with the threatened revolt in Philadelphia demanded that Muhlenberg assume a low profile in the face of the outcry against pietistic heresy.

On August 24, 1760, Muhlenberg first met the newly arrived Swedish provost, Charles Magnus Wrangel.[63] From the start the two men, so alike in temperament and theology, struck up a close friendship which provided them with badly needed mutual support. Three weeks later, on September 15, 1760, Muhlenberg attended the first conference of the colonial Swedish Lutheran church summoned by Wrangel. The provost read instructions from Upsala which ordered fraternal amity between Swedish and German Lutherans and strongly suggested that their pastors attend each other's conferences. On Wrangel's request for an opportunity to meet the German Lutheran clergy of Pennsylvania, Muhlenberg agreed to resurrect the dormant ministerium.

In his letter of invitation to the ministerium meeting to be held in Providence on October 19–20, 1760, Muhlenberg promised that the manner of conducting business would be decided by those present and that every effort would be taken to avoid ambitious rivalry.[64] The purpose of the meeting was

> that we poor preachers may at least have such freedom in our congregations as to be able now and then to meet, to tell one another our troubles, to partake of the Lord's Supper together, to decide on cases of conscience, to edify and comfort one another with accounts concerning the progress of the Kingdom of God, and to afford mutual encouragement under difficult official burdens.[65]

To allay potential congregational objections to the renewal of the ministerium, Muhlenberg explained that no lay delegates would be invited, though they could attend on their own if so inclined, since this was to be merely a fraternal gathering of pastors. In reality it was a resumption of the old ministerium, this time excluding even nominal lay participation. Muhlenberg had been badly burned by the congregational revolts in Lancaster and Germantown. He was now determined to guarantee, even more than before, the supremacy of the ministry. The first step was to weed out lay influence at the central governing level. Then he would attempt to curb the individual congregations.

There were several reasons why Muhlenberg decided to resume ministerium meetings. In the first place, Wrangel's request for such a meeting gave him an opportunity to hold one without arousing suspicion on the part of the laity. Equally important, Wrangel's friendship gave Muhlenberg the backing of the colonial Swedish Lutheran church in his assertion of authority. Then too, Gerock had not, as Muhlenberg had feared, provided a rallying point for a challenge to his position. Indeed he expressed openly his fellowship with the Hallensians and attended the 1760 meeting. Finally, the revolt begun by the Germantown dissidents and their threat to institute similar uprisings in the other congregations, rapidly subsided. By 1763 the congregation had reunited with the ministerium. Thus by 1760 conditions were right for another attempt by Muhlenberg to impose central control on Pennsylvania Lutherans.

The thirteenth meeting of the ministerium, held in 1760, was attended by both Halle men and independents. Present were Wrangel, Muhlenberg, Handschuh, Schaum, Kurtz, Gerock, Weygand, John Caspar Stoever, and William Kurtz, John N. Kurtz's son, and a catechist at Tohickon. The first question debated was the wisdom of continuing annual meetings. This was unanimously decided in the affirmative, with the provision that the gatherings be rotated among the various congregations to stress their relative equality.[66]

Catechization of German youth next occupied the attention of the pastors. It was resolved that in *Kinderlehre,* catechists should follow closely the text of Luther's catechism but take pains to avoid rote memorization of the text. Instead it should be explained to the children in terms fitting their age and maturity level. Since, too, a child's love of the word of God had to be nourished, it was resolved that the Bible should not be used as a textbook to teach secular subjects in the schools. To do so would give the child the same distaste for scripture that he might feel toward school work.[67]

Preachers were advised to seek the level of the congregation in their sermons and not use them as occasions to display their theological erudition. Nor should they use the sermon to mention individual problems with specific congregants. Such matters were to be settled in private.[68] On the matter of the Lord's Supper, it was urged that legalism be avoided and that the pastor stress the necessity for genuine repentance as opposed to the *ex opere operato* interpretation of the sacraments. Before being admitted to the Lord's Supper, moreover, the pastor was to arrange a private meeting with each declared communicant to investigate the state of his or her soul.[69]

Finally it was determined that the office of ministerium president be reinstituted. This time, Muhlenberg accepted the job instead of arranging for a stand-in, as had been Brunnholtz.[70]

With the ministerium now fully operative once more, Muhlenberg set about the task of consolidating pastoral control over individual congregations. His target became the Philadelphia congregation. During the Germantown troubles, a dissident element hostile to Muhlenberg had risen in Philadelphia. When Handschuh succeeded the late Brunnholtz in Philadelphia in 1757, discontent spread. By 1760 Handschuh had managed to split the congregation in two, the church council supporting him, the others backing Muhlenberg. This prompted Muhlenberg to resurrect his 1742 call and move back to the city as *pastor primarius* in 1761. Though he quickly quelled the unrest, Muhlenberg realized that a formal constitution was necessary which would insure stability through firm pastoral control, yet concede something to lay ambitions for a voice in church matters. The result was the Constitution of 1762 which he wrote for St. Michael's Church. Since St. Michael's was one of the original congregations, it was not subject to the restrictions made on congregations newly arrived in the ministerium. This constitution remedied this situation.

Chapter one concerned the duties of pastors, "faithful stewards of the mysteries of God." They were admonished to execute faithfully divine services, to distribute the sacraments to those who wished them, though they retained the freedom to disbar those whom they felt unworthy of reception, and to visit the sick.[71] Pastors were placed in charge of the parish school and were to preside over the church council of which they were members *ex officio*. The pastor was also obligated to keep from his pulpit unordained itinerants and to help out pastorless congregations in the ministerium as much as his duties allowed.

One real innovation concerned the dismissal of a pastor accused of wrongdoing. This right was removed from the congregation. Instead, a series of steps were outlined to remedy any such situation. In the first place, charges could only be brought against a pastor by the testimony of two or three witnesses of irreproachable character.[72] If convicted of the charge by two-thirds of the church council, the council was to admonish the pastor to mend his ways. Should this not avail, the council would summon the closest neighboring pastor of the United Congregations and repeat the charge and admonition in his presence. Failing this, the matter had to be referred to an extraordinary or regular session of the ministerium for final disposition.[73] Should the ministerium find the charges valid, it was empowered to suspend the guilty pastor from his office, stop all benefices he enjoyed, and assign another of the college of pastors to serve the congregation until a replacement could be found.

In the election of pastors, too, the congregation lost its independence of action. If the congregation was vacant, both the church council and the senior preachers of the united congregations were to consider possible replacements. When both had settled on an individual, he was to be invited to preach a trial sermon. After this, the candidate was voted on by both council and communicating members, a two-thirds vote of each being necessary for election. Once elected, and after he had subscribed to the church constitution, the new pastor was installed by a pastor united with the ministerium. Should, however, no suitable candidate be found or available among the united congregations, then the congregation had the right to appeal to a European consistory for a candidate, with the ministerium's consent. Such a candidate must be properly examined, regularly ordained, well educated in Lutheran doctrine, and must have led an edifying life before he was accepted by the ministerium.[74] Finally, the preacher was obligated to abide by the liturgical agenda adopted by the ministerium until such time as that body found fit to alter or amend it.

The second chapter dealt with the external government of the congregation. The church council, consisting of fourteen permanent trustees, six elders, and six *Vorstehers,* presided over by the pastor, constituted the governing body of the congregation. Among the trustees named by the constitution were Muhlenberg, Handschuh, and Henry Keppele. These men were to hold office for life until it was proved that they were unsuited for the job, or they themselves resigned. In that event, successors were to be elected by a two-thirds vote of the congregation.

Elders, too, were elected by majority vote. Responsibility for selecting the electoral slate was in the hands of the church council which chose eighteen candidates. On the appointed election day, each communicating member of the congregation was allowed to vote for six candidates from the eighteen-man slate, the six with the largest plurality being elected. These men were then installed in office by the pastor for a three-year term with the right of reelection.[75]

Electoral procedures for the six *Vorstehers* followed that of the elders with the exception that elections were staggered so that only one-half of them left office every two years. Unlike the office of elder, a person who had been elected *Vorsteher* could not refuse to serve unless released from this obligation by paying a considerable donation to the church treasury.[76]

Congregation matters of any import could only be decided by a two-thirds majority of the entire church council. Once passed, any such decisions had to be submitted to the communicating members of the congregation for their ratification, again by two-thirds vote.

The third and final chapter concerned the duties and rights of congregation members. Perhaps its most significant innovation was the establishment of graduated steps of action against unruly congregants or those living in gross sin. The process was to be privately initiated by the pastor, then turned over to the church council. Should the sinner still refuse to repent, he or she was to be excommunicated by the whole council. The constitution, moreover, was to remain in effect until amended or abrogated by a two-thirds vote of both council and communicating members.

This constitution shows Muhlenberg's genius for adaptation for it secured his main goal, pastoral and ministerial preeminence, without sacrificing lay participation in church matters. While effective control over pastors was removed from the congregation and given to the ministerium, the congregation still retained considerable autonomy over its own affairs. Here, too, however Muhlenberg effected a compromise. Leadership remained with the council, but the congregation retained a right of veto over acts it disliked. The council retained some control over the choice of its membership by its right to nominate candidates, but the congregation received a share in the choice by its right to elect. Muhlenberg's insistence on a two-thirds, rather than a simple, majority ensured that decisions would not be the result of mere emotion or whim but would truly represent the mind of both council and congregation. In all, the Constitution of 1762 was a tribute to Muhlenberg's administrative ability.

By the close of 1762, then, Muhlenberg had once again established the ministerium as the effective governing body of the United Congregations and had initiated congregational constitutions which would transfer effective control from layman to pastor while still retaining a lay voice in church affairs. With these actions, his ecclesiastical polity was essentially constructed. As Muhlenberg extended the scope of his activities throughout the middle colonies and into the northern part of the southern colonies, congregational membership in the ministerium continued to increase. Throughout his active years of ministerial career, the ministerium functioned without a written constitution. Decisions were reached on an *ad hoc* basis with the guidance of the senior of the ministerium, Henry Melchior Muhlenberg. But the foundation he laid was solid enough. After 1762 there was no really effective challenge to the supremacy of either pastor or ministerium, nor to Muhlenberg's own authority.

In 1781 the ministerium finally adopted a carefully written constitution which embodied Muhlenberg's ideals of government. By that time, however, the founder had withdrawn into semiretirement at his Providence home and was no longer active in the ecclesiastical body he had organized.

NOTES

[1]Henry Melchior Muhlenberg, *The Journals of Henry Melchior Muhlenberg in Three Volumes*, trans. Theodore G. Tappert and John W. Doberstein, I (Philadelphia: Muhlenberg Press, 1942), p. 69. Hereafter referred to as *I Journals*.

[2]Ibid., p. 68.

[3]Ibid.

[4]John Ludwig Schulze, ed., *Reports of the United German Evangelical Congregations in North America, Especially in Pennsylvania*, I, trans. C. W. Schaeffer (Reading: Pilger Book Store, 1882), p. 141. See also the formula of the call to Schaum and Kurtz in Johann Ludwig Schulze, ed. *Nachrichten von den vereinigten-Deutschen Evangelish-Lutherischen Gemeinen in Nord-America, absonderlich in Pennsylvanien*, I (Allentown: Brobst, Diehl & Co., 1886), p. 88. Hereafter referred to as *Nachrichten*.

[5]Muhlenberg to Francke in Schulze, p. 172. Letter dated December 12, 1745.

[6]Ibid., p. 174.

[7]Ibid.

[8]Ibid.

[9]Muhlenberg to Conrad Weiser, Providence, August 6, 1747, reproduced in original German and translation in Abdel Ross Wentz, "A Muhlenberg Letter and the Ministerium of Pennsylvania," *Lutheran Church Quarterly* 20 (October 1947): 418.

[10]Ibid.

[11]Ibid., p. 421.

[12]Ibid., p. 431; this, for example, is the position of Wentz.

[13]Ibid., p. 422.

[14]*I Journals*, p. 193.

[15]The Church Agenda of 1748 is found in *Nachrichten*, I, pp. 211–16.

[16]*I Journals*, p. 201.

[17]Ibid.,; see also Robert Fortenbaugh, *The Development of the Synodical Polity of*

the Lutheran Church in America, to 1829 (Philadelphia: Privately printed, 1926), p. 42.

[18]"Examination and Ordination of the Catechist Kurtz," questions submitted to John N. Kurtz on August 12, 1748, in Schulze, pp. 209–10.

[19]Ibid., p. 210.

[20]"Biographical Sketch of John Nich. Kurtz," in Schulze, pp. 213–14.

[21]*"Revers* of John N. Kurtz," in Schulze, pp. 208–09.

[22]Ibid., p. 215.

[23]Ibid., pp. 215–16.

[24]Ibid., pp. 216–17.

[25]Ibid., p. 217.

[26]Ibid.

[27]*I Journals*, p. 201.

[28]Ibid., p. 202.

[29]Ibid.

[30]Evangelical Lutheran Ministerium, *Documentary History of the Evangelical Lutheran Ministerium of Pennsylvania and Adjacent States: Proceedings of the Annual Conventions from 1748–1821, compiled and translated from Records in the archives and from the written protocols* (Philadelphia: Board of Publication of the Evangelical Lutheran Church in North America, 1898), p. 9. Hereafter referred to as *Documentary History.*

[31]Ibid.

[32]Ibid., p. 10.

[33]Ibid., pp. 10–11.

[34]Ibid., p. 11.

[35]Ibid.

[36]Theodore G. Tappert, "John Caspar Stoever and the Ministerium of Pennsylvania," *Lutheran Church Quarterly* 21 (April 1948): 180. The letter, dated January 20, 1747, is presented in full in translation.

[37]Ibid., p. 181.

[38]Concerning, for example, his explanation of his actions in interfering with Wagner's Tulpehocken pastorate, Muhlenberg said:

> Mr. Wagner, however, took great offense and said that I had secretly wanted to dismiss him, though he certainly should have known that the little congregation had addressed itself to me before he ever came to this country; that it had accepted him only for the interim; and that up to this time they had left the supervision to me and through me had applied for help from our Reverend Fathers. Moreover, he is unable to produce a regular call to this country. He came of his own accord and conceit and offered himself and even forced his way in. I was also obliged by the intricate circumstances of this free country to exercise supervision until the Lord in His providence has unraveled the circumstances and opened the door for us. (*I Journals*, p. 171)

[39]*Documentary History*, p. 11.

[40]Ibid.

[41]Ibid., p. 12.

[42]Francke to Muhlenberg, March 26, 1749 at Halle, in *Nachrichten* I, p. 324.

[43]Ibid., p. 325.
[44]*Documentary History,* pp. 24–25.
[45]Ibid., p. 26.
[46]Ibid.
[47]Ibid., pp. 29–30.
[48]Ibid., p. 31.
[49]Ibid., p. 39.
[50]Fortenbaugh, pp. 48–49.
[51]William J. Mann, *The Life and Times of Henry Melchior Muhlenberg* (Philadelphia: G. W. Frederick, 1887), pp. 299–300.
[52]*I Journals,* p. 238.
[53]Ibid., p. 240.
[54]Ibid., p. 261.
[55]"Report of the Congregation in Lancaster," in *Nachrichten,* II, p. 680.
[56]Muhlenberg to Francke, August 24, 1753, in *Nachrichten,* I, p. 701.
[57]Ibid., p. 702.
[58]Ibid.
[59]Ibid.
[60]Ibid., p. 703.
[61]Arthur M. Bowser, "The Great Awakening of the Evangelical Lutheran Church in the Middle Colonies, 1742–1764," Master's thesis, Pennsylvania State University, 1968, p. 49.
[62]Handschuh to Ziegenhagen, Germantown, June 18, 1754, in *Nachrichten,* II, p. 79.
[63]*I Journals,* p. 431.
[64]*Documentary History,* p. 44.
[65]Ibid., pp. 44–45.
[66]*Documentary History,* p. 51.
[67]Ibid., pp. 51–52.
[68]Ibid., p. 54.
[69]Ibid., p. 56.
[70]"Church Constitution of the German Evangelical Lutheran Congregation in Philadelphia," in *Nachrichten,* II, p. 436.
[71]Ibid.
[72]Ibid., p. 437.
[73]Ibid.
[74]Ibid.
[75]Ibid., p. 438.
[76]Ibid., p. 439.

[7]

Muhlenberg: The Compleat Politician

Concerned as he was primarily with the welfare of the church and the spiritual needs of his flock, Henry Melchior Muhlenberg did not directly involve himself in provincial Pennsylvania politics. This is not to say that he lacked interest in political affairs for, on the great issues of his day, Muhlenberg's presence was felt, though only vaguely, as a shadow in the background. Rather than commit himself publicly, he far preferred to have his views expressed indirectly through others. Though it would be unfair to dismiss him as a political manipulator, it is extremely difficult to pin him down on any specific issue because he usually avoided any direct stand.

Part of the explanation for Muhlenberg's reticence in matters political stemmed from his European Lutheran background with its emphasis on the separate but equal nature of the two swords, church and state, and its willingness to defer to the judgment of the ruler in secular matters.[1] Much of his reticence, however, was derived from conditions which existed in English America.

When Muhlenberg began his American ministry in 1742, he faced a chaotic jumble of conflicting congregational interests, intensified by American voluntarism. Muhlenberg's first task was to impose some central ecclesiastical control over hitherto independent congregational councils and to assert his authority in church affairs. Thus it was inexpedient for him to risk alienating his congregants by assuming political leadership as well since that could only have served to divide further an already disunited church.

Among the Germans of Pennsylvania, moreover, political influence was exerted by the Philadelphia publisher, Christopher Sauer, a champion of German sectarian and English Quaker pacifism, who, from the moment of Muhlenberg's arrival, became his implacable foe. Any direct entry onto the political scene would have placed Muhlenberg in a head-on confrontation with the powerful Sauer, which he wished to avoid.

Finally, until the French and Indian War, no real occasion had arisen to cause Pennsylvania Germans to assume an active political role. Located in the back country and distinguished from their neighbors by language and customs, German colonists tended to consider politics a purely English affair. Due to Sauer's influence, they had been content to back the Quaker element in the Pennsylvania assembly which retained unchallenged control over that body until the death of its leader, Speaker and Chief Justice John Kinsey, in 1750. After Kinsey's death, the political situation in Pennsylvania became more fluid. William Allen replaced Kinsey as chief justice, while Isaac Norris became speaker of the assembly and leader of the secular Friends who were willing to compromise on matters of conscience for the sake of political expediency. Israel Pemberton assumed control over the rigid, umcompromising religious Friends, while Benjamin Franklin, elected to the assembly in 1751, began his long career as a political manipulator.[2] For a quarter of a century, Pennsylvania politics revolved around the conflicting interests of these men, along with Richard Peters, an Anglican minister who served as province secretary to the Penns as well as a counsellor to the governors of Pennsylvania. During these same years, provincial politics boiled down to questions of defense and proprietary prerogatives, both of which were staunchly opposed by Quaker pacifists.

Franklin had first risen to political eminence during King George's War when, as a member of the governor's party, he organized an all-volunteer militia known as the Associators, in the face of the persistent refusal of the assembly to vote a defense bill. In his recruiting pamphlet, *Plain Truth,* Franklin had issued a special appeal to "the *brave* and *steady* Germans,"[3] to take up arms for provincial defense. He had, however, run into Sauer's opposition and found scant support for his scheme from among Pennsylvania Germans who still strongly supported the Quaker assembly. From this time on, Franklin's apprehensions about the huge, unassimilated mass of Germans, composing nearly one-half of Pennsylvania's population, increased. Unable as most were to understand English, Germans could be reached only through the press of Sauer, and the gospel Sauer preached to them was one of Quaker pacifism. Thus the Germans formed the base of Quaker voting strength. Moreover, Franklin bemoaned the fact that the only other channel to the Germans, their clergymen, even had they been willing, could not exercise any control over their unruly countrymen.

> Their own clergy have very little influence over their own people who seem to have an uncommon Pleasure in abusing and discharging the Minister on every trivial occasion. Not being used to Liberty they know not how to make a modest use of it. . . . They seem not to think themselves Free till they can feel their Liberty in abusing and insulting their teachers. Thus they are under no restraint from ecclesiastical Government.[4]

Unable to crack the German vote, Franklin began to devise plans for their complete disfranchisement. In *Observations on the Increase of Mankind,* written in 1751 but not published until four years later, Franklin warned that Pennsylvania was in danger of becoming a German province dominated by the "Palatine Boors."[5] Moreover, Franklin warned an English friend, Richard Jackson, in 1753 that German refusal to join the Associators during King George's War indicated that they were at heart disloyal to the crown and might join with the French in a new outbreak of hostilities.[6]

In response to Franklin's statements, Peter Collinson presented seven proposals on the German problem to Parliament, submitting them first to Franklin for his views. The first proposal, to establish free English schools among the Germans, met with his hearty approval. Indeed Franklin had himself suggested such a step to Jackson.[7] The second and third proposals, disqualifying from holding public office all who could not speak English, and invalidating any legal document written in any language other than English, also won his approbation. Franklin, however, disapproved of the fourth and fifth proposals, the suppression of all German printing houses and the prohibition of the importation of German books, as too harsh. Encouraging intermarriage between Germans and English by government subsidies, the sixth proposal, would not work, Franklin felt, for

> the German women are generally so disagreeable to an English Eye, that it wou'd require great portions to induce Englishmen to marry them. Nor would the German Ideas of Beauty generally agree with our Women: *dick und starke,* that is, *thick & strong,* always enter into their Description of a pretty Girl; for the value of a Wife with them consists much in the Work she is able to do.[8]

To the last proposal, the prohibition of further German immigration into Pennsylvania, Franklin gave great praise.

Though Franklin failed to have political disabilities levied against the Germans, he did see one of his schemes for Anglicizing them, the establishment of free English schools, come to fruition. Actually these schools, which came to be known as charity schools, had originally been conceived of by the Reverend Michael Schlatter, a colonial Pennsylvania German Reformed clergyman, who saw a great need for education for religious purposes among his Pennsylvania flock. Schlatter had attempted to raise educational funds from Thomas Penn in 1750 by warning him that "the Large body of Germans that inhabits your territorie are in danger of growing savage, if there are not some wise methods taken to reclaim them."[9] He further pointed out that German history proved that "their uncultivated Tempers has often made Sovereigns tremble on their thrones, because it was often attended with Rebellion and Revolt."[10] The answer, Schlatter felt, was to introduce order among the Germans by establishing adequate schools.

In 1751 Schlatter traveled throughout Holland raising money for his school plan. Through the efforts of the Reverend David Thompson, an English clergyman living in Holland, the subscription campaign spread to the British Isles where the king and royal family contributed generously. By 1753 the "London Society for the Propagation of Christian Knowledge among the Germans in Pennsylvania" was formed on the advice of the Reverend William Smith.

Under Smith, however, Schlatter's religious motives were replaced by political considerations. The schools, Smith argued, would assimilate the Germans into the general population and make it unlikely that they would ally with France in the event of war.[11] Smith later offered a further reason for the schools. By 1756 he dreamed of the establishment of an American episcopate with himself as first bishop. As a prelude to that, Smith sought a merger of the Lutheran and Anglican churches in America, a scheme which would be furthered by the charity schools.[12]

In presenting the society's goals, Schlatter's religious and charitable motives were stressed. Funds were to be used to assist "pious and industrious Protestant ministers that are or shall be regularly ordained and settled among the said Germans."[13] The society pledged itself to establish schools for the "pious education" of German youth of all denominations and for those English children who lived among them.[14] Subjects were to be chosen which were "useful to advance industry and true godliness."[15] Among these were English, German, writing, elementary accounting, psalm-singing, and catechism. For the last subject, the society proposed to print in both English and German the particular catechism used by each denomination. Though the education of boys received the greatest attention, provision was made for instructing girls in reading and sewing.[16]

The society in England acted chiefly as a fund-raising organization. Day-to-day administration of the project within Pennsylvania was entrusted to a central board, called the trustees gen-

188   MISSIONARY OF MODERATION

eral, which included James Hamilton (governor of the province), William Allen (chief justice), Richard Peters (province
secretary), Benjamin Franklin, Conrad Weiser, and William
Smith. They in turn appointed Schlatter supervisor or visitor of
the schools. In an effort to drum up local support, immediate
supervision was entrusted to assistant or deputy trustees, parents
or parishioners, who lived close to the schools and whose function was to visit them monthly or quarterly to see that they were
fulfilling their duties. Schlatter was to visit each of the schools
four times a year, while the trustees were expected to pay an
annual visit.

Locations of the schools depended on local interest and the
availability of funds. Should particular congregations wish to
offer their school houses for its use, the society would fund the
project provided that the school was inter-denominational in
character and English was taught in conformity with the society's
stated goal "which is to qualify the Germans for all the advantages of native English subjects."[17] The society further promised
to hire particular teachers recommended by each school, including ministers, provided that they were properly qualified.

Muhlenberg, though he did not lend his name to the project,
was quick to seize advantage of its financial benefits without
incurring any of its political liabilities. His own New Hanover
congregation joined with the Reformed in offering the Lutheran school house for the project and the first of the charity
schools was located there.[18] Eventually eight other schools were
established, including those servicing Lutheran congregations at
Lancaster, York, Providence, and Reading. Though Muhlenberg recognized the political ends of the movement, they did not
seem to disturb him. Unlike some of his German contemporaries, Muhlenberg was favorable to the concept of Anglicization. Indeed he pioneered in the effort to preach sermons in
English in the Lutheran church. As he wrote to Halle:

> From this it may be seen that the noble patrons are earnestly
> intent on preparing our Germans to become faithful subjects
> and good members of the Church, which is highly proper.[19]

Though Muhlenberg gave the charity schools at least covert

support, their reception among the German community as a whole was decidedly cool. Christopher Sauer showed outright hostility, roundly denouncing Schlatter as a turncoat for suggesting to Penn that there was reason to doubt German loyalty. The whole idea, Sauer charged, was a scheme concocted by Franklin, Smith, Peters, Schlatter, and Muhlenberg to enslave the Germans. The politicians in the group—Franklin, Peters, and Allen—Sauer claimed in a letter to Conrad Weiser, wished to use the schools as a vehicle to gain German votes which would elect them to the assembly. Once elected, they could pass their cherished militia law to protect their own property with the lives of their fellow citizens. Schlatter, Smith, and Muhlenberg, Sauer professed to believe, would be rewarded for their support of the scheme by having the assembly secure a fixed salary for ministers so that "it will not be requisite, in future, to write begging letters to Halle."[20] Sauer also suggested that Germans did not want charity or wish to ape the manners of their English neighbors and that the charity schools were backed by the Masons.

When in 1755 the trustees general purchased a press from Benjamin Franklin and began publishing an anti-Sauer, anti-Quaker, German language newspaper, the *Philadelphische Zeitung,* Sauer's attacks increased. The depth of Muhlenberg's involvement in the movement can be measured by the fact that the new paper's editor was none other than the Reverend John Frederick Handschuh, his own Halle colleague.

Sauer's determined opposition achieved its aim of thoroughly discrediting the charity schools in the eyes of Pennsylvania Germans. Had Muhlenberg come out into the open in their defense with the full weight of his authority, the outcome might have been different. He was, however, preoccupied by congregational revolts in Lancaster, Germantown, and Philadelphia, so Michael Schlatter was forced to bear the brunt of the attack. Schlatter fell into disfavor among the members of his own Reformed coetus. A fellow Reformed clergyman, the Reverend William Stroy, wrote to Holland that the movement was a front for Anglican dominance and that the trustees were "Zinzendorfers, Quakers, Separatists, perchance even Deists."[21] He further charged that the schools were useless to the Reformed church "for the only objective of these schools is to extend the English Language among the Germans, and so the object is a political one."[22] This opposition voiced by the Reformed coetus deeply angered Muhlenberg who wrote in reply:

> Should a parcel of whimsical heads have so much influence as to deprive a number of poor children of the intended charity? To give offense to so many well-minded Germans in America? To provoke the illustrious Society and the Honorable Trustees to just indignation? And to make a German printer and his associates laugh and hollow[sic]? I think in my humble opinion, it be against the intention of the German benefactors and the charitable scheme to force and press the charitable gifts upon some people, of what denominations soever, who count themselves to be rich and have need of nothing."[23]

Stung by coetus opposition, William Smith withheld funds from the Reformed while liberally distributing them to Muhlenberg because of his hoped-for Anglican-Lutheran merger. By 1757 Schlatter was so thoroughly discredited that he resigned his school superintendency to enlist as a chaplain in the French and Indian War.

The charity schools continued until 1763 when all subsidies were terminated. Muhlenberg's regret at the end of the project was sincere: "Thus this arrangement, which has for several years contributed especially to the good of the poorest German Protestants and their children, has come to an end."[24] The net result of the school experiment was to cause the Germans to resist further assimilation and to embitter even more relations between them and their English neighbors.

Believing that they would soon reap political benefits from their charity school scheme, the proprietary faction, to which all the members of the trustees general belonged, had hastily naturalized many Germans in time for the October, 1754, elections.[25] They were, however, bitterly disappointed. Urged on by Sauer, the Germans voted in droves for the Quaker faction which won a landslide victory to retain control over the assembly.[26] Proprietary leaders then urgently appealed to Parliament for disenfranchisement of the Germans in the face of increased French threats.[27]

These appeals were based, again, on the possible disloyalty of the Germans in the event of war with France because of their suspected Catholic sympathies. Part of the source for this suspicion came from Moravian missioners who were wont to spend weeks in the wilderness caring for the Indians, dressed in long black robes with prominent crucifixes hung about their necks.[28] Uninformed Englishmen thus suspected that they were Jesuits though it is highly improbable that many of them had ever seen a member of that dreaded Roman Catholic religious order. To them, Moravian missionary activity, in particular their journeys into the wild, were merely excuses to communicate in secret with the French and their Jesuit priests who lurked in the Ohio wilderness. Added to this was the peculiar monastic existence at the Ephrata Cloister with its practice of celibacy which was again confused with Catholicism.

At this time, the governor and assembly were as usual busily locked in a battle over militia funds for provincial defense, in particular, to aid the expedition of General Edward Braddock. Exasperated at the assembly's intransigence and eager to further his own career as well, William Smith, newly appointed provost of the College of Philadelphia, published a pamphlet in February, 1755, entitled *A Brief State of the Province of Pennsylvania*. In it Smith accused the assembly of acting independently of the mother country and declared that Pennsylvania's frontiers would never be secured until the Quaker assembly was unseated, Quakers were barred from holding political office, and Germans were disfranchised.[29] At Franklin's urging, young Joseph Galloway issued *An Answer to An Invidious Pamphlet, Intitled, A Brief State of the Province of Pennsylvania*. Galloway argued that the Proprietary party had sought to discredit both Quakers and Germans in order to seize control of the assembly for its own selfish purposes and to cover up the blunderings of Governor Robert Hunter Morris.[30]

With Braddock's defeat in July, 1755, the whole of the Pennsylvania frontier lay exposed. Still, despite the warnings and pleas of the Proprietary Party, the frontier Germans joined their urban brethren in giving the Quakers another landslide victory in the elections held that year. Once more assembly and governor clashed over defense. While the assembly did vote to raise £50,000 in bills of credit, it was made contingent on a tax to be levied on all Pennsylvania properties, including the proprietary estates. Governor Morris, on orders from the Penns, vetoed the bill, reaffirming the right to proprietary exemption. The deadlock continued until late October when Indian raids erupted all across the frontier. Immediately the Quakers voted a £60,000 defense bill but once again included a tax on proprietary estates.

As disaster spread on the frontier, Morris offered to compromise and sign a tax bill whose rates were determined by commissioners appointed by himself while the proprietary tax clause was to remain in suspension until received and reviewed by the crown. This the Quakers would not accept. The assembly changed its mind only when the Penn family voluntarily contributed £5,000 for provincial defense. Also serving to goad the Quakers into action was the growing discontent of defenseless frontier Germans and Scotch-Irish who felt betrayed by their erstwhile Quaker allies. On November 25, 1755, some four hundred German frontiersmen marched peaceably on the assembly to demand protection.[31] Faced with the possibility of violence and bloodshed should it continue to procrastinate, the assembly finally voted a £60,000 defense bill which omitted the noxious proprietary tax. But the Quakers would not give in on a regular militia. Instead Franklin once more raised a volunteer militia which Morris unhappily accepted.

During the winter of 1755–1756, a series of defensive forts were erected along the frontier under the supervision of Franklin and Weiser; yet the Indian raids continued. The difficulty was that the Quakers still refused to raise a regular militia, and the king had disallowed Franklin's voluntary association as unconstitutional. Caught between a choice of incurring royal wrath or violating their consciences, the religious Friends, led by Israel Pemberton, withdrew from the assembly in 1756. Franklin filled their places with Anglican cronies thus gaining firm control over the Quaker party.[32] When the assembly ran into additional trouble with newly appointed Governor William Denny on the same issue of proprietary taxation, Franklin was dispatched to London to bring the whole matter before the Privy Council.

With the accession of William Pitt to the office of prime minister in 1757, British troops took over much of the burden of provincial defense. Brigader General John Forbes reduced Fort Dusquesne on November 25, 1758, bringing the French and Indian War to a virtual conclusion so far as Pennsylvania was concerned. In its political effects, though, the war had a profound, ongoing significance, for the old German-Quaker alliance had been seriously jeopardized by assembly refusal to provide for frontier defense. Much of the actual suffering had been borne by the Germans and Scotch-Irish. Additional frontier difficulties could conceivably make them political bedfellows, united in opposition to the Quakers. Moreover, the Quaker party was now led by the despised Franklin whose comment about Palatine boors was not soon forgotten. Finally, the death of Christopher Sauer in 1758 had deprived the Quakers of their staunchest German political ally. The time was ripe, therefore, for the Germans to assume an active political role of their own and to cease functioning as mere Quaker appendages.

In Sauer's place, men like Conrad Weiser and Provost Charles Magnus Wrangel came to the fore as spokesmen for the Germans, and they espoused the Proprietary, not the Quaker, cause. Wrangel in particular, who arrived from Sweden in 1760, became Muhlenberg's closest friend and confidant.[33] Muhlenberg seems to have followed Wrangel's lead in politics as Wrangel followed Muhlenberg's ideas on church government and organization.[34] And though Muhlenberg continued to refuse to commit himself publicly on political issues, it is evident from his journals that he backed Wrangel's stands in private.

The spark that ignited the German tinderbox resulted from Pontiac's uprising in 1763 when Indian raids once more bedeviled the frontier. Two groups of Indians supposedly remained loyal to the province as they had been during the French and Indian War. One group, the Conestogas, had been wards of the province, dwelling at Conestoga Manor in Lancaster County, since a 1701 treaty with William Penn.[35] By 1763 there were only twenty members of the tribe surviving. A second group, the Moravian Indians, numbering about 140, who had been converted by the Brethren, dwelt near the Moravian settlements in Northampton County.

In 1763 a resident of Paxtang (Paxton) township, near Conestoga Manor in Lancaster County reported that he had seen an Indian flee into the manor after murdering his mother. Frustrated by the assembly's refusal to provide them with adequate defense and enraged over the continuing massacres, a group of fifty-seven men from Paxton, known as the Paxton Boys, took matters into their own hands, descending on the manor and killing and scalping the six hapless Indians they found there.[36]

When news of the Paxton Boys' actions reached Lancaster, the surviving members of the tribe were rounded up and placed in protective custody in the town jail. Not to be deterred, the Paxton Boys broke into the jail on December 27, 1763, and murdered the remainder of the tribe.

After learning of the massacre of the Conestogas, Governor John Penn issued warrants for the árrest of the Paxtons on murder charges and ordered the Moravian Indians moved to Providence Island in the Delaware River for their security. Finally, at the insistent urgings of the assembly and after repeated threats from the Paxton Boys, the Indians were removed to Philadelphia. The Paxton Boys now marched on the provincial capitol causing Governor Penn to proclaim a state of armed rebellion while the assembly extended the Riot Act of George II to the province.[37] When, however, the governor called for volunteers to defend the threatened city, the Germans refused to enlist, bringing on them the suspicion that they were in league with the rebels.

As Muhlenberg explained it, German sympathies did indeed lie with the rebels for they, like the men from Paxton, had suffered from Indian raids on the frontier. Not only did they believe that the Moravian Indians had killed German settlers during Pontiac's uprising but that the Moravians and Quakers had used the Indians as spies. Nor could the Germans help but contrast the defense and comfort extended to the Indians by the Quakers with the indifference shown to the white frontiersmen's pleas for help. As Muhlenberg summarized the situation:

> That is the general *tone* among some. They would unhesitatingly and gladly pour out their possessions and their blood for our most gracious king and [D: his] officers, but they would not wage war against their own suffering fellow citizens for the sake of the Quakers and Herrnhuters and their creatures or instruments, the double-dealing Indians.
> It is difficult in such a crisis to say anything or give any judgement in such a strange republick which has caught a fever, or, rather, is suffering from *colica pituitosa.*[38]

On February 5, 1764, Muhlenberg met with Wrangel, the Swede Reverend Johann Haeggblad, and the Lutheran Reverend Paul Brycelius to formulate what they should say about the Paxton crisis. Muhlenberg's opinion was that a public stand should be avoided.[39] On the following day, however, Wrangel informed Muhlenberg that the governor's vexation with the Germans was increasing because of their continued refusal to bear arms. The provost now felt it was necessary to urge their congregations to cooperate. Muhlenberg begged to be excused because of illness, so Wrangel went about the Philadelphia Lutherans while Brycelius rode ahead to Germantown "to warn the elders of our congregation there not to join the approaching rebels, but rather to stand on the side of the government."[40] Brycelius was then to attempt to locate the Paxton Boys, among whom, it was believed, were many Germans, and try to reason with them.[41]

When Brycelius finally met up with the rebels, most of whom were Scotch-Irish, he was favorably impressed by their "decent and substantial" character.[42] The rebels, he reported to Wrangel and Muhlenberg, had assured him that they merely wished to escort the Indians out of the province and were willing to post a bond guaranteeing that they would not kill them. The purpose of the march, they also claimed, was to air to the assembly the grievances of the frontiersmen. For his part, Brycelius seems to have made them agree to negotiate rather than to attempt to storm Philadelphia by force of arms.

On February 7, 1764, Governor Penn dispatched a blue ribbon negotiating team consisting of Wrangel, Franklin, Attorney General Benjamin Chew, Mayor Thomas Wilting, Joseph Galloway, William Logan, and Daniel Roberdeau to Germantown. Wrangel rode ahead to prepare the way for the talks. The Paxton Boys' complaints were specific and to some degree justified. They claimed that they had received no help from Philadelphia during the Indian massacres, but when they attempted to defend their own lives and homes they were insulted by the Quakers and denounced as murderers. While the Quakers did nothing for their fellow citizens on the frontier, they kept the Indians lodged in Philadelphia in luxury. Finally the Paxton Boys pledged their continued loyalty to king and province but asked redress of their grievances.[43]

Muhlenberg expressed his satisfaction that the governor had decided to negotiate rather than fight.[44] The negotiations were successful in that the Paxton Boys disbanded once assured that their grievances would be remedied. But the Quakers were unwilling to let the matter drop. They passed through the assembly an act which would shift the murder trial to the counties of Bucks, Chester, or Philadelphia should the Paxton Boys be apprehended. Since these were Quaker strongholds, which, because of representative gerrymandering were able to control the legislature, a popular outcry was raised over the act.[45] Sympathizers of the Paxton Boys presented a complaint in behalf of the "Frontier Counties of Lancaster, York, Cumberland, Berks and Northhampton" which was, in effect, a manifesto of frontier grievances against the Quaker assembly, especially decrying the lack of representation by the frontier counties.[46]

The Paxton incident drove yet another wedge between the Germans and their one-time Quaker allies. The final break came in 1764. In that year a new political crisis developed in Pennsylvania centered around the long-standing dispute between the assembly and proprietors over proprietary rights. For decades the Penns had fought with the assembly to obtain their quitrents either in sterling or provincial paper currency at the London rate of exchange. Instead, the assembly insisted on issuing paper money which it forced on the Penns at face value. In 1764 the Privy Council resolved the dispute in Penn's favor by empowering him to refuse to accept the paper money at par.[47]

Using proprietorial mismanagement of the province and their subversion of rights as an issue, Franklin and the Quaker party countered this latest proprietary victory by a massive campaign to gain royal government for Pennsylvania, kicking it off with "Resolves Upon the present Circumstances of this Province, and the Aggrievances of the Inhabitants thereof," introduced in the assembly on March 10, 1764.[48] The committee, which was appointed to prepare grievance resolves, reported some twenty-six to the assembly on March 24, 1764. They were immediately adopted. Resolves twenty-five and twenty-six spelled out the Quaker demands: Pennsylvania should become a royal province, and the assembly should adjourn to consult its constituents on whether to ask the king to assume protection and government of the province.[49]

Immediately on adjournment, Franklin launched his bid for popular support for royal government with his *Cool Thoughts on . . . Our Public Affairs* which was joined by Galloway's more radical *Address to The Freeholders and Inhabitants of Pennsylvania.*

Muhlenberg was sorely grieved by this latest deadlock among the province's officials for so long as the assembly remained in adjournment, the new militia bill went unpassed and the frontier settlers were once more defenceless and exposed to Indian attacks. When, however, a frontiersman urged him to send a circular letter to the united preachers asking that they warn their congregants not to sign the Quaker petition for royal government, which he claimed was a trick to leave the frontier unguarded, Muhlenberg replied that "We preachers could not permit ourselves to interfere in such critical, political affairs."[50]

By May 14, 1764, the Quakers had collected 3,500 names in favor of royal government. At this point the proprietary forces, bolstered by the addition to their ranks of John Dickinson, counterattacked. The Reverend William Smith turned provincial Anglican and Presbyterian pulpits into forums for anti-royalist opinion while appealing to the Germans for support. Angered over Quaker failure to defend the frontier, fearful that royal government might lead to the establishment of the Church of England and the diminution of their religious and political freedoms, and nourishing an intense personal dislike for Franklin, the German church people rallied to Smith's cause.

Wrangel, on July 25, 1764, gave Muhlenberg a petition to the king which asked for the retention of proprietary government, requesting that Muhlenberg circulate it among his deacons and elders.[51] This he did. Meanwhile the German publisher, Heinrich Miller, presented a broadside, "Durch Germanicus," calling for the retention of proprietary government and the defeat of Franklin in the October election.[52]

On August 11, 1764, Muhlenberg's Philadelphia church council subscribed its names to the proprietary petition. The following day Muhlenberg allowed a German-speaking English justice of the peace to circulate a similar petition in church, after services, to the rest of St. Michael's congregation.[53] Since the Proprietary party had placed a trustee of St. Michael's, Henry Keppele, on its ticket, Muhlenberg felt an even stronger attraction to the anti-Quaker cause.

It seems likely, too, that Muhlenberg had reached some sort of a deal with Smith, granting him some benefits in exchange for German votes in the October elections. On August 20, 1764, Smith, the Reverend Jacob Duche, Muhlenberg, and Wrangel jointly presented a petition to the governor asking for a greater number of German justices of the peace in the frontier areas.[54] In September of the following year, St. Michael's was granted a charter by the governor. Thus Muhlenberg was well compensated for whatever support he did lend the proprietary cause.

The elections of October 3, 1764, represented a sharp setback for the Quaker and royalist causes. Both Franklin and Galloway went down to narrow defeats, though the Quakers retained enough seats in their gerrymandered districts to retain control of the assembly. In addition, the first German in the province's history, Henry Keppele, won election to the assembly. Muhlenberg added his own postmortem to the campaign:

> There was great rejoicing and great bitterness in the political circles of the city, since it was reported that the German church people had gained a victory in the election by putting

our *trustee,* Mr. Henry Keple, into the *assembly,* a thing which greatly pleased the friends of the *Proprietors,* but greatly exasperated the *Quakers* and German *Moravians.* Never before in the history of Pennsylvania, they say, have so many people assembled for an election. The English and German Quakers, the Herrnhuters, Mennonites and Schwenckfelders formed one party, and the English of the High church and the Presbyterian Church, the German Lutheran, and German Reformed joined the other party and gained the upper hand—a thing heretofore unheard of.[55]

When it became evident that Franklin would not retain his assembly seat, the Quakers devised a plan to send him to England as provincial agent. Again the Germans rallied to defeat their old antagonist. Some sixty to seventy members of St. Michael's signed a petition urging the assembly not to appoint Franklin, but to no avail.[56]

In their own post-election analysis, it became clear to the Quakers that the defection of the German church people had cost them the election. Soon they were busy attempting to mend their political fences and rebuild the old alliance which had kept them in power for so many years. On February 15, 1765, Muhlenberg was visited by John Hughes, a member of the inner clique of the Quaker party, and soon to be appointed stamp agent for Pennsylvania, and Henry Pawling, a defeated judge. When they attempted to win Muhlenberg over to their position on royal government, he replied that the Germans had merely followed the advice given by Christopher Sauer during the last decade. Sauer's pro-Quaker arguments, Muhlenberg claimed, had been to safeguard against subversion of the liberties granted the province by Charles II. Should any minister speak against Sauer, he was regarded as a traitor. Now the shoe was on the other foot, and it was the Quakers who were threatening to abolish the ancient rights through the obtainment of royal government. Hence a proprietary faction fought to preserve these liberties and, said Muhlenberg, "This I and my friends commended, because for twenty-two years I have never heard anything else but that one must implore God the Lord and the King for the preservation of the vested liberty of conscience, etc."[57]

When Hughes remarked that it seemed strange that Germans would object to government by a king who was German and had been Lutheran, Muhlenberg replied:

> We are and shall remain loyal subjects of His Britannic Majesty regardless of whether the province is governed indirectly by the *Proprieteur's* governors or directly by His Majesty's governors as in other royal *Provinces*. But as concerns the priceless religious and civil privileges granted to this *province* by king Charles II of glorious memory, and protected and confirmed by all succeeding kings, a people would certainly be foolish not to supplicate God and the king for their continuation when a part of the provincial government desired to give them away and demand a new form of government.[58]

Finally, when questioned by Hughes on why the Germans had run their own candidate and had forsaken their traditional Quaker alliance, Muhlenberg answered:

> When all our members were called by our church council to attend a meeting in the large schoolhouse on election day, and they unaminously decided it would be a good thing if several of our German citizens were elected to the *Assembly*, I approved it because we German citizens are not bastards but His Majesty's loyal subjects and naturalized children. We have to bear taxes and *onera* just as much as the English inhabitants, and therefore we have the right and liberty to have one or more German citizens in the Assembly and to learn through them what is going on.[59]

In the elections of 1765, the Quaker party once more gained the upper hand, leaving Muhlenberg to bemoan the fact that he "was able to do no more than to plead in secret at the throne of grace."[60] With the onset of the Stamp Act crisis, however, he resumed his cautious, nonpolitical stance. It was one thing to struggle with a provincial political faction but quite another to directly confront his majesty's government.

When a British ship arrived in Philadelphia harbor bearing the hated stamps on October 5, 1765, Muhlenberg was requested to toll the bells of St. Michael's in mourning along with those of the High Church and the state house. He answered that he had not the authority to do so without the advice of his church council. When, however, the council requested his guidance in their decision, Muhlenberg replied:

> Be subject to the authorities that have power over you. The proposed movements in regard to the landing of stamp materials will be noticed and reported in detail in the newspapers. Since, apart from this, we Germans are already being painted black enough by the envious opposing party in England, we would be sensible to guard ourselves against this act; this is good advice to the wise. We would do better to remain quiet and let the English act as they see fit. As much as possible, let us warn our members not to appear at the State House and to have nothing whatsoever to do with any uprising or tumult.[61]

The congregation did as Muhlenberg advised, and St. Michael's bells remained conspicuously mute, much to the annoyance of the English colonists, Muhlenberg, however, wrote: "I was glad that it had not been done, for the English . . . are prone to incite and egg the Germans on and then put the blame on us."[62] Still, the Stamp Act crisis proved to be only a prelude to a far greater conflict which Muhlenberg sincerely dreaded, open rebellion of the colonies against the mother country.

As tensions increased between Britain and her restive colonies, Muhlenberg became even more determined to avoid any public expression of his political opinions. This became increasingly difficult to accomplish for as the leader of the numerous German church minority he was, in fact, whether he willed it or no, an important political person. His attempted silence only led both sides in this dispute to suspect him and made them more determined than ever to smoke him out.

When, for example, he undertook a journey at Halle's request to visit Lutheran congregations in Georgia from September 1774 to March 1775, rumors spread about his supposed Tory inclinations. First he was accused of seeking colonial-wide establishment of the Church of England which he would then join to collect a tithe. Then, somewhat contradictorily, it was said that George III had converted to Roman Catholicism and old Muhlenberg had sailed to England to celebrate for him a popish mass. At the very least it was believed that he had been tarred and feathered, publicly displayed in a cart, and then driven from Philadelphia in disgrace.[63]

Muhlenberg bridled at such malicious gossip but held his tongue. What refutations he made were done privately or confined to his journal. While in Reading he encountered a Virginia German who, aware of the talk, bluntly asked him "why the German Lutheran preachers have brought about such a grave tragedy, have betrayed the liberty of the country, and have caused this grave war?" Muhlenberg hotly denied that he was either a Tory or a traitor. Indeed he appears to align himself with the patriot cause: "My dear friend," he replied, "you are not correctly informed. I and most of my colleagues have friends and relatives—and children—here in America. We cherish civil and religious liberty as a precious gift vouchsafed to us by God."[64]

As public opinion veered toward war, many colonies began to raise armed militia. Such martial actions were, in Muhlenberg's view, legitimate measures of self-defense: "It is not as if the inhabitants wished to injure anybody, or invade the rights of others, for they wish to defend their civil rights and the liberty of conscience given them by God."[65] Great Britain, he felt, "had rejected the Christian religion and, along with it, has lost light and right, has been struck with blindness in a just judgement, and has become ripe for humiliation."[66] God would use her as a scourge against American sinfulness; then, in the full measure of time, when her purpose was played out, she would be cast aside. Still, up to the final break, Muhlenberg hoped that the mother country would return to her senses; that the sight of well-armed, determined, and thoroughly enraged colonials might compel her to compromise as she had done in the past.[67]

With crisis succeeding crisis, Muhlenberg's sanguine expectations of reconciliation waned. During the early part of 1776, he seriously began to consider the possibility of removing himself from Philadelphia. The city was, after all, the very seat of rebellion for there the Continental Congress sat. To remain and yet maintain silence on the issue of revolution would be impossible. Moreover, Muhlenberg realized, as did any sensible person, that Philadelphia would be attacked by the British in case of open war. Hence, in March 1776, he purchased a home in Providence which was both conveniently near and comfortably distant from the metropolis. Within a week of the proclamation of American independence, he betook both himself and his family to this pastoral retreat, "to remain there," as he explained "until a better solution offered itself."[68]

Safe in Providence Muhlenberg felt himself free from political pressures. Yet he continued to maintain a keen interest in political and especially in military matters. That this interest reflected an American viewpoint is evidenced by the journals.

The journals are, however, problematic. In a sense they were an official record of his American ministry. As such they served as the basis for his annual reports to Halle which published them in a missionary newsletter, the *Hallesche Nachrichten,* designed to raise funds for American Lutheran congregations. Obviously what Muhlenberg sent to Halle, he heavily edited to suit his own purposes. The reverend fathers in Europe knew of Muhlenberg only what he intended they know. He also used his journals as a repository of his financial records as well as of synodical documents and proceedings. To this degree then they were semipublic papers and not merely a private diary. Hence Muhlenberg was both cautious and circumspect, one is tempted to say byzantine, about what he recorded. It could, after all, be used against him at a future date. Despite all this, the journals do indicate that Muhlenberg was never as neutral as he sometimes professed but leaned decisively toward the colonial cause. This, of course, would also explain his anxiety over the fate of these documents. Several times he began preparations to ship them to safety as the British drew near to Providence, an action scarcely necessary if they were innocent of rebel ruminations.

In the journals one finds evidence that Muhlenberg thought the American cause was just. Britain's object was "to make serfs of the inhabitants of America by force and to reap what they have neither plowed nor sown," while the Americans were trying "to defend the rights and privileges granted and stipulated to them by God the Highest and by former crowned heads."[69]

Muhlenberg, moreover, despite his protestations, did not entirely remain aloof from political matters. He did, for example, play a minor role in the adoption of the revolutionary Pennsylvania constitution which, in British eyes at least, might appear inappropriate for one either loyal to the king or professing strict neutrality. On September 17, 1776, he traveled to Philadelphia to confer with the Reverend William Smith, Anglican rector, about the constitution, several portions of which troubled them. The new government demanded no specific profession of Christian faith from office holders, granted full freedom of worship and conscience to any religious sect, but neglected to confirm ecclesiastical charters granted under previous proprietary governments. Smith and Muhlenberg decided to petition the new government only on the last point—that their existing charters be confirmed, as eventually they were. But the first two points were adopted much to Muhlenberg's anger. In a venomous passage he recorded his displeasure:

> Very well you smart chief-fabricators with your refined taste, you have acted very cleverly in allowing nothing concerning a Savior of the World ... to slip in. For that is too old-fashioned. . . . your ingenious edifice is founded on quicksand and will not survive many stormy winds and rains. Your heathen morality has putrid sources and your wild and untainted flesh abhors the salt of Christian morality.[70]

Muhlenberg does not appear to have had a high opinion of revolutionary Pennsylvania leadership. At one time he refers to it in apocalyptic terms as "the beast with horns."[71] At other times he sees it riddled with atheists, deists, and naturalists. The main object of his disaffection was possibly Benjamin Franklin, Pennsylvania's most influential politician and a renowned deist with whom Muhlenberg had previously tangled. As has been noted, Franklin's express dislike of Pennsylvania Germans united them in seeking his defeat in the provincial election of 1764. The role his erstwhile adversary played in the formation of the Pennsylvania government during the Revolution might be another reason for Muhlenberg's noninvolvement on a public level.

In private, however, he was deeply involved in the revolutionary struggle. Throughout the war Muhlenberg received detailed accounts of battle results, troop movements, losses of men and supplies, which he carefully transcribed in his journals. He rejoiced when "our armies," as he wrote in an unguarded moment, won and bemoaned colonial setbacks. For example, upon learning of the failure of Burgoyne's campaigns against Forts Edward and Stanwix, he noted that "God, in His providence has not yet been willing to hand over the poor inhabitants, especially the defenseless women and helpless children, to the rage of the barbarians."[72] During 1777, when the British occupied Philadelphia, the American army encamped a few miles distant from his home. Muhlenberg constantly entertained colonial officers, once receiving a personal briefing on the progress of the war, in return for breakfast, from General "mad" Anthony Wayne, a man not given to over-familiarity with Tories. American armies stored supplies in his cellars and Muhlenberg diligently observed days of fast and prayer prescribed by Congress, condemning the "members of sullen sects [who] declared their consciences were oppressed if they were expected to observe a day which was appointed only by men."[73] He denounced conscientious objectors who refused to pay a tax to the revolutionary government in lieu of military service[74] and vigorously applauded the arrest of wealthy Quakers on charges of treason:

[they] have critized and fought against the defensive measures of the Americans, both publicly and privately, in writing and orally, have refused to contribute their share even in money, have spoken for and rendered every possible assistance to the enemy, etc., they cannot be tolerated as members of a *republic* but must be excluded and be deprived of protection. . . . they did not suffer for Christ's sake but on account of their transgressions as traitors.[75]

Muhlenberg continually denounces British atrocities on civilians and prisoners of war alike. At one point he suggests that Americans could stop this British barbarism by giving "the measure which is measured out to them. For the Americans have more prisoners and so far these have been held and treated humanely."[76]

One could also argue on the basis of guilt by association that

Muhlenberg was a patriot. Certainly an astonishingly large number of his relatives actively supported the struggle for independence. One son, Peter, fought as a brigadier-general; another, Frederick, served in both the Pennsylvania Assembly and the Continental Congress. Francis Swaine, his son-in-law, and Peter Weiser, his brother-in-law, also saw military action. Yet Muhlenberg remained on intimate terms with all these "rebels."

It is true that he initially opposed the involvement of his two sons, but only because it meant abandoning their ministerial careers and exposure to great personal risks. "There are" Muhlenberg mused when he heard of Peter's appointment to the rank of brigadier-general "greater and better deeds than murdering men." But, he continued, "for everything there is a season . . . a time to kill and a time to heal."[77] The time, he realized, had come to fight. In November of 1778 Peter sought his father's advice on whether he should stay in the army or go to the side of his pregnant wife. Muhlenberg emphatically urged him to stick to his duty:

> In times of war . . . a crafty and powerful enemy cannot be restrained by midwives; this must rather be done with God's help by men who have the vocation, skill and heart for it . . . the circumstances make it clear that neither resignation nor furlough could occur without great risk and harm.[78]

For their part, both the British and their Hessian mercenaries were convinced that Muhlenberg was a rebel, a conviction which caused them assiduously to seek his capture. On several occasions, as British troops neared his home, Muhlenberg prepared to flee. His son-in-law, the Reverend John Christopher Kunze, who had remained in Philadelphia to minister to the city's Lutherans, was forbidden by the British to communicate with the rebel patriarch. As Kunze dryly noted "the [British and Hessian] officers are rather unfavorably informed concerning my father-in-law."[79]

Shortly after this incident, Muhlenberg did produce a quasi-public refutation of the charges against him. It is this document, reproduced in his journal, which serves to buttress the opinion that he was either a Tory or a genuine neutral.[80] Close investigation of the letter and the circumstances under which it was written, however, refute this.

On December 4, 1776, Muhlenberg's son Frederick, then a Lutheran clergyman in New York, wrote to inform him that a Hessian officer in the city was allegedly circulating a letter supposedly from the Reverend Gottlieb Anastasius Freyling-hausen, director of the Halle Institute. Though Frederick's information was all hearsay, as he had not himself seen the letter, it was supposed to be directed to the Pennsylvania Minis-terium and warned Halle pastors to have nothing to do with the rebels.

Nearly a year later, on November 5, 1777, Muhlenberg's daughter Margareta Kunze wrote from Philadelphia that the same letter had surfaced there, again in the hands of Hessian officers. Muhlenberg was exceedingly puzzled because he had not received, nor did he ever receive, the letter. But presuming that it was genuine, which it was, and upset because the British were making use of it to argue that Muhlenberg had violated its orders, he chose to reply.[81] This he did in a long letter to David Grim, a prominant Lutheran merchant who had contacts with the Lutheran court preacher in London, Reverend Friedrich Wilhelm Pasche. The reply was sent unsealed to Kunze who would in turn relay it to Grim. It appears that Muhlenberg was in this way trying to kill two birds with one stone. Well aware that the British read all mail entering Philadelphia, he hoped that its contents, once perused by a military censor, would diminish their ardent desire to imprison him. If Grim later forwarded it to Germany via London, he would also be let off the hook at Halle which was probably picking up reports through the Hes-sians of his political meddling.[82] They could, after all, cut off his supply of men and money if they were convinced he was disobeying orders.

On the surface the letter seems to exude Tory views, but a surface impression is misleading. Muhlenberg was a desperate man. As he saw the situation: "Things look black for me for I am caught between two fires and I am still unable to see the outcome which divine providence will ordain for me."[83] As Muhlenberg realized from the arrests of his close clerical friends, the Reverends Michael Schlatter, German-Reformed minister, and Jacob Duche, an Episcopalian priest, the British felt no qualms about imprisoning men of the cloth. He had also heard that "their treatment of preachers is barbarous and merciless."[84] The letter then is best interpreted as an effort to avoid imminent arrest by emphasizing, perhaps even exaggerating, his previous loyalty and surface neutrality.

Muhlenberg begins his explanation with a complaint that Hessian officers were condemning him without justice or trial as a rebel. To counter this, Muhlenberg pointed out his strong ties to George III and the House of Hanover. He emphasized that he, as a Hanoverian, was doubly a subject, by birth and by naturalization, that he had studied at the royal university, received his call through London Court Preacher Ziegenhagen, and that "up to this time I have neither broken nor transferred my oath of fealty."[85] This could be a Machiavellian argument, technically true but beside the point. Obviously Muhlenberg had two oaths of loyalty to George III, the first as elector of Hanover, the second as king of Great Britain. He could renounce Britain's king and still keep his oath to the House of Hanover. It should be noted that Muhlenberg does not, in his apologia, refer to George III as His Britannic Majesty, a form he uses elsewhere, but simply as His Royal Majesty. It would have been extraordinary had Muhlenberg escaped Pennsylvania's mandatory oath to the state and Congress. Providence was a small village. He could never have neglected to swear allegiance without being noticed, nor would American military officers have felt so free to visit him and impart to him sensitive military information had he not done so. In all probability, then, he did renounce his oath to George as British sovereign.

Muhlenberg next tackled an embarrassing blemish on his self-proclaimed abhorrence of the public political spotlight. In 1766 he had indeed taken a public stance in delivering and later printing a tract which he explained was "for the use of our German inhabitants" and in which he "emphasized loyalty and due obligation toward our rightful king, the whole royal house, and all governments."[86] What he neglects to mention is that his topic was a thanksgiving for the repeal of the Stamp Act and that it had received general distribution.[87]

Muhlenberg then related in great detail the rumors spread by "a few God forsaken, crafty persons, who well knew that I was a loyal subject of the lawful government" to the effect that he was a Tory selling out his country to the king.[88] Instead, he insisted, throughout his tenure in Philadelphia during the troubled year 1775 he had studiously avoided involvement in the rebel cause. For emphasis' sake he recounted an incident that happened in July of 1775 when a member of the revolutionary Congress attempted to draw him into a declaration of rebel sentiments by writing and publishing an exhortation to colonial Germans warning them that their liberties were in grave danger from the king. According to Muhlenberg, he curtly replied:

> Sir, as far as I know, all of the intelligent members of our Lutheran congregations are loyal subjects of His Royal Majesty, our sovereign, and such a statement as is desired is not befitting to preachers; political matters are usually published through the newspapers.[89]

Supposedly when Congress arranged to have such a declaration circulated through Lewis Weiss, a German lawyer, Muhlenberg joined with the Philadelphia German Reformed pastor, the Reverend Caspar D. Weyberg, in protesting "publicly with petitions and fair words that the document should not, and could not pass under the names of the preachers nor as having our approval."[90] Curiously this incident is recorded only in this letter copied into his journals on January 22, 1778, three years after it was supposed to have occured. Journal entries for the month of July 1775 do not mention it. Instead, under date of July 20, 1775, Muhlenberg notes that he celebrated at St. Michael's Church in Philadelphia a day of repentance and prayer proclaimed by the Continental Congress.[91] Obviously there is something peculiar about the whole incident.

When independence was proclaimed, Muhlenberg told Grim: "robbed of my former protection, old and worn out, unwilling to exchange my oath of loyalty except by compulsion, another victim of the enraged people, I betook my sick wife to the country . . . here I thought I should have a solitary, quiet, private life."[92] That quiet life, of course, did not turn out to be so solitary for, as previously noted, he had plenty of rebel visitors in the country. It is equally likely that Muhlenberg fled from the city to escape the British as to avoid renouncing his oath of loyalty to the king. That it occurred to him that this might well be the British view is attested to by his admission that "perhaps a wrong construction was put on the fact that I retired from Philadelphia to the country."[93] Certainly had Muhlenberg desired to function as a preacher subject to the king he could have easily treked the few miles back to Philadelphia while it still remained in British hands.

Peter Muhlenberg's military career would also, to understate the matter, have raised suspicions about his father's loyalty. This Muhlenberg explained away by the fact that "he was two hundred and fifty miles away from me and entered [the army] contrary to my will and warning."[94] Yet a mere ten months after he wrote this, as has been seen, he talked Peter out of resigning from the army. To butress his point that fathers and sons are not responsible for each other and often hold different political views, Muhlenberg brought up Benjamin Franklin's son William, governor of New Jersey, who became a Tory while his father remained a rebel. This is, of course, true. Yet it is also true that Franklin then disowned his son, a thing Muhlenberg never did.

The letter closed with Muhlenberg's denial that he had ever received Freylinghausen's letter, but he assured Grim nonetheless that all Halle pastors had always acted in full accord with its admonition: they had remained neutral.

This then is the basis for the claim that Muhlenberg was either neutral or a Tory during the Revolution; he stated as much to Grim. Actually he said no such thing. As has been observed, what he wrote was deliberately ambiguous, was intended to prevent his imminent arrest, and could be explained in such a way as to harmonize with the view that he was a patriot. There is, moreover, no evidence that Grim ever received the letter. Muhlenberg, it seems, had second thoughts about the wisdom of the project. In admirable cloak and dagger fashion, on February

4, 1778, Muhlenberg enclosed a note to his daughter Margareta Kunze, in a letter addressed to a woman in Philadelphia. The note, written in Latin to thwart military censors who, it was hoped, had been deprived of a classical education, told her to send the letter to Grim if her husband thought it expedient. "If not, I beg and beseech you to hide the one you have, lest your poor father, wishing to avoid Charybdis, fall into Scylla."[95]

From the onset of bloodshed, it appears that Muhlenberg recognized that, given the British attitude, independence was irrevocable, reconciliation impossible. Thus he noted in his journal on October 4, 1776 that Lord Howe had called on all Americans to return to their ancient allegiance. His comment:

> It is easy to proclaim: come to allegiance, swear loyalty anew, and you shall find grace and pardon. On the other side, however, it is also proclaimed: Beware of a power that breaks solemnly sworn compacts, that makes you slaves or serfs by cunning and violence, that binds you *in all cases whatsoever,* that feeds idlers and rakes with your property gained by your sweat and blood, and desires to rob you of the rights and liberties bestowed upon your children and children's children by God and former crowned heads.[96]

Muhlenberg continued to reason that peace could be achieved on British terms only if *all* colonists renounced independence and surrendered voluntarily, a patent impossibility. Should only a portion of the population heed Lord Howe's decrees, then civil war would erupt in America between Patriots and Tories, a situation even worse than revolutionary warfare.

On June 14, 1778 Muhlenberg recorded the peace terms proposed by the ill-fated Carlisle Commission which granted the colonies anything they desired short of outright independence. This too, he felt, would fail:

> Oh a thousand pities that only a half or a third of such proposals were not made three, two, or even one year ago, or that no attention was paid in the homeland to the petitions submitted by *Congress!* Thus much bloodshed between mother, children and relatives, and the horrible destruction, etc., could have been avoided. How can *Congress* repeal *independence* now that a treaty has been concluded with France?[97]

Besides, Muhlenberg was convinced at a very early date, even during the setbacks of the first years of the war, that with God's help America would be victorious:

> ... Although the American cause has been precarious, adverse, and gloomy, as if decline and collapse were unavoidable, a mightier, invisible Hand has intervened and unexpectedly helped.[98]

Finally, on March 25, 1783, after seven long years of bloodshed, Muhlenberg recorded the end of the war and penned his thoughts on the new nation.

> Now one can, of course, reasonably conclude from this success that it was the will of the Supreme Ruler of heaven and earth that there should be *independence,* and not otherwise. But whether this was God's active or passive will, His gracious or His permissive will, only the future will show, according as men use *independence* well or abuse it.[99]

With peace at hand and independence secured, Muhlenberg feared the new nation would soon forget the true meaning of its long struggle with Great Britain. "plenty of histories of the Revolution *pro* and *contra* will come out," he prophesied; "but if the authors do not understand or believe in the dominion of divine governance and providence . . . they will get no further than secondary causes."[100] The primary causes were for him theological, and the Revolutionary War was best interpreted in biblical terms. After all, God's nature had not changed since the days when there were kings in Israel. He was still the lord of history. His ghostly hand whose wall writing had doomed the kingdom of Balthassar had most recently been directed against the kingdom of George III. It too had been weighed in the balance and found wanting. And so the kingdom was lost, at least its American part.

For Muhlenberg God had sent the Revolution, an "extraordinary war in ancient, heathen Barbaric mode, which manifests little or nothing that is humane . . ." as a punishment for the irreligious behavior of both Great Britain and her colonies.[101] God had used Britain as a rod to scourge America. When she had served his divine purposes, he would cast the rod into the fire for the sins of the mother were greater than those of the child. Great Britain had richly earned such rejection for, puffed up with pride, she gloried in her own strength and throughout the war had committed "heaven-crying sins and wickedness upon the defenseless and the helpless."[102] The Americans, on the other hand, had fought in a Christian manner, not to conquer but in self-defense. They had respected prisoners of war; the British had abused them. Congress had rendered due subordination to God, calling upon the nation to fast and repent after defeats and to offer thanksgiving for victories. The most important sign that God's grace was with America lay in the nature of the colonial commander-in-chief. To Muhlenberg George Washington was "a gentleman [who] does not belong to the so-called world of society, for he respects God's Word, believes in the atonement through Christ, and bears himself in humility and gentleness."[103] So impressed was he by the general that he baptised his grandson, the child of his daughter Maria and Francis Swaine, George Washington Swaine in his honor.[104]

Muhlenberg considered Washington not only the father of his country but its savior as well. Under date of April 3, 1783, Muhlenberg records "an incident which might have led to a great misfortune if God in His mercy and forbearance had not prevented it through his servant G[eorge] W[ashington]."[105] After provisional peace terms had been agreed upon by Britain and the colonies, an incipient revolt broke out within the American army. Certain officers refused to demobilize unless Congress immediately voted them back pay and a life-long pension. Because Congress lacked the funds to do this there was a great danger that "an armed army would have marched from one state to another and levied upon the defenseless inhabitants until they had had enough or until some stronger monarchical power imposed *dependence* upon us."[106] Through Washington's intervention the revolt was avoided. Two months later the general laid down his own arms and bade Congress a dignified farewell prompting Muhlenberg to again extol his Christian spirit.[107]

Only divine intervention could, in Muhlenberg's opinion,

explain the astonishing victory won by ragged colonial citizen soldiers against the world's mightiest military power. By God's grace, America was independent; but continued national existence depended on God's providence and America's faithfulness to his commands. As he phrased it:

> Our transient political independence does not free us for a moment . . . from the *dependence* and the duties which we owe to God, our Redeemer, our neighbors, and ourselves.[108]

Dependence, in Muhlenberg's mind, meant faithful adherence to true Christian doctrine and leading lives of sobriety, hard work, and duty. Otherwise God's hand would once more be lifted against his rebelious people. That such punishment was imminent he saw evidenced by postwar American behavior, for

> the true Christian religion still has few roots and assured fruits in America. The pity is that too many do not understand the word *independence,* and do not want to understand it, because they think now that they are also independent of the Saviour of the world and His laws and are left to themselves.[109]

Throughout his life Muhlenberg viewed society through European spectacles. To him it should be static, patriarchal, class-conscious, and agrarian. Each person had a calling in life which bound one to a certain social standing in which one must remain. Each level of society was linked to the others by almost feudal ties of duty and deference. Authoritarianism permeated Muhlenberg's world view and was reflected in his concept of civil and ecclesiastical governments. Most decidedly, he was innocent of harboring democractic tendencies. As he warned his son Frederick, one should beware of *vox populi* which "was very changeable and often shifted to extremes."[110] Indeed in most cases *vox populi* was equivalent to *vox diaboli.* Democracy for Muhlenberg meant social leveling and attendant chaos.

It was precisely these leveling tendencies that he opposed in the new American state for they threatened to bring down in ruins the social fabric to which he was accustomed. Excessive liberty would result only in license.

Muhlenberg first noted signs of leveling in ecclesiastical affairs. Throughout the revolutionary period tension had been rising between Pennsylvania Presbyterians and Anglicans. The Presbyterian clergy, of course, had been in the vanguard of revolutionary enthusiasm. Ministers from the Church of England, in particular the Reverend William Smith, had also supported the American cause, though with considerably less ardor. Partly this was due to the peculiar relationship between the British crown and the Anglican church. Partly it stemmed from Pennsylvania political realities.

During the struggle over royal government, Lutherans, Presbyterians, and Anglicans had all joined together in support of the Proprietors. By 1768 this alliance was in disarray. It foundered on the shoals of William Smith's ambition which inspired him to launch a spirited campaign to secure a native Anglican bishop for America. Obviously Smith felt he was the best qualified to serve in so lofty an office. Presbyterians, however, were determined to thwart Smith's scheme.

Both sides debated their case in the *Pennsylvania Gazette.* For his part, Smith argued that a bishop was necessary to create a native ministry which alone could establish colonial Anglicanism on a firm footing. Presbyterian opposition, he charged, stemmed from their determination to keep the Church of England weak so that they could become the majority religious body. Presbyterians, on the other hand, argues that Smith's intention was to hang about American necks "that yoke of spiritual bondage and jurisdiction . . . [over the dissenting churches] which neither they nor their fathers could bear."[111]

Smith and his fellow Anglicans were not alone in their dislike and suspicion of Presbyterians. Quakers had hated them since 1764 when the Paxton Boys had sent the governor of Pennsylvania their "Declaration of the distressed and bleeding Frontier Inhabitants" which blamed all the frontier woes of the province on Quaker misleadership. The Friends struck back with an uncharacteristic vengeance, denouncing the Scotch-Irish Paxtons as having the "same Spirit with the blood-ran, blood-thirsty Presbyterians, who cut off King Charles his Head."[112] Quakers branded the sons of the Kirk as "Quarrelsome, Riotous, Rebellious, dissatisfied with the publick Establishment," and as enemies to royal government.[113] It was further charged "that in the Annals both of ancient and modern History, Presbyterianism and Rebellion, were twin-Sisters . . . and their Affection for each other, has ever been so strong, that a separation of them never could be effected."[114]

Muhlenberg's attitude toward the Presbyterians was ambivalent. He greatly admired their flexibility which made them the fastest growing denomination in America. As he noted in his journal for 1765, William Tennant's Log College at Neshaminy and the seminary at Princeton had turned out several hundred native ministers who "get along on meager salaries and know how to adapt themselves to circumstances here. Nor are they subject to hyponchondria, for their *cursus theol[ogicus]* is not extensive but goes directly *ad rem;* they are not required to toil over a multitude of questions in *futuram oblivionem,* which only cause all manner of *obstructiones* and flatulence anyhow."[115] Still Muhlenberg never felt completely comfortable with Presbyterians for he thought that they "push the doctrine of absolute predestination and the hypotheses connected with it too far, and their pastoral staff is well tipped with steel."[116] This distrust might explain Muhlenberg's actions during the Stamp Act crisis when, as has been noted, he refused to join his Presbyterian and Anglican colleagues in tolling the bells of St. Michael's in mourning over the landing of a consignment of stamps at Philadelphia. Oddly enough, this occurred on October 5, 1765, exactly four days after the provincial elections of October 1st when he had noted that: "the German sectarians and English Quakers and their large following gained the upper hand in the election, and the English and German church people lost out. I was able to do no more than to plead in secret at the throne of grace that the invisible, omnipotent, all-ruling hand of God might direct the circumstances to His honor and the best welfare of His kingdom."[117] Thus, despite his obvious sympathies for the Proprietary Party, he deserts them and assumes a position akin to that of the Quakers. Mistrust of Presbyterian-led revolutionary protest against constituted authority would explain this. Muhlenberg might have considered the Stamp Act unwise, particularly because it provided for double taxation for

German-language newspapers and documents, but he disapproved of other than legally constituted avenues of protest to overturn it. Revolutionary acts could be tolerated only as a last-ditch extreme measure to be employed after all other possibilities had been explored. Even then they would be justified only in defending absolutely essential rights and privileges. In such a case they would not really be revolutionary at all but essentially defensive measures. His decision to abandon the Proprietary Party was probably further strengthened by the recall of Provost Charles Magnus Wrangel on September 13, 1765. It was Wrangel who had persuaded Muhlenberg to become politically active in the first place. With his influence withdrawn, Muhlenberg lapsed into a much more congenial public neutrality in Pennsylvania politics.

Muhlenberg's journals for 1768 contain no direct reference to the episcopate controversy. But under date of November 6, 1768, he does accuse the Church of England of "suffering severely from *passiones hystericae;* . . . at least we feel the effects of the hysteria here . . . for in her paroxysms she disciplines her children with an iron fist instead of a glove and does not see where she strikes."[118] The reference is to the Lutheran church in Culpepper, Virginia. Muhlenberg had sent them a minister, Johannes Schwarback, who, since he had not obtained episcopal ordination as provincial law required, was unable to perform such official acts as marriages. For these the Lutherans had to enlist the aid of an Anglican clergyman. Moreover, because the congregations had to pay a tax to support the Anglican clergy, they were unable to adequately provide for their own minister. Muhlenberg viewed this law as extremely unjust so it is probable that he would have strongly opposed the creation of an American episcopate with the consequent threat of colonial-wide establishment of the Church of England. Still he remained on good terms with Smith and the English church whose Society for the Propagation of the Gospel contributed funds to American Lutheran congregations.

Smith meanwhile was having his problems. Though he supported the American cause during the Revolution, he was still suspected of secret Tory inclinations. In December, 1775, Smith delivered an address before the Continental Congress lauding General Richard Montgomery who had been killed during the assault on Quebec. Unfortunately, John Adams thought Smith's oration too lukewarm, "an insolent performance,"[119] and persuaded Congress not to publish it, causing the Anglican divine to bring it out at his own expense. Smith later urged reconciliation with Great Britain in a series of articles signed "Candidus." This caused him in 1779 to lose his position as provost of the Philadelphia Academy, a post he had held since 1755. Pennsylvania's assembly voided the institution's charter on the grounds that it had violated its charter rights by abandoning its nondenominational character. It then absorbed the academy into the newly created and Presbyterian controlled University of Pennsylvania. Muhlenberg leaves no doubt that he supported Smith in this controversy which he viewed as an example of Presbyterian aggression. As he explained in a 1784 letter to Wrangel, then in Sweden:

> He [Smith] maintained the academy on its original basis even in the difficult period when the British were occupying Philadelphia, although they knew that he was an adherent of the American side. But when the Engl[ish] were gone, the Presb[yterian] politico-Christiani, especially Dr. [John] Ew[ing], etc., brought about a revolution with the help of the ass[embly] or the tribuni plebis, elected new trustees, founded a university, drove Prov[ost] Sm[ith] from his office and his home, and created baccal[aurei] art[ium], mag[istri], doct[ores] med[icinae et] juris, and finally also d[octors of d[ivinity].[120]

Smith then moved to Chestertown, Maryland where he founded a new school, Washington College. But Presbyterians continued to hound him. As Muhlenberg noted: "an opponent to the project—presumably a Presbyterian—immediately appeared and attacked this project in the English newspaper as a crimen laesae majestatis and demanded that the state assembly curb and restrain the proposed Episcopal institution."[121] However, as he wrote, since other denominations had their own schools and as the new state constitutions guaranteed religious freedom to all sects, the new college should not be hindered. Besides, Muhlenberg warned, "most of the government and offices have hitherto been in the hands of Presbyterians and still are. If this sort of thing continues, the sparks may grow into flames and result, if God in His grace does not prevent it, in a religious war."[122]

Muhlenberg did write to Smith on December 31, 1782, praising him and defending his actions when provost of the academy. To his intense annoyance, Smith publicized this letter in his continuing struggle against the Pennsylvania Assembly's decision. For his part, Muhlenberg decidedly wished to avoid a quarrel with Smith's enemies who he said "are great and learned wise men of the world and heroes of controversy and are quite ready to give one who plays the truth a rap on the head with the fiddlestick."[123]

Another activity of Smith earned Muhlenberg's deep displeasure. In 1784 Smith initiated a campaign to reestablish the Episcopal church in Maryland. This Muhlenberg saw as an impossible and imprudent effort to restore the status quo ante Revolution, something that neither could nor should be done. The following year the industrious Smith succeeded in having the Maryland Assembly consider the imposition of a poll tax which would be used to pay the salaries of all clergymen regardless of denominational affiliation. In effect, this amounted to the establishment of all religions, at least all of those belonging to Christianity. Again Muhlenberg dissented echoing the words of Pastor Johann Andreas Krug that "such compulsion [was] inadvisable and unnecessary for it would tend to make laborers in the kingdom of Grace lazy and sloathful."[124] It would also, especially if enacted throughout the colonies, give to state governments whose Christian character Muhlenberg deeply suspected complete control over religion in America.

For his remaining days Muhlenberg looked with disfavor on the University of Pennsylvania and its "refined" leaders. When his son-in-law, the Reverend John Christopher Kunze, was awarded the degree of Doctor of Divinity from that institution in 1783 Muhlenberg sarcastically wrote:

Loathsome and contemptible as the German scholars were to the English Presbyterian politico-theologians here in former times, so much the more do they for obvious reasons flatter them now, because the right to elect to positions of honor depends upon the people, their legal advisers, and the majority of their votes. *Tempora mutantur,* etc. Hitherto they compared us Germans with sauerkraut and foul cheese, now their tastes have changed; but these are petty things. . . During the *Revolution* the refined Presbyterian leaders wrested control of the Academy and its *estate* from the heads of the Episcopal church, and now they feel obliged out of love to make friends of the mammon of unrighteousness and to hand out titles of honor[125]

When, in the following year, Muhlenberg was informed that he too had been awarded a Doctor of Divinity by the university, he suggested it confer its honors on those who had earned them "and not waste them on an old, decrepit, deaf, lame and unlearned Mühlenberg, who, despite his depraved, flattering egotism and by virtue of a true self-knowledge, still does not consider himself worthy to be called an accomplished catechist, driller, or preacher, much less a D.D."[126]

The older he grew, the more delight Muhlenberg took in poking fun at secular intellectuals. In 1784 he noted that American "philosophers" were experimenting with balloon flying machines. This he satirically lampooned as a waste of time and money for "there are no means of subsistence or treasures to be had beyond, the atmosphere, nor is there any air there that is fit for human beings; these Daedali will thus be making waxen wings for themselves and their sons, and like Phaeton will want to rule the sun."[127] One wonders what Muhlenberg thought of the dignified Mr. Franklin racing through a Philadelphia field in a thunderstorm with a kite aloft, sentiments which are unfortunately not recorded in his journals.

Presbyterian aggressiveness was not the only sign Muhlenberg observed of what to him was religious degeneracy. To his horror, in 1787 an English woman from Rhode Island along with two of her followers showed up in Philadelphia. Evidently she was preaching that she was the incarnation of Jesus Christ in his second coming and that her disciples were the two witnesses referred to in St. John's Book of Revelation. These "apes of Satan," as Muhlenberg labeled them, had actually found some incredulous citizens to follow them which further convinced him that excessive tolerance in matters of religion merely led to irreligion. "Is not this annoying and scandalous that such insolent lies and jokes of Satan should be tolerated as an unquenchable offense in a so-called Christian Republic?"[128]

In 1786 Muhlenberg commented on a spate of religious reformations: the creation of Unitarianism with its denial of the Trinity, the democratic changes adopted by the Protestant Episcopal church to make it more appealing to Americans. All these he dismissed as "heresies" fostered by "the unfeeling foe of God and man [who] moves the machines and his comedians behind the curtain, and makes use of the old maxim of the world, *divide et imperabis.*"[129]

As religious doctrine was in decline so, too, Muhlenberg felt, were the hoary old decent social customs. The sobriety and simplicity characteristic of colonial days were yielding to a new sophistication in morals and manners which he heartily disliked. Mere social pleasures he still rejected as profitless dissipations. Thus he could sternly admonish his maid Catharina Haag because she had accepted an invitation to attend a "frolick" "where cornhusking will be rewarded with drink, games, or dancing."[130] When his daughter-in-law Hanna, the wife of General Peter Gabriel Muhlenberg, entertained some neighbor ladies for tea and gossip, Muhlenberg ridiculed this newfangled fad and warned: "if poverty and need come as a consequence, such table companions will remain afar off."[131]

Nor did the younger generation escape his censure. Muhlenberg had never held an overly high opinion of youth, in particular American youth, for he had always been exceedingly puritan in his outlook. Youth were unruly by nature, given to sinfulness and frivolity, and in need of stern parental guidance to tame and educate them and to save their souls. All Americans, he felt, spoiled their children shamefully but particularly was this true in urban areas where children were "permitted all freedom and frivolity, for there is no strict policing or discipline."[132] In 1764 Muhlenberg had recorded the onset of incipient juvenile delinquency in his own congregation in Philadelphia. When distracted deacons ordered several voluble young men to shut up during religious instructions, "the impudent rascals had clenched their fists at them and poured out English curses such as 'Go to H——l!' 'You son of a b——ch!' 'God d——nn you!' etc. And what is more, they said that their parents would protect them against the deacons."[133] Thoroughly enraged, Muhlenberg excoriated the parents from the pulpit informing them that unless they forced their offspring to mend their ways, he would have them arrested should they dare to disrupt future catechism classes. Better yet, he mused with obvious anticipation, he would bind cords into a scourge and whip the monsters from the church. Twenty years after this incident, Muhlenberg still confronted unruly adolescents, this time his own grandchildren whom he instructed during his semiretirement. One day in 1783, while teaching his grandchildren about the body's five senses, Muhlenberg asked one, a five year old, which one you see with. "The tongue," the child quickly replied. Why not mused Muhlenberg since most Americans appeared to concentrate all their senses on the tongue or sensual pleasure and refined taste. What resulted was "Sick bodies and the minds of dwarfs or moles."[134]

Four years later, when baby-sitting John Peter Gabriel's son, Muhlenberg smacked the child with a rod for coming home late whereupon the incorrigible youngster, who appears to have inherited his father's temper, shouted out that he would now stay out late again tomorrow. This caused Muhlenberg to again lament the laxness of parents:

> If parents do not in time break the inborn, wicked selfishness and self-will which are inherited from Adam, the children will become thorns . . . in their sides and ultimately the rule of God will place reins and bits in their mouths—for example, the pushing of a barrow in Philadelphia., the pillory, the gallows, or all sorts of incurable diseases will occur as consequences of their unbridled sins."[135]

Even if the children escaped the gallows, it appeared that their elders should not. Postwar America increasingly seemed to Muhlenberg to be a society on the verge of anarchy, infested with highway men, burglars, and murderers.[136] Part of this was the result of seven years of continual warfare with its attendant disintegration of social institutions. A generation grown accustomed to burning, pillaging, and bloodshed was wont to continue it even after peace came. Some of the soldiers who could not adjust to mobolization and the tedium of normal life took to crime. The war, too, had caused great disruption in law-enforcement agencies. The result was that:

> both in cities and in the country there is a daily increase of breaking into homes, of street robberies, of theft, murder, etc., so that one is hardly safe at night, either at home or on a journey, unless God's gracious providence protects city and house.[137]

Lawlessness touched close to home in 1783. A desperado named Joseph Doane had been imprisoned by Pennsylvania authorities. His gang now threatened to kidnap and hold for ransom Frederick Augustus Muhlenberg, then speaker of the assembly, until their chief was released. Because Frederick journeyed through the sparsely settled country each weekend from Philadelphia to visit his father's home in Providence, he was particularly vulnerable to capture. For a time an armed guard escorted Frederick on his travels while his father lived in fear of his son's life. As he bitterly wrote in his journals: "So it is commonly with such so-called honorable offices in the great world: grapes from thorns and figs from thistles, stench for thanks."[138]

Along with the rise in crime, the economy went into depression, again from the dislocations of the war. Muhlenberg continually complained of the massive inflation and consequent devaluation of the currency which especially harmed the middle class, himself included. With prices rising as well they were being squeezed out of existence. Meanwhile Americans, despite decreased incomes, were increasing consumption, purchasing on credit, living above their means which could only result in eventual impoverishment.[139] With war's end Europe was flooding the new nation with cheap goods. American craftsmen and artisans, unable to compete, went out of business.[140] Politics offered no stable career for the cost of getting elected frequently exceeded the income produced by the office and, once elected, officials were mercilessly abused by a licentious electorate.[141] Muhlenberg also warned against the pitfalls of becoming a merchant or shopkeeper. Profits were small, made smaller still by cut-throat competitive practices designed to undersell and bankrupt your rivals. Moreover clerical help was expensive, merchandise rapidly aged and depreciated, and debtors defaulted with depressing regularity.[142] The only solution, "the most innocent way of living in this part of the evil world" so Muhlenberg felt, "is still the patriarchical way."[143] He strongly advised his children to move to the country, raise cattle, and grow crops. That way they would at least be assured of food and a suitable environment in which their children could grow.

European immigration was, to Muhlenberg, merely increasing America's economic woes. Most of the newcomers refused to soil their hands in manual labor, preferring instead a white collar or professional job for which there was already an over abundance of applicants. As a result "the prisons are almost always full of debtors and loafers."[144] Many Hessian soldiers stranded in America at the conclusion of the war pretended to be preachers to earn a living. They caused Muhlenberg numerous headaches as they gradually infiltrated congregations formerly provided for by the ministerium.[145] In desperation Muhlenberg wrote: "one would like to shout to the Europeans: Stay in your own country and get along somehow! *ora et labora.*"[146]

Things did not appear much brighter on the political scene. Congress, weak as it was under the Articles of Confederation, was unable to pursue a strong foreign policy or gain the respect of European states. Nowhere was this weakness felt as strongly as on the Ohio frontier. Here, after Congress had opened the land to settlement, Indians went on the warpath. Muhlenberg felt that only two solutions were possible under the circumstances. Congress could purchase this land from the local tribes, but sufficient funds were unavailable. Thus only by sending an overpowering military force to crush the Indians could the frontier be made safe for settlement.[147] In this harsh attitude Muhlenberg reflected the prejudices of Pennsylvania Germans who, as frontiersmen, had too frequently borne the brunt of bloody Indian attacks. He had no love for the Redman. By August, 1785, Muhlenberg noted that the Ohio Indians were being incited to rise against the United States by the British in Canada who offered bounties for the scalps of whitemen delivered to Fort Niagara.[148] During the following year, Georgia's Indians had also gone on the warpath incited by the Spanish in Florida.[149] Congress seemed powerless to stop them. When General James Clark finally mounted an attack on the Indians, his mission failed "because his soldiers rebelled, and some subordinate officers were partly to blame for it."[150] Militarily and politically the new nation appeared utterly impotent to assert and defend its sovereignty.[151]

Meanwhile social and political anarchy inexorably spread at home as licentious and irresponsible behavior paralyzed government at all levels. A typical journal entry for 1784 notes that:

Conditions in the political government here in our state of Penns[ylvania] appear to be terribly distressing. The state assembly adjourned early, its members disbanding in contention, and the council of censors also ended in disunity without accomplishing much and perhaps, as it is said, merely pouring oil into the fire.[152]

Americans, he wrote, should take seriously the lesson from the twelfth chapter of Matthew: a house divided against itself cannot long stand. Above all else, unity was needed at home. Instead, dissension spread all the more. In October, 1786, Muhlenberg anxiously recorded news of the rebellion of Daniel Shays and his followers against the government of Massachusetts. "These," he wrote, "are harbingers of anarchy and its consequences."[153] His greatest fear was that Shay's rebellion was just the opening salvo in a coming civil war. "If God in His grace does not avert it, this wild fire might cause a conflagration in the rest of the *independent* states because combustible materials, both physical and moral, are heaped up here."[154] Pennsylvania, his own beloved state, was, he felt, tottering on the brink of the same madness which threatened to engulf New England.[155] In an effort to explain the situation in America as he saw it, Muhlenberg constantly used the following parable:

A cock was scratching upon a manure heap and found a costly diamond. He did not know its value and kept pushing it here and there, unable either to break it or swallow it. He called his hens, but they likewise did not know what to do with it. Unexpectedly a jeweler came riding by and saw the diamond from a distance. He dismounted and took possession of it, giving the cock and hens a handful of his horse's feed which they swallowed with eager appetite, and thus remained in their assigned sphere.[156]

The diamond symbolized independence; the cock stood for colonial leaders; the hens, the people. The jeweler represented either a foreign nation or a home-grown dictator. As for the moral of the tale: unless Americans curbed their excesses, they would lose their newly won independence.

By the beginning of 1787, Muhlenberg and his wife were both in a precarious state of health which he gloomily likened to the health of his nation. All three, he feared, were *in extremis*.

Muhlenberg's wife, Anna Maria, had been subject to epileptic seizures since 1766, seizures which gradually became so frequent and severe that she required constant watching. In 1781, for example, Anna Maria was cooking beets over an open fire when she suffered a fit, first falling face down into the kettle of boiling water, then tipping the scalding contents of the pot over the left side of her body. She was horribly scalded and barely recovered. Muhlenberg's own health was rapidly deteriorating. In July of 1778, while attending an artilleryman's funeral, his hearing had been permanently damaged by the noise of a farewell volley. From that time on he suffered from vertigo and a roaring in his ears. In his last years this annoying condition was complicated by dropsy.

Accustomed as he was to a strenuous and active life, Muhlenberg suffered acutely from the indignities imposed upon him by illness and age. He sadly recounted an incident when he went into his garden during the winter to attend to necessary bodily functions and, overcome by dizziness, fell into the snow. Lacking strength to raise himself up he was reduced to calling for help until a neighbor responded.[157] On another occasion Muhlenberg tried to help his wife to a chair during one of her seizures but instead fell helplessly to the floor with her.[158] "Both of us," he moaned "are *inutilia terrae pondera*, or we are like the fig tree which consumes sap and bears no fruit."[159] The inexorable

death of most of his friends depressed Muhlenberg ever more
and increased his feeling of isolation and melancholy. He expressed this mood in February of 1787 to the pages of his
journal:

> Dark without and within. I looked through the so-called
> album which I brought with me from Europe and found to my
> confusion the excellent greetings, admonitions, and consola-
> tions which various counts, barons, citizens, theologians, etc.
> inscribed between 1735 and 1742. I suppose that most, if not
> all, of these blessed persons have died before 1787 and are
> now flourishing in the joy and glory of their Redeemer, where
> they are enjoying what no eye here hath seen. Meanwhile I,
> wretched man that I am, remain here in this dangerous
> wilderness of temptation. Who shall deliver me from the body
> of this death?[160]

Three months later he poignantly prayed in his native tongue:
"Mach End, O Herr, mach Ende."[161] By then the end was indeed
very near.

On September 29, 1787 Muhlenberg recorded the last entry
in his journals, fittingly another pastoral notation that he had
baptized a fifteen-month-old girl. The following day he entered
upon his last illness. For a week Muhlenberg suffered pain so
intense that he was unable to sleep. Finally, early on Sunday
morning, October 7, 1787, surrounded by most of his family, he
died peacefully in his seventy-sixth year. At approximately the
same time, General Washington, whom Muhlenberg once ad-
miringly referred to as a "rejuvenated Joshua,"[162] had joined
with other conservative colonial leaders to put an end to the
anarchy Muhlenberg had so strongly denounced. A constitutional convention had convened in Philadelphia in May of 1787.
On September 17, the convention approved the newly written
Constitution. Then, on September 28, two days before Muhlenberg's last illness, Congress had issued a call for state ratifying
conventions. Had he lived, Muhlenberg would assuredly have
supported the Constitution's adoption for it created the strong
central government he had known must come if the nation were
to survive. Washington's inauguration as head of the new
government would have convinced him that God in his mercy

and wisdom had decided to save the Republic. In Muhlenberg's absence, his two sons, Peter and Frederick, represented his sentiments as they rallied Pennsylvania's Germans behind the document. And so his missionary efforts ended after forty-five years of uninterrupted and fruitful labor. He had accomplished much for his adopted country and richly deserved the title of patriarch universally accorded him by his coreligionists. His tombstone in the churchyard of Agustus church in Providence, Pennsylvania bears the following inscription: "Qualis et quantus fuerit, non ignorabunt sine lapide futura saecula," which freely translates as "Even if he lacked a monument of stone, future generations would still know how great a man he was." This is literal truth for his greatest memorial is American Lutheranism itself, a living monument to his life and works.

NOTES

[1]See Robert C. Schultz, ed., *Luther's Works,* 3 (Philadelphia: Fortress Press, 1967), "The Christian in Society," p. 26.

[2]Dietmar Rothermund, *The Layman's Progress: Religious and Political Experience in Colonial Pennsylvania, 1740–1770* (Philadelphia: University of Pennsylvania Press, 1961), pp. 84–85; see also Dietmar Rothermund, "The German Problem of Colonial Pennsylvania," *Pennsylvania Magazine of History and Biography* 84 (January 1960): 8.

[3]Glenn Weaver, "Benjamin Franklin and the Pennsylvania Germans," *William and Mary Quarterly,* Third series, 14 (October 1957): 539.

[4]Quoted in Ralph Ketcham, ed., *The Political Thought of Benjamin Franklin* (Indianapolis: Bobbs-Merrill Co., 1965), p. 77.

[5]"Why should the Palatinate Boors be suffered to swarm into our settlements and by herding together establish their language and Manners to the Exclusion of Ours? Why should Pennsylvania, founded by the English, become a Colony of Aliens who will shortly be so numerous as to Germanize us instead of anglicizing them, and will never adopt our language or Customs anymore than they can acquire our complexion?" cited in Arthur D. Graeff, *The Relations Between the Pennsylvania Germans and the British Authorities (1750–1776)* (Philadelphia: Privately printed, 1939), p. 24.

[6]The French who watch all advantages are now [themselves] making a German settlement back of us in the Illinois Country, and by means of those Germans they may in time come to an understanding with ours, and indeed in the last war

our Germans shewed a general disposition that seems to bode us no good; for when the English who were not Quakers, alarmed by the danger arising from the defenceless state of our Country entered unanimously into an Association within this Government and the Lower Countries [counties] raised Armed and Disciplined [near] 10,000 men, the Germans except a very few in proportion to their numbers refused to engage in it, giving out one among another, and even in print, that if they were quiet the French should they take the Country would not molest them. (in Ketcham, p. 78)

[7]Ibid.

[8]Quoted in Rothermund, "German Problem," p. 12.

[9]Ibid., p. 13.

[10]Ibid.

[11]See the letter of Smith to the London Society, dated December 15, 1753, in William R. Steckel, "Pietist in Colonial Pennsylvania: Christopher Sauer, Printer," Ph.D. dissertation, Stanford University, 1949, p. 183.

[12]Smith to the Bishop of Oxford, in ibid., p. 185.

[13]Henry Harbaugh, *The Life of Rev. Michael Schlatter; with a full Account of his Travels and Labors among the Germans in Pennsylvania, New Jersey, Maryland and Virginia; Including His Services as Chaplain in the French and Indian War, and in the War of the Revolution, 1716–1790* (Philadelphia: Lindsay & Blakiston, 1857), p. 270.

[14]Ibid.

[15]Ibid., p. 272.

[16]Ibid., p. 273.

[17]Ibid., p. 277.

[18]Ibid., pp. 296–98.

[19]Ibid., p. 265.

[20]Sauer to Conrad Weiser, September 6, 1755, in ibid., pp. 293–94.

[21]Ibid., p. 302.

[22]Ibid., pp. 301–2.

[23]Ibid., pp. 298–99.

[24]Henry Melchior Muhlenberg, *The Journals of Henry Melchior Muhlenberg in Three Volumes*, I, trans. Theodore G. Tappert and John W. Doberstein (Philadelphia: Muhlenberg Press, 1942), p. 648. Hereafter referred to as *I Journals*.

[25]Graeff, p. 56.

[26]Theodore Thayer, *Pennsylvania Politics and the Growth of Democracy, 1740–1776* (Harrisburg: Pennsylvania Historical and Museum Commission, 1953), p. 37.

[27]Ibid.

[28]Graeff, p. 70.

[29]Thayer, pp. 39–40.

[30]Ibid., p. 41.

[31]Graeff, pp. 136–37.

[32]Thayer, p. 56.

[33]*I Journals*, p. 604.

[34]Rothermund, *Layman's*, p. 103.

35Graeff, p. 189.
36Ibid., p. 191.
37Ibid., p. 196.
38Henry Melchior Muhlenberg, *The Journals of Henry Melchior Muhlenberg in Three Volumes*, II, trans. Theodore G. Tappert and John W. Doberstein (Philadelphia: Muhlenberg Press, 1945), p. 19. Hereafter referred to as *II Journals*.
39Actually, what Muhlenberg said is open to debate. He merely indicated that the principle which should guide their actions was found in Romans: 13:1–2, Titus 3:1, 1 Peter 2:13–14, and Proverbs 24:21. All of these texts boil down to the same thing—be obedient to the authorities that actually govern you. It could also mean not to interfere in their business. Since the militia to be raised was a voluntary one, there was no need for the German clergy to take a stand.
40*II Journals*, p. 20.
41Further evidence of Muhlenberg's sympathies is manifest in his description of the Quakers arming themselves against the Paxton Boys. "These pious sheep, who had such a tender conscience during the long Spanish, French and Indian War, and would rather have died than lift a hand for defense against the most dangerous enemies, were now all of a sudden willing to put on horns of iron . . . and shout and smite a small group of their poor, oppressed, driven, and suffering fellow inhabitants from the frontier." (Ibid., p. 20)
42*II Journals*, p. 22.
43Ibid.
44Ibid., p. 24.
45Graeff, pp. 201–2.
46Ibid., p. 202.
47James H. Hutson, "The Campaign to Make Pennsylvania a Royal Province, 1764–1770, Part I," in *Pennsylvania Magazine of History and Biography* 94 (October 1970): 431.
48Ibid., p. 435.
49Ibid., p. 437.
50*II Journals*, pp. 54–55.
51Ibid., pp. 102–3.
52Graeff, p. 215.
53*II Journals*, p. 107.
54Ibid., p. 111.
55Ibid., p. 123.
56Ibid., p. 140.
57Ibid., pp. 190–91.
58Ibid., p. 191.
59Ibid., p. 192.
60Ibid., p. 262.
61*II Journals*, p. 272.
62Ibid., p. 274.
63Ibid., p. 693.

64Ibid., p. 694.

65Ibid., p. 699.

66Ibid., p. 701.

67Ibid., p. 700.

68Ibid., p. 722.

69Ibid., p. 735.

70Ibid., pp. 747–48.

71Ibid., p. 751.

72*III Journals,* p. 70.

73Ibid., p. 28.

74Ibid., p. 61.

75Ibid., pp. 75–76. Muhlenberg's harsh position is partly explained by the extreme antipathy he felt toward German sectarians and Quakers both of which held pacifism. Throughout the journals he refers to them as pious sheep with over-tender consciences.

76Ibid., p. 97.

77Ibid., p. 17.

78Ibid., p. 196.

79Ibid., p. 101.

80Theodore G. Tappert, in "Henry Melchior Muhlenberg and the American Revolution," *Church History* 11 December 1941: 284–301, concluded: "When the war began he had Tory leanings without being a Tory in the full sense of the word. As the war progressed he seems by almost imperceptible stages to have become somewhat reconciled to the cause which two of his sons embraced, but his doubts and fears and misgivings were never absent." (p. 301)

Paul A. W. Wallace, *The Muhlenbergs of Pennsylvania* (Philadelphia: University of Pennsylvania Press, 1950), also holds the idea of Muhlenberg's gradual conversion to the American cause: "By 1777, they were all, the boys and their father together, united in their American loyalty. But, whereas the boys had never been anywhere else, their father had to think his way to that position." (p. 109)

81Freylinghausen's instructions appeared in the 15th edition of the Halle Reports published in 1776 and reproduced in Johann Ludewig Schluze, ed., *Nachrichten von den Vereinigten Deutschen Evangelisch-Lutherischen Gemeinen in Nord-America, absonderlich in Pennsylvanien* (Philadelphia: G. C. Eisenhardt, 1895), vol. 2, p. 708.

22Freylinghausen emphasized that he was convinced from what pastors Kunze and Helmuth wrote that neither they nor the other Halle fathers had conducted themselves improperly in the crisis. It is noteworthy that he fails to mention Muhlenberg, by far the senior of the Halle fathers.

83*III Journals,* p. 133.

84Ibid., p. 77.

85Ibid., p. 124.

86Ibid.

87The title of Muhlenberg's pamphlet was *A Testimony of the Goodness and Zeal of*

God toward His Covenant People in the Old and New Times and of the Ingratitude of the People toward Him, given at the Occasion of the Thanksgiving in Consequence of the Repeal of the Stamp Act, August 1, 1766 (Philadelphia: H. Miller, 1776).

[88]*III Journals,* p. 124.

[89]Ibid., p. 125.

[90]Ibid.

[91]*II Journals,* p. 703.

[92]*III Journals,* p. 125.

[93]Ibid.

[94]Ibid.

[95]Ibid., p. 129.

[96]*II Journals,* p. 746.

[97]*III Journals,* p. 163.

[98]Ibid., p. 69.

[99]*III Journals,* p. 534.

[100]*III Journals,* p. 587.

[101]Ibid., p. 134.

[102]*II Journals,* p. 768.

[103]*III Journals,* p. 149.

[104]Ibid., p. 275.

[105]Ibid., p. 535.

[106]Ibid.

[107]Ibid., p. 553.

[108]Ibid., p. 650.

[109]Ibid., p. 534.

[110]Ibid., p. 375.

[111]Theodore Thayer, *Pennsylvania Politics and the Growth of Democracy, 1740–1776* (Harrisburg: Pennsylvania Historical and Museum Commission, 1953), p. 135.

[112]James H. Hutson, *Pennsylvania Politics, 1746–1770: The Movement for Royal Government and Its Consequences* (Princeton: Princeton University Press, 1972), p. 96.

[113]Ibid., p. 98.

[114]Ibid.

[115]*II Journals,* p. 295.

[116]Ibid., p. 181.

[117]Ibid., p. 272.

[118]Ibid., p. 375.

[119]Alan Heimert, *Religion and the American Mind: From the Great Awakening to the Revolution* (Cambridge, Mass.: Harvard University Press, 1966), p. 440.

[120]*III Journals,* p. 625.

[121]Ibid., p. 647.

[122]*III Journals,* p. 647.

[123]Ibid., p. 546.

[124]Ibid., p. 660.

[125]Ibid., p. 551.

126Ibid., p. 597.
127Ibid., pp. 604–5.
128Ibid., p. 128.
129Ibid., p. 707.
130Ibid., p. 619.
131Ibid., p. 746.
132*II Journals,* p. 89.
133Ibid., p. 90.
134*III Journals,* p. 572.
135Ibid., p. 744.
136Ibid., pp. 537–38.
137Ibid., p. 746.
138Ibid., p. 561.
139Ibid., p. 682.
140Ibid.
141Ibid., p. 650.
142Ibid.
143Ibid.
144Ibid., p. 630.
145Ibid.
146Ibid.
147*III Journals,* p. 607.
148Ibid., p. 683.
149Ibid., p. 721.
150Ibid., p. 724.
151Ibid., p. 731.
152Ibid., p. 618.
153Ibid., p. 719.
154Ibid., p. 730.
155Ibid., p. 733.
156Ibid., pp. 607–8.
157Ibid., p. 702.
158Ibid., p. 677.
159Ibid., p. 736.
160Ibid., p. 730.
161Ibid., p. 738.
162Ibid., p. 607.

Conclusion

It is evident that Henry Melchior Muhlenberg was more than just a pragmatic opportunist with a genius for organization. Pragmatic he was and organizational ability he possessed in abundance, but these qualities stemmed from a deep-rooted moderation which caused him to seek the middle way between extremes abhorrent to him.

This moderation in theological matters resulted from his exposure to both orthodoxy and pietism during his formative years. The best features of both traditions combined in his own person to produce a distinctive brand of Lutheranism rigid enough to retain traditional dogmas, yet flexible enough to adapt to and flourish in a strange new environment. His theological moderation caused him to espouse the godly life but only if it was mediated and expressed through the institutionalized channels of the structured church. Unlike many of his clerical contemporaries, Muhlenberg never lost sight of the incarnational nature of his charges. Men and women are spirits, it is true, but spirits encased in fleshly bodies. Both natures had to become pastoral concerns. Muhlenberg's contribution to American Lutheranism on a theological level was precisely this blending of piety and orthodoxy which created a common doctrinal basis on which most could agree. Because he eschewed the enthusiastic bent of revivalism and insisted that revivalistic practices be manifested only within an ordered liturgical framework, Muhlenberg spared American Lutheranism the schisms which rent other denominations after the awakenings of the 1740s. In this he succeeded where many of his coetaneous counterparts failed.

The key to Muhlenberg's thought, political, social, or theological, is his felt need for order. As he phrased it in an admonition to his unruly congregants:

> God . . . is a God of order. Whoever fears Him, loves order for God's sake. If we wish to be Evangelical Christians and congregations, we must hold to and observe Christian Evangelical order. But if we wish to become enthusiasts and sectarians, we must not call ourselves Evangelical Lutherans."

This sentiment reflects Muhlenberg's cosmological views. God created and preserves the universe and put within it natural laws, a divine order, according to which things function. In such a structured universe, each person or thing has its assigned place be it inferior or superior. Ultimately all creation is subordinate to the will of the creator. Thus, beyond the surface discordance of seemingly widely divergent elements, there exists an overall harmony for all creation emanating from a single source and groping its way back to the one from which it came. All things then are interconnected precisely in their diversity.

Given this theological and cosmological orientation Muhlenberg was forced to combat Moravian pan-denominationalism on the one hand and orthodox exclusivity on the other. Muhlenberg's Lutheran church remained denominationally distinctive yet open to counterplay and contact with other churches for his insistence on the uniqueness of Lutheranism as a religious experience was coupled with a truly ecumenical vision of Christianity. For Muhlenberg the genuine church of Christ manifested itself within the various denominations, all of which retained their doctrinal and liturgical individuality while joining together in a common mediation of God's word. Muhlenberg's city of God was a genuinely pluralistic society reached by many different paths. Thus Muhlenberg held that genuine Christian union need not result in a blurring of doctrinal lines until doctrine itself became meaningless and Christianity degenerated into humanitarianism. Instead he wished to preserve the theological contributions of every genuinely historical manifestation of the spirit of God. This, however, did not prevent him from rejecting as false manifestations those sects whose doctrine stood in contradiction to the historical revelation of God.

Because American Lutheranism was of such recent origin and had developed without benefit of organized ecclesiastical authority, Muhlenberg's American ministry was devoted primarily to imposing order and establishing ministerial primacy. His organizational contributions to his church form a lasting legacy, but these were made possible only because of the theological premises which underlay them.

Muhlenberg's great passion was the good of the church and the welfare of souls. The state he viewed as sharing with the church a complementary yet independent role in the economy of salvation. Hence he was extremely reluctant to intervene in purely secular affairs and did so only when the state appeared to interfere in the life of the spirit. His conception of the state, of course, was also influenced by his cosmology. Just as order permeates the universe, so too the city of man must be an ordered society, one in which each person remains within his or her appointed sphere and wherein all classes of people jointly strive toward salvation. It was the resultant chaos and leveling tendencies of the revolutionary and confederation eras that turned him first against the British authorities and then against the government of the Articles of Confederation. Neither could preserve the ultimate necessity for existence, order. Neither, therefore, had a legitimate claim to secular authority.

Henry Melchior Muhlenberg was, then, a far more important personage then colonial historians have traditionally made him out to be. To be sure he does not belong among the legendary "founding fathers" who were in the vanguard of the forces that created a new nation—men such as Washington, Franklin, and Jefferson. But, if not in the vanguard, surely he can be assigned to the middle ranks. His sons Peter and Frederick made major lasting contributions to the formation of the republic. So too did Muhlenberg. It was he who Americanized Lutheranism and brought ethnic Germans into the mainstream of American life. It was he who curbed the excesses of the awakening movement and so helped to prevent religious fragmentation. Finally it was he who firmly planted the Lutheran church in the soil of the New World. The spirit of toleration and moderation which he advocated in theological as well as secular concerns enabled Lutheranism to adapt itself to a pluralistic American environment and assume its rightful place in the emerging denominational structure of American Protestantism.

Bibliography

PRIMARY SOURCES

Evangelical Lutheran Ministerium. *Documentary History of the Evangelical Ministerium of Pennsylvania and Adjacent States: Proceedings of the Annual Conventions from 1748–1821, compiled and translated from records in the archives and from the written protocols.* Philadelphia: Board of Publication of the General Council of the Evangelical Lutheran Church in North America. 1898.

Franklin, Benjamin. *The Political Thought of Benjamin Franklin.* Edited by Ralph Ketcham. Indianapolis: Bobbs-Merrill Co., 1965.

Fresenius, Johann Philip. *Nachrichten von Herrnhutischen Sachen.* Vol. 3. Frankfurt: Heinrich Ludwig Brönner, 1748.

Harbaugh, Henry. *The Life of Rev. Michael Schlatter: With a full Account of his Travels and Labors Among the Germans in Pennsylvania, New Jersey, Maryland and Virginia: Including His Services as Chaplain in the French and Indian War, and in the War of the Revolution, 1716–1790.* Philadelphia: Lindsay & Blakiston, 1857.

Hart, Simon and Kreider, Harry J., eds. and trans. *The Lutheran Church in New York and New Jersey, 1722–1760.* New York: United Lutheran Synod of New York and New England, 1962.

Hinke, William J., ed. *Life and Letters of the Rev. John Philip Boehm, Founder of the Reformed Church in Pennsylvania, 1683–1749.* Philadelphia: Publication & Sunday School Board of the Reformed Church in the United States, 1916.

Muhlenberg, Henry M. *The Journals of Henry Melchior Muhlenberg in Three Volumes.* Edited by Theodore G. Tappert and John W.

Doberstein. Vol. I. Philadelphia: Muhlenberg Press, 1942. Vol. II, 1945; Vol. III, 1958.

———. *Heinrich Melchior Muhlenberg: Partriarch der Lutherischen Kirche Nordamericka's, Selbstbiographie, 1721–1743. Aus dem Missionsarchive der Franckeschen Stiftungen zu Halle.* Edited by W. Germann. Allentown: Brobst, Diehl & Co., 1881.

Schulze, Johann Ludwig, ed. *Nachrichten von den vereinigten Deutschen Evangelisch-Lutherischen Gemeinen in Nord-America, absonderlich in Pennsylvanien.* Vol. 1. Allentown: Brobst, Diehl & Co., 1886. Vol. 2. Philadelphia: P. G. C. Eisenhardt, 1895.

———. *Reports of the United German Evangelical Lutheran Congregations in North America, Especially in Pennsylvania,* Vol. 1. Translated by C. W. Schaeffer. Reading: Pilger Book Store, 1882.

———. *Reports of the United German Evangelical Lutheran Congregations in North America, Specially in Pennsylvania.* Translated by Jonathan Oswald. Vol. 1. Philadelphia: Lutheran Publication Society, 1880. Vol. 2, 1881.

Van Laer, Arnold J. H., trans. and ed. *The Lutheran Church in New York, 1649–1772: Records in the Lutheran Church Archives at Amsterdam, Holland.* New York: New York Public Library, 1946.

Zinzendorf, Lewis von. *Sixteen Discourses on Jesus Christ Our Lord: Being an Exposition of the Second Part of the Creed Preached at Berlin by the Right Reverend, Lewis, Bishop of the Ancient Brethren's Churches.* Translated from the High Dutch. 2d ed. London: William Bowyer, 1750.

SECONDARY WORKS

Books

Bittinger, Lucy Forney. *German Religious Life in Colonial Times.* Philadelphia: J. B. Lippincott Co., 1906.

———. *The Germans in Colonial Times.* Philadelphia: J. B. Lippincott Co., 1901.

De Schweinitz, E. *The Moravian Manual.* Philadelphia: Lindsay & Blakiston, 1859.

Eisenberg, William E. *The Lutheran Church in Virginia, 1717–1962.* Roanoke, Virginia: Trustees of the Virginia Synod of the Lutheran Church in America, 1967.

Fortenbaugh, Robert. *The Development of the Synodical Polity of the Lutheran Church in America, to 1829.* Philadelphia: Privately printed, 1926.

Graeff, Arthur D. *The Relations Between the Pennsylvania Germans and the British Authorities (1750–1776).* Philadelphia: Privately printed, 1939.

Hamilton J. Taylor. *A History of the Church Known as the Moravian Church, or the Unitas Fratrum, or the Unity of the Brethren, During the Eighteenth and Nineteenth Centuries.* Bethlehem: Times Publishing Co., 1900.

Hopkins, Joseph G., ed. *Concise Dictionary of American Biography.* New York: Charles Scribner's Sons, 1964.

Hutson, James H. *Pennsylvania Politics 1746–1770: The Movement for Royal Government and Its Consequences.* Princeton, N. J.: Princeton University Press, 1972.

Jacobs, Henry Eyster. *A History of the Evangelical Lutheran Church in the United States.* New York: Christian Literature Co., 1893.

Knittle, William Allen. *Early Eighteenth Century Palatine Emigration.* Philadelphia: Dorrance & Co., 1937.

Knox, Ronald. *Enthusiasm: A Chapter in the History of Religion: With Special Reference to the XVII and XVIII Centuries.* New York: Oxford University Press, 1950.

Kreider, Harry Julius. *Lutheranism in Colonial New York.* New York: Privately printed, 1942.

Kretschmann, Ernst T. *The Old Trappe Church: A Memorial of the Sesquicentennial Services of Augustus Evangelical Lutheran Church, Montgomery County, Pa.* Philadelphia: Printed by the congregation, 1893.

Kuhns, Oscar. *The German and Swiss Settlements of Colonial Pennsylvania. A Study of the so-called Pennsylvania Dutch.* New York: Henry Holt & Co., 1901.

Kurtz, Nicholas. *Church History.* Translated by John Macpherson. Vol. 3. New York: Funk & Wagnalls, 1890.

Langton, Edward. *History of the Moravian Church.* London: George Allen & Unwin, Ltd., 1956.

Lewis, A. J. *Zinzendorf the Ecumenical Pioneer: A Study in the Moravian Contribution to Christian Mission and Unity.* Philadelphia: Westminster Press, 1962.

McNeill, John T. *Modern Christian Movements.* Philadelphia: Westminster Press, 1954.

Maland, David. *Europe in the Seventeenth Century.* New York: St. Martin's Press, 1966.

Mann, William J. *Life and Times of Henry Melchior Muhlenberg.* Philadelphia: G. W. Frederick, 1887.

Palatine Society of the United Evangelical Lutheran Church of New York and New England. *The Palatines of New York State: A Compilation of the History of the Palatines who first came to New York State in 1708–1722.* Johnstown, N. Y.: Palatine Society, Inc., 1953.

Pfatteicher, Helen E. *The Ministerium of Pennsylvania: Oldest Lutheran Synod in America, Founded in Colonial Days.* Philadelphia: Ministerium Press, 1938.

Qualben, Lars P. *The Lutheran Church in Colonial America.* New York: Thomas Nelson & Sons, 1940.

Reichel, Levin Theodore. *The Early History of the Church of the United Brethren, Commonly Called Moravians, in North America, A.D. 1734–1748.* Nazareth: Moravian Historical Society, 1888.

Rothermund, Dietmar. *The Layman's Progress: Religious and Political Experience in Colonial Pennsylvania, 1740–1770.* Philadelphia: University of Pennsylvania Press, 1961.

Sachse, Julius Friedrich. *The German Pietists of Provincial Pennsylvania, 1694–1708.* Philadelphia: Printed by the author, 1895.

Schmauk, Theodore Emanuel. *The Lutheran Church in Pennsylvania, 1638–1800.* Lancaster: Pennsylvania German Society, Vols. 11 (1901) and 12 (1902) of *Proceedings and Addresses.*

Schmidt, Martin and Jannasch, Wilhelm. *Das Zeitalter des Pietismus.* Bremen: Carl Schünemann Verlag, 1965.

Schultz, Robert C., ed. *Luther's Works.* Vol. 3. Philadelphia: Fortress Press, 1967.

Stoeffler, F. Ernest. *The Rise of Evangelical Pietism.* Leiden: E. J. Brill, 1965.

Tappert, Theodore G. "Orthodoxism, Pietism and Rationalism, 1580–1830." *Christian Social Responsibility: A Symposium in Three Volumes. Vol. II. The Lutheran Heritage.* Edited by Harold C. Letts. Philadelphia: Muhlenberg Press, 1957., pp. 36–88.

————, trans. and ed. *Pia Desideria.* Philadelphia: Fortress Press, 1964.

Thayer, Theodore. *Pennsylvania Politics and the Growth of Democracy, 1740–1776.* Harrisburg: Pennsylvania Historical and Museum Commission, 1953.

Wallace, Paul A. W. *The Muhlenbergs of Pennsylvania.* Philadelphia: University of Pennsylvania Press, 1950.

Wedgwood, Cicely V. *The Thirty Years War.* New Haven: Yale University Press, 1939.

Weinlick, John R. *Count Zinzendorf*. New York: Abingdon Press, 1956.

Wentz, Abdel Ross. *A Basic History of Lutheranism in America*. Philadelphia: Muhlenberg Press, 1955.

Wolf, Edmund Jacob. *The Lutherans in America: A Story of Struggle, Progress, Influence and Marvelous Growth*. New York: J. A. Hill & Co., 1889.

Articles

Benz, Ernst. "Pietist and Puritan Sources of Early Protestant World Missions." *Church History* 20 (June 1951): 28–55.

Conrad, Leslie, Jr. "The Importance of Preaching in the Great Awakening." *Lutheran Quarterly* 12 (May 1960): 111–20.

DeLevie, Dagobert. "Patriotic Activity of Calvinists and Lutheran Clergymen During the American Revolution." *Lutheran Quartlery* 8 (November 1956): 319–40.

Feer, Robert A. "Official Use of the German Language in Pennsylvania." *Pennsylvania Magazine of History and Biography* 76 (July 1952): 394–405.

Fortenbaugh, Robert. "Ecclesiastical Orders in American Colonial Lutheranism." *Lutheran Church Quarterly* 20 (1947): 274–96.

Gibson, James E. "The German Academy or Seminary in Philadelphia, 1773–1777." *Lutheran Church Quarterly* 14 (January 1941): 84–97.

Hutson, James H. "The Campaign to Make Pennsylvania a Royal Province, 1764–1770, Part I." *Pennsylvania Magazine of History and Biography* 94 (October 1970): 427–63.

————. "The Campaign to Make Pennsylvania a Royal Province, 1764–1770, Part II." *Pennsylvania Magazine of History and Biography* 95 (January 1971): 28–49.

James, George F. "In Memoriam: John Martin Boltzius, 1703–1765, Patriarch of the Georgia Lutherans." *Lutheran Quarterly* 17 (May 1965): 151–66.

Mellick, Andrew D., Jr. "German Emigration to the American Colonies, Its Cause, and the Distribution of the Emigrants." *Pennsylvania Magazine of History and Biography* 10 (1886): 241–50 and 375–91.

Richards, George W. "Henry Melchior Muhlenberg and Michael Schlatter." *Lutheran Church Quarterly* 15 (July 1942): 274–84.

Ritter, John N. "Muhlenberg's Anticipation of Psychosomatic Medicine." *Lutheran Church Quarterly* 19 (April 1946): 181–88.

Rothermund, Dietmar. "The German Problem of Colonial Pennsylvania." *Pennsylvania Magazine of History and Biography* 84 (January 1960): 3–21.

Schaeffer, C. W., trans. "Muhlenberg's Defense of Pietism." *Lutheran Church Review* 12 (1893): 349–75.

Schindler, Carl J. "The Psychology of Henry Melchior Muhlenberg's Pastoral Technique." *Lutheran Church Quarterly* 16 (January 1943): 50–59.

Schmidt, Martin. "Pietism." *New Encyclopedia of the Lutheran Church* 3 (1965): 1898–1906.

Suhr, Heinrich P. "Muhlenberg's Opinion on the Introduction of English in the Swedish Churches, 1761." *Lutheran Church Quarterly* 13 (January 1940): 79–85.

Tappert, Theodore G. "Henry Melchior Muhlenberg and the American Revolution." *Church History* 11 (December 1942): 284–301.

———. "John Caspar Stoever and the Ministerium of Pennsylvania." *Lutheran Church Quarterly* 21 (April 1948): 180–84.

———. "The Muhlenberg Tradition in the Nineteenth Century." *Lutheran Church Quarterly* 15 (1942): 394–403.

———. "Was Ecclesia Plantanda Muhlenberg's Motto?" *Lutheran Quarterly* 5 (August 1953): 308–11.

Von Lany, Milan, trans. "Instructions for the Swedish Mission in America, 1758." *Lutheran Church Quarterly* 13 (January 1940): 75–79.

Weaver, Glenn. "Benjamin Franklin and the Pennsylvania Germans." *William and Mary Quarterly,* Third Series, 14 (October 1957): 536–59.

Wentz, Abdel Ross. "A Muhlenberg Letter and the Ministerium of Pennsylvania." *Lutheran Church Quarterly* 20 (October 1947): 417–24.

Theses and Dissertations

Bowser, Arthur M. "The Great Awakening of the Evangelical Lutheran Church in the Middle Colonies, 1742–1764." Master's thesis, Pennsylvania State University, 1968.

Ensign, Chauncey David. "Radical German Pietism (ca. 1675–ca. 1760)." Ph.D. dissertation, Boston University, 1955.

Glatfelter, Charles H. "The Colonial Pennsylvania German Lutheran and Reformed Clergymen." Ph.D. dissertation, Johns Hopkins University, 1952.

Lodge, Martin Ellsworth. "The Great Awakening in the Middle Colonies." Ph.D. dissertation, University of California at Berkely, 1964.

Scheidt, David Lee. "Linguistic Transition in the Muhlenberg Tradition of American Lutheranism." Ph.D. dissertation, Temple University, 1963.

Steckel, William R. "Pietist in Colonial Pennsylvania: Christopher Sauer, Printer." Ph.D. dissertation, Stanford University, 1949.

Wolf, Richard Charles. "The Americanization of the German Lutherans, 1683–1829." Ph.D. dissertation, Yale University, 1947.

Index

245